Indigenous Writes

A Guide to First Nations, Métis
& Inuit Issues in Canada

Indigenous Writes
A Guide to First Nations, Métis & Inuit Issues in Canada

Chelsea Vowel

HIGHWATER PRESS

HighWater Press gratefully acknowledges for their financial support the Government of Canada through the Canada Book Fund, the Canada Council for the Arts, the Manitoba Book Publishing Tax Credit, and the Manitoba Department of Culture, Heritage & Tourism.

LIBRARY AND ARCHIVES CANADA CATALOGUING IN PUBLICATION

Vowel, Chelsea, author
    Indigenous writes : a guide to First Nations, Métis, and Inuit issues in Canada / Chelsea Vowel.

Includes bibliographical references.
Issued in print and electronic formats.
ISBN 978-1-55379-680-0 (paperback).--ISBN 978-1-55379-684-8 (pdf)

    1. Native peoples--Canada. I. Title.

E78.C2V69 2016   971.004'97   C2016-903683-9
                                        C2016-903684-7

HighWater Press is an imprint of Portage & Main Press
Printed and bound in Canada by Friesens
Cover and interior design by Relish New Brand Experience

21 20 19 18 17   3 4 5 6 7

 THE DEBWE SERIES

Exceptional Indigenous Writing from Across Canada

 HIGHWATER PRESS

 FSC
www.fsc.org
MIX
Paper from responsible sources
FSC® C016245

100-318 McDermot Avenue
Winnipeg, MB, Canada R3A 0A2

Toll free: 1-800-667-9673
www.highwaterpress.com

Dedicated to ninâpêm, José Tomás Díaz Valenzuela, kisâkihitin mistahi.

Contents

kinanâskomitinâwâw/Acknowledgments

In addition to all the amazing people I have cited as sources and resources in this book, I have some specific acknowledgments to make.

I want to start by thanking Darrel Dennis for giving me the motivation I needed to finally sit down and get this book done. ay-ay.

To my husband, kinanâskomitin mistahi. The only reason I got this book done in three months with a newborn in the house is because he is an amazing and present father. I have been writing and teaching and speaking and travelling for a few years now, none of which would have been possible without my husband's help. He will downplay his role, but this work took a village, and nîcimos is the reason the village didn't burn down around our ears.

ninanâskomâwak all our amazing daughters: Isidora, Arlis, Emily, Neve, and sâkowêw. They are the light and joy of this life.

ninanâskomâw my fellow otipêyimisiw-iskwêw kihci-kîsikohk, Molly Swain, for reading the whole manuscript as I produced it, helping me to avoid classist and ableist language (two areas I continue to really struggle with, as ingrained as these things are), and asking me the questions that helped me go back and make things a little more clear when necessary. Also, Molly is my cohost on Métis In Space, honorary okâwiya (auntie) to my kids, and, basically, an all-around mood-lifter. Her visits during the course of my work on this book kept my mood positive, and my humour intact!

ninanâskomâw Shauna Mulligan for organizing my endnotes. That might sound underwhelming, so let me clarify how important this was! As I point out in the Introduction, I didn't just want to present readers with a bunch of my opinions and the digested portions of my research. A huge part of this book, perhaps the most important part, is the curated resources I've included with every chapter. Making sure those resources are properly cited, and as accessible to readers as possible, was absolutely vital. I was doing a very poor job of this, so having Shauna step in was a huge reason this book actually got completed.

ninanâskomâw Romeo Saganash for being the catalyst of sorts for my writing on these issues. He is the one who first tweeted out my article on Attawapiskat, and things haven't been the same since!

ninanâskomâwak Chris Andersen, Jennifer Adese, Adam Gaudry, Zoe S. Todd, Rob Innes, and Darren O'Toole – all of whom are brilliant and hilarious Métis scholars. Their vital feedback and thought-provoking conversations (and rants) have been wonderful sources of inspiration and energy.

And, of course, ninanâskomâwak my parents for their love and support, my sister, Cathleen, who always has my back, and my brother, Teagun, who is out there in the world doing exactly what he wants to be doing.

Introduction

How to Read This Book

After teaching in the Northwest Territories and Alberta for a few years, I applied to law school at the University of Alberta. Education has always been my passion, but I felt I needed additional skills to be able to better understand and articulate some of the problems I was dealing with on a daily basis in the classroom. I wanted to be able to advocate more effectively for my students – most of whom are Indigenous – and I wanted to know how to go about making institutional changes. I thought studying law would give me insights I lacked.

I was right, but the most valuable education I received was not the one I'd been expecting.

I began law school in 2006. To say it was difficult is an understatement. Oh, it wasn't the crushing workload or the competitive peers, and it wasn't even studying law while raising two daughters. It was the world-view that informed every course. I thought I was prepared for this – after all, I had spent 17 years in the Canadian system of education. I had forced myself to read all the great European philosophers, and I thought I already understood the world-view. Yet, as I squirmed uncomfortably through each Property Law session, it dawned on me that although I had been exposed to these ideas before, they had never been laid before me so clearly and concretely – and boy, were they different from the way I had been raised to see the world!

I didn't know how to process any of this until, one day, I went to get a pint with a couple of classmates. It sounds like the beginning of a joke: "A Métis, a Liberal, and a Conservative walk into a bar...." Well, they actually were members of these political parties and were the first people I'd ever met who knew that much about Canadian politics. By now, I've mythologized these conversations because they had such a profound impact on me, but, at the time, it was just three people debating topics they'd learned in class.

This was an opportunity to sit down with people who were my friends and who had very clear yet different political beliefs from my own. We weren't out to prove each other wrong or "win" anything. We were trying to understand and be understood. We wanted to leave these conversations as friends. Our discussions about Indigenous issues were unlike anything I'd ever experienced before because they were *respectful*. There were times when emotions ran high because the issues we were discussing were challenging, and very personal. When you are talking about the relationship between Indigenous peoples and Canada, it is very difficult for the conversation not to get personal if you live on these lands. Nonetheless, despite the fact we had very deep political differences – and I mean Mariana Trench-sized differences – all three of us managed to really listen to what the others were saying, and to be truly heard in return. For me, these conversations were life changing and are the part of my legal education I value the most.

We did not come out of those conversations in full agreement – and in many situations we had to agree to disagree – but we did come out of them with a deeper understanding of one another's concerns and beliefs.

Those conversations are the reason this book exists. Each one of the pieces presented here is written as though you and I are sitting down together having a discussion. Obviously, the conversation is one-sided (as I am trying to present my point of view to you), but always, in the back of my mind, I am speaking to friends. Sometimes, I invoke the counterarguments or questions I was actually presented with or that I have had in subsequent conversations with others. They are not the only counterarguments or questions that are possible, but when I present them it is because I believe they are questions many people have on these topics. I am not trying to put words in your mouth, and I am certainly not trying to represent Liberal or Conservative viewpoints; I do not claim to understand the political ideologies involved well enough to do that. I am trying to make myself understood, and it is entirely up to you to evaluate this information as you will.

My writing will not always be received as polite – I warn you now. I am indeed impatient with certain claims, and I have been battling the same stereotypes for nearly two decades. This can wear on a person. Sometimes, I am going to be straight-out sarcastic and brusque. It is extremely important readers of this book remind themselves we probably do not know one another in real life – what I am saying, dismissing, or getting a little snarky about is not something personal to you, the reader. Instead, I am reacting to wider social beliefs. Basically, this is not about you as a person. It can't be, because, as I pointed out, we are strangers. If you start to get the eerie feeling that I am peering out from these pages and fixing you with an accusatory stare, go back and see if I've actually named you. From time to time, I *will* name names, so if yours is not there, you can relax. More significantly, if you need me to always be polite in order to read what I've written here, please ask yourself whether my tone is more important than learning about these issues. I do try my best to keep things light, but these topics are not easy ones, and I am genuinely trying to communicate with you.

The writings in this book are divided into five broad, interrelated themes: the terminology of relationships; culture and identity; myth-busting; state violence; and land, learning, law, and treaties. Each chapter is meant to stand on its own, and I have made it a priority to provide readers with as many additional resources as possible on each topic.

In fact, I worked as hard on the endnotes as I did on some of the chapters for three reasons: (1) I wanted to make sure to acknowledge my learning has been aided by many brilliant people, and this book would not have been possible without all they have thought about, tried, and shared. That I am able to articulate any of what is in this book is a result of my interaction with those minds. (2) I want you to be able to pull out a chapter you are interested in and have the full sources cited even if they refer to things mentioned in other chapters. (3) I want you to have a curated list of books and websites to explore as you wish. This book should only be the beginning of your exploration of these topics.

I want this book to spark further conversations in your home, in the classroom, and in community groups. Sometimes, emotions are going to run high; that is an inevitable part of these vital conversations. When we remind ourselves we are speaking to other human beings who have families, who face diverse challenges, and who have diverse aspirations for a better life, it becomes easier to process those emotions. What we cannot do is pretend the subject matter is anything but difficult. Sometimes, we will simply have to agree to disagree. At the end of the day, we are all still going to have to figure out how to relate to one another. We begin that process by understanding the fundamental issues.

PART 1
The Terminology of Relationships

1

Just Don't Call Us Late for Supper

Names for Indigenous Peoples

Any discussion needs a certain number of terms that can be understood by all participants; otherwise, communication ends up even messier than usual. I've read a lot of books about Indigenous peoples, and it seems every single one spends some time explaining which term the author will use in the rest of the text, and why he or she chose that particular term. I've tried avoiding that sort of thing when talking to people, but it absolutely always comes up.

I find it somewhat easier to start with a list of what you should definitely *not* be calling us – a little housecleaning of the mind, if you will. Surprisingly, there are a great number of people who still think the use of some of these terms is up for debate, but I would sincerely like to help you avoid unintentionally putting your foot in your mouth. So, between us, let's just agree the following words are never okay to call Indigenous peoples:

- savage
- red Indian
- redskin
- primitive
- half-breed
- squaw/brave/buck/papoose

This is not an exhaustive list, and there are plenty of other slurs we do not need to mention that are obviously unacceptable. I do not intend to spend any time discussing how the above terms might *not* be offensive, because engaging in a philosophical sidebar about whether words have inherent meaning tends to end in recitals of

Jabberwocky;[1] before you know it, you've wasted half the night trying to translate it into Cree, yet again. Or, so I've heard.

A lot of people who would like to talk about Indigenous issues honestly do not want to cause offence, and get very stressed out about the proper terms; so, it is in the interest of lowering those people's blood pressure that I'm now going to discuss various terms in use out there.

First, there is no across-the-board agreement on a term. The fact that all Indigenous peoples have not settled on one term really seems to bother some people. I would like those people to take a deep breath, and chill out. *It's okay.* Names are linked to identity, and notions of identity are fluid.

For example, did you have a cute nickname when you were a young child? I did. My parents called me "Goose Girl." Twenty-five or so years later, if my employer called me "Goose Girl," it would be awkward at best. There are terms of endearment that my friends and family call me that would sound very strange coming out of the mouth of someone I just met.

When meeting new people, we tend to err on the side of formality to avoid giving a poor first impression. So it is with identifiers for Indigenous peoples. Terms change; they evolve. What was a good term 20 years ago might be inappropriate now, or it has been worn out through constant repetition – like every hit song you used to love but can no longer stand to listen to. There is also an issue of terms becoming co-opted and changed by government, industry, or by pundits searching for new ways to take potshots at us. Sometimes, a term is abandoned because it has become so loaded that using it suggests tacit agreement to some bizarre external interpretation of who Indigenous peoples are.

Indigenous peoples are incredibly diverse; there are all sorts of internal arguments about which terms are best, what they actually mean, why people should reject this and that, and so on. What I'm okay with you calling *me* might really annoy someone else. If you were hoping this chapter was going to help you avoid that completely, I want to be upfront with the fact that you will leave disappointed. Be aware: no matter how safe you think a term is, someone somewhere might get upset if you call them that. No one can give you a magical pass so you never have to re-examine the terms you are using – not even your Native friend.

Be prepared to listen to what people have to say about the term you use, and to respect what they suggest you call them instead. This is surprisingly easy to do, and goes a very long way in keeping the dialogue useful. I mean, it would be a bit off to deliberately keep calling someone "Susie" when she's asked you to call her "Susan," right?

Here are some of the names in use:

- Indian
- NDN
- Aboriginal
- Indigenous
- Native
- First Nations
- Inuit
- Métis
- Native American (more in the United States than in Canada)
- the name of a particular nation (Cree, Ojibway, Chipewyan, and so on)
- the name of a particular nation in that nation's original language (nêhiyaw,[2] Anishinaabe, Dene sųłiné, and so on)

Notice that I always capitalize the various terms used to describe Indigenous peoples. This is deliberate; the terms are proper nouns and adjectives referring to specific groups. "To capitalize or not to capitalize" ends up being a heated debate at times, but I feel it is a measure of respect to always capitalize our names when writing in English. This is my rule of thumb: if I can swap out "Indigenous" with "Canadian" (which is always capitalized), then I use the big *I*. I also capitalize names for non-Indigenous peoples throughout this book.

The term *Indian* is probably the most contentious. There are a couple of theories about where the term originated,[3] but that's not the point. In Canada, *Indian* continues to have legal connotations, and there is still an *Indian Act*[4]; so you'll see it used officially, as well as colloquially. There is also a long history of this term being used pejoratively – two good reasons why it doesn't sit well with everyone.

However, it is also a term that is often used internally. Please note this does not mean it's always okay for others to use the term. I tend to suggest that avoiding this term is probably for the best, unless someone is specifically referencing the *Indian Act*. There is a level of sarcasm and challenge often associated with its internal use that is easy to miss, and most likely cannot be replicated. If you are interested in avoiding giving offence, this term is one you might want to drop from your vocabulary.

NDN is a term of more recent origin, in heavy use via social media. This shorthand term has no official meaning and is very informal. If you say it aloud it just sounds like *Indian*, so its use really only makes sense in text-based situations. NDN is more of a self-identifier than anything.

I know *Native American* is very popular in the U.S., and it is still in use as a way of self-identifying among some older people here in Canada. It's a weird thing to hear in our Canadian context, though; and *Native Canadian* is just silly.[5] *American Indian* is another term that is very rarely used in Canada outside of references to the American Indian Movement (AIM).

Aboriginal (never *aborigine*) is a term of fairly recent origin, being adopted officially in the *Constitution Act, 1982,* to refer generally to First Nations, Inuit, and Métis peoples.[6] It has become the most common official term used here in Canada. I now tend to use this term only within its legal context because, although it is not offensive per se, its use is incredibly generic and made increasingly obnoxious by overuse – once again, like a hit song you can no longer stand to hear. If you use this term, please try to remember it is not a proper noun. Do not, for example, refer to people as Aboriginals, but rather as Aboriginal peoples. Also, please avoid the possessive. Referring to Indigenous peoples as Canada's Aboriginals is likely to cause an embarrassed silence.

Indigenous tends to have international connotations, referring to Indigenous peoples throughout the world rather than being country-specific.[7] It can be both a legal and colloquial term; like *Aboriginal*, it includes First Nations, Inuit, and Métis peoples. At this moment, it is my favourite term to use and will be my go-to throughout this book. It is possible that in five years I will look back at my use of this term with shame, but future me can just hush because present me doesn't really have a better word. An added bonus is that it is almost impossible to accidentally use this term as a proper noun. *Indigenouses* doesn't exactly roll off the tongue, does it?

Throughout this book, I use the term *Indigenous* to refer specifically to First Nations, Métis, and Inuit living in what is now called Canada. By using it this way, I do not intend to deny indigeneity to those who are indigenous to other places in the world. When I say *non-Indigenous* in this book, I mean only "not-Indigenous-to-this-place-called-Canada."

You might also wonder why I keep saying Indigenous *peoples* instead of Indigenous *people*; after all, isn't *people* already plural? Many epic nonphysical battles were fought for the inclusion of that *s* on the end of people, and I'm going to honour the sweat and tears that put it there. It speaks to the incredible diversity of Indigenous peoples as hundreds of culturally and linguistically distinct groups, rather than one homogenous whole. It also speaks to the kind of pedantry I will not be successful in confining to this chapter – my apologies in advance.

Native is another tricky term. For some people it refers only to First Nations, and for others (myself included) it's another catchall term, but a much more informal one than *Aboriginal* or *Indigenous*. I don't want to suggest this is an internal term that can never be used by non-Indigenous peoples, but it does have some historically pejorative connotations that you may wish to avoid (e.g., *going native*). Many people also contest this use of the term because they want to employ it as well (e.g., native of Alberta, native to Canada). Many Indigenous peoples use the term and are okay with it, but it's a bit like *Indian* in that you are more likely to step on toes if you go throwing it around.

Now for some more specific, yet still quite general, terms. *First Nations* refers to that group of people officially known as Indians under the *Indian Act,* and does not include Inuit or Métis peoples. Because many First Nations people share similar issues – related to reserves, status, and so forth – it's a good general term for a very diverse group of Indigenous peoples.

Inuit has pretty well replaced *Eskimo* in regular parlance here in Canada, and using *Eskimo* here is probably going to get you dirty looks. *Eskimo* is still a term used in Alaska, however, because it includes both Iñupiat and Yupik peoples while Inuit does not. Thus, *Eskimo* did not make it onto my "never say this" list. Just make sure you're in Alaska when you're saying it.

Métis is a term that is not as common in the U.S. as it is in Canada, although there are absolutely Métis people there. In terms of official recognition, however, it is a uniquely Canadian name. There is a chapter in this book that delves into Métis identity in great detail; but, for now, just be aware the Métis are also an Indigenous people.

These are some of the terms being used right now, so pick your poison.

Notice I did not suggest the term *Canadian* at any point. This is a deliberate exclusion. Many Indigenous peoples do not identify as Canadian because, at no point, did they or their ancestors consent to becoming Canadian. The issue is much more complex than this, of course, but it is important to be aware of the situation. Some Indigenous peoples have no problem identifying as *Canadian,* so this is not an across-the-board rejection of the term; just something to think about.

If you want to move beyond general terms, and I definitely encourage that, the learning curve can be a bit steep at first. Over the years, various groups of Europeans used their own names for Indigenous peoples; sometimes, a single group of people can be known by two, or three, or more different names! If you aren't aware that a number of different terms refer to the same group of people, it can be incredibly difficult to sort out. If you were to sit down and make a list of all the different names every Indigenous group in Canada has been given by Europeans (sometimes based on bastardized versions of the names *other* Indigenous peoples called them), you would have a substantial and basically unusable document.

For example, the Algonquin are an Anishinaabe people related to the Odawa and Ojibwe. Over the years, they have been called Attenkins,[8] Algoumequins,[9] Alinconguins,[10] and at least a dozen other variations that are not immediately recognizable as referring to the same people. To muddy the waters even further, Indigenous peoples are sometimes grouped linguistically (according to languages). For example, the Algonquin are classed by linguists as being part of the Algonquian language group that includes about 30 languages, such as Blackfoot, Cree, and Mi'kmaq! Such a slight spelling difference, but beware these linguistic groupings because they collapse extremely different cultures into one linguistic category.

Then, you have names that sound similar but refer to very different peoples, like the Chipewyan (Dene sųłiné) and the Chippewa (another name for Ojibwe), which are two very distinct groups.

There are often multiple names in use. One person can call herself Assiniboine, Stoney, Nakota Sioux, Stone Sioux, Asinipwât, Nakoda or Nakota, and Îyârhe Nakoda – all names that have been used for the same group of people. In addition to the group name, people will also identify themselves by which community they come from; in this case, it could be the Alexis Nakota-Sioux Nation in Alberta. Many of our communities have undergone name changes, too; so, depending on what generation you are in, you may use different names for the same community!

The names are going to continue to change. Many Indigenous communities have discarded their European-language names for Indigenous place names. The eastern James Bay Cree communities in Quebec were each known by an English and a French name, and have officially renamed almost all of their communities in Cree. One community, now Whapmagoostui in Cree, is still known by many as Great Whale River or Poste-de-la-Baleine. There is a sizeable Inuit population there, as well, so the community is also named Kuujjuaraapik. You can see how this can quickly get confusing for people who are not familiar with the history of the area.

Do not despair! No one can be expected to know all of the different names for every single people and community across Canada. A really powerful and beautiful start would be to simply learn the names in use, both historic and contemporary, for the Indigenous peoples in the area where you live. Much as place names are changing (or reverting), the names we call ourselves are changing, as well, and the trend is to use the name we originally called ourselves in our languages. If you get confused, don't be scared to ask! You just might get an interesting history lesson of the area you are in, because names are so inextricably linked to that history.

I hope this helps. My intention is not to simplify the issue, but rather to make people more aware of how complex and, sometimes, confusing names can be. More important, we now have some terms we can work with as we explore these issues together.

NOTES

1. Douglas R. Hofstadter, *Gödel, Escher, Bach: An Eternal Golden Braid* (New York: Basic Books, 1980; New York: Vintage Books, 1980), http://www76.pair.com/keithlim/jabberwocky/poem/hofstadter.html. I could spend hours discussing how a successful translation of Lewis Carroll's nonsense poem, *Jabberwocky*, into an Indigenous language would herald a kind of linguistic health I aspire to. On the difficulties of translating this poem into other languages, see Hofstadter.

2. I will not be capitalizing Cree words throughout this book. I used a standardized written Cree and, within this system, words are never capitalized. Although this book is in English, I want to respect nêhiyawêwin conventions as much as possible.

3. Straight Dope Science Advisory Board, "The Straight Dope: Does 'Indian' Derive from Columbus's Description of Native Americans as 'una Gente in Dios'?" *The Straight Dope,* last modified October 25, 2001, accessed December 2, 2013, http://www.straightdope.com/columns/read/1966/does-indian-derive-from-columbuss-description-of-native-americans-as-una-gente-in-dios. Here, you will find a great discussion of the various possible origins of the term *Indian.*

4. *Indian Act*, RSC. 1985, c.I-5.

5. Robert Sawyer, *Hominids* (New York: Tor, 2003). I think Robert Sawyer uses the term *Native Canadians* in all his books because it is more familiar to his readers in the United States than First Nations would be. Don't worry, Robert, I'm still a fan!

6. *Constitution Act, 1982*, schedule B of *Canada Act, 1982* (UK), c 11, s 35.

7. United Nations, *United Nations Declaration on the Rights of Indigenous Peoples: Resolution Adopted by the General Assembly*, October 2, 2007, A/RES/61/295, accessed December 1, 2012, http://www.refworld.org/docid/471355a82.html.

8. Clinton, Vol. 6 in *New York Documents of Colonial History* (1855), 276.

9. Samuel de Champlain, chap. 2 in *Oeuvres* (1870), 8.

10. Nicolls, Vol. 2 in *New York Documents of Colonial History* (1853), 147.

2

Settling on a Name
Names for Non-Indigenous Canadians

This book is very much about relationships – historical, contemporary, and future relationships. Unfortunately, the historical and contemporary relationships between Indigenous peoples and non-Indigenous peoples in Canada have, at times, been very strained. In order to form healthier and more positive relationships into the future, there needs to be dialogue between all peoples living on these lands.

Dialogue requires terminology we can use to name one another, so we can recognize how certain events impacted/impact us differently, as well as what we have in common as diverse peoples. The previous chapter was all about the multitude of terms and names that are used to speak about Indigenous peoples. Those terms shift and change over time, and will continue to do so, but it seems obvious having a vocabulary we can use is absolutely necessary if we wish to have a discussion about Indigenous issues.

There are terms to choose from when speaking of the wide range of non-European peoples who have immigrated to Canada over successive generations; terms that have official status, as well as terms preferred by these communities themselves. Terms related to identity among non-European populations have shifted and changed with time and also require checking to find out which terms are acceptable right now.[1]

There are really no sanctioned and widely accepted terms with which to refer to "the non-Indigenous peoples living in Canada who form the European-descended sociopolitical majority" in a generalized sense comparable to the term *Indigenous peoples* or any of the generalized labels for other non-Indigenous peoples. In great part, this is due to the fact that the majority tends to have the power to sanction and widely accept terms, and does not really have much cause to refer to itself.

When I cast about for a term to use to refer to "the non-Indigenous peoples living in Canada who form the European-descended sociopolitical majority," I do so because it makes no sense to ignore the fact that these peoples exist. Naming these peoples is just as important as naming Indigenous peoples if we are going to talk about how the past informs the present.

Can you sense my hesitancy here to pick a name? Perhaps this will help to clarify why that hesitation exists; take a gander at some of the terms that do get used to name "the non-Indigenous peoples living in Canada who form the European-descended sociopolitical majority":

- White
- non-Native, non-Aboriginal, non-Indigenous
- European
- settler, settler colonials

First off, there aren't many terms to choose from, and the second bullet lists terms that are based entirely on a "not-this" dichotomy, which almost always rubs people the wrong way as they are inherently exclusionary.

It is fairly easy to come up with reasons why all of these terms fail to be properly descriptive and shouldn't be used. I once had someone explain it to me like this: she said, "When I try to find a word to refer to you with, I'm just naming you. When you call me White, or a non-Native settler, you're blaming me for something I didn't do. Right away we're at odds."

I get that. I really do. However, I'm not actually trying to put us at odds, and using a term is not inherently about blame. What I'm trying to do is talk about us in a wider context than the first person and second person singular. We all need terms to use, or we cannot have a discussion. Terms are what I'm looking for, not offensive labels.

Unfortunately, when I ask for terms preferred by "the non-Indigenous peoples living in Canada who form the European-descended sociopolitical majority," I almost always receive names that blend these peoples in with everyone else. Now, that is perfectly fine in many situations, but when specificity is required, it is unhelpful.

For example, I've been asked to just say "Canadian," but Canadian is a category of citizenship and is so general as to be useless when we're trying to understand the history of this country. Canadian as a national identity did not exist until hundreds of years after contact. While this term works for contemporary discussions of all non-Indigenous peoples living in Canada, it does not help us discuss the particular situation of those who are descended from the original European settlers here.[2] While some people do argue that people living today have no connection to those first

Europeans in the 15th and 16th centuries, we cannot escape our history so easily. The social and political systems that currently exist in Canada are a direct result of the European-based cultures that first arrived in the Americas all those centuries ago.

Some people do prefer *non-Native, non-Aboriginal,* or *non-Indigenous,* but again these terms include everyone who is not-us. This can be useful when centring the conversation on Indigenous peoples, and these terms will show up at times throughout this book. However, sometimes we need to talk about our history and our present in ways that highlight how the differences between the many groups of peoples living in Canada have actual impacts on our lives. I mean, really, having that discussion is the whole reason I've written this book. I want to find some common ground, but not by pretending our differences are irrelevant.

For the most part, when I do need to refer specifically to "the non-Indigenous peoples living in Canada who form the European-descended sociopolitical majority," I've decided on the term *settler.* I feel it is the most accurate relational term and helps to keep the conversation more focused than the term *White.*

The history of the category of White is a powerful and complex one, and although it is still very much officially recognized,[3] it seems to invite more argument than any other term. I do not agree that *White* is a pejorative term or that it can be equated with racist terms for other groups because, frankly, there is no history of systemic oppression that has been enforced against people included in the category of White in Canadian history. However, give and take is needed. In the last chapter, I asked us to agree not to use certain terms. In my experience, the term *White* bothers many people, so, in the spirit of give and take, I will use a different term as much as possible. This is not an attempt to avoid naming Whiteness as a system of power and privilege; I will still be speaking to that very much as we go.

I pointed out that I feel *settler* is a relational term, rather than a racial category, which is another way in which it is more useful. Since I have chosen this term, I suppose I do need to explain what it means, or at least what I am using it to mean. For me, it is a shortened version of *settler colonials.* Settler colonialism is a concept that has recently begun to be explored in-depth,[4] and it essentially refers to the deliberate physical occupation of land as a method of asserting ownership over land and resources.[5] The original settlers were of various European origins, and they brought with them their laws and customs, which they then applied to Indigenous peoples and later to all peoples who have come to Canada from non-settler backgrounds. This does not refer only to those European people with sociopolitical power, but also to those of lower classes who settled here to seek economic opportunity.

The term *settler* has also been used to refer to people who continue to move to Canada and settle here. This is often done to highlight the fact that settlement, as a facet of colonialism, continues. In that way, it is a useful term, but it also obscures the way in which colonialism outside of Canada has created conditions that have given many peoples little choice but to seek homes elsewhere – including in Canada. Like European-descended peoples of the lower classes, who were more pawns than power-brokers in the early years of colonization in Canada and the United States, non-European peoples displaced by colonization in their own lands are folded into the settlement process when they arrive here – even as they are often denied equal social privileges. However, non-European migrants do not have the power to bring with them their laws and customs, which they then apply to the rest of the peoples living in Canada – no matter what some alarmists like to claim. The dominant sociopolitical structures in place remain European in origin and, as Indigenous peoples are well aware, they are not so easy to change.

While a strong argument can be made that non-European-descended peoples who come to live in Canada are also settlers, I am going to eschew the term here in favour of *non-Black people of colour*. This term will not be completely satisfactory either, because some non-European peoples are also able to access Whiteness, but it is a heck of a lot better than the term *newcomers*, which completely erases the history of communities that have existed in Canada for hundreds of years.

I want to be very clear that the term *settler* does not, and can never, refer to the descendants of Africans who were kidnapped and sold into chattel slavery.[6] Black people, removed and cut off from their own indigenous lands – literally stripped of their humanity and redefined legally as property – could not be agents of settlement. The fact that slavery has been abolished does not change this history. Although Black people are not all indigenous to the Americas, the Americas are home to the descendants of enslaved African peoples.[7]

We are left with three broad, unsatisfactory, but possibly usable categories: settlers (the non-Indigenous peoples living in Canada who form the European-descended sociopolitical majority), non-Black persons of colour (hereafter, non-Black POC), and Black people. These categories will be used when necessary to point out the different ways in which peoples experience power and/or oppression in Canada. When I am referring to all peoples who are non-Indigenous to the Americas, of any background living in these lands today, I will use the term *Canadians*. However, the fact that this book focuses most of its attention on colonial structures of power means we don't get to explore Indigenous/Black/non-Black POC relationships in great detail.

If this is boring the pants off you, please put them back on if you are reading this in public, and be comforted by the fact that this conversation is going to get more interesting soon. I promise. I just want to make one more point before moving on to more excellent discussions.

Frank Wilderson III points out that it is too simplistic to think of oppression in binaries: settler versus Indigenous, settler versus Black, or settler versus everyone else.[8] The complexities involved become more obvious when one considers that Indigenous is not really a racial category; there are many mixed-race Indians.

These oppressions can overlap, and this is important to understand in the context of settler colonialism. Just as it is true that Indigenous peoples can participate in anti-Black racism, and reinforce oppressive structures based on that racism, it is also true that other non-Indigenous peoples can buy into and reinforce settler colonialism by supporting the occupation of land and exploitation of resources as a method to achieving greater civil and social equality. Reinforcing anti-Black racism or settler colonialism does not undo the marginalization faced in other aspects of life, but the complexity of the relationships between all peoples living here is something we cannot lose sight of.

The point is it's messy, complicated, and I'm not going to solve it in this chapter; all I want is to highlight the fact that just as terms are needed to refer to Indigenous peoples, terms are also needed to refer to settlers. I'm not trying to be a jerk here; I just can't keep using really long descriptive sentences to dance around calling people "settlers." I do have a lot to say about power, names, and who gets to decide who is called what, but to be honest, even I'm bored at this point. The only reason I brought up this unsatisfying conversation was to reiterate what I said in the Introduction. I am not trying to be deliberately provocative, and I mean no disrespect when I use the term *settler*. I cannot prove this to be true, so it has to be taken on faith, and read in that light.

I decided I wanted to round this section out with something much more interesting: terms Indigenous peoples have in their own languages for non-Indigenous peoples!

Not all Indigenous peoples have names for Black and non-Black POC. It seems to depend on how much contact there was between these groups before serious language decline began. Some of the names that do exist replicate 19th-century racial essentialism, referring to skin colour (such as the Cree word *kaskitêwiyâs* or the Lakota term *hásapa*, both of which mean "black flesh/skin"). In Otoe, the word for Black person is *wą'shithewe*, which literally translates as "black person."[9] In Hupa, the term is *mining'-ɫiwhin*, which means "black faces."

In the eastern Arctic, Inuit describe Black people as "portagee" or "portugee," which one linguist believes is a variation of *Portuguese,* so used because of contact between Inuit and whalers from Cape Verde.[10] Other names are more traditionally descriptive, referring to observed characteristics. Where I am from in Alberta, a Chinese person is called "sêkipatwâw," which means "s/he has braids." This gives you a fairly good idea of when this name began to be applied to describe the appearance of early male Chinese migrants.[11] Another name is *apihkês,* which actually means "spider." I have been told this refers to weaving skill. Southeast Asians are sometimes referred to as "nêhiyahkân," which means "Cree-like" or "almost Cree."

Indigenous languages, like all living languages, are capable of growth and change. Radmilla Cody is Black and Indigenous, and a former Miss Navajo Nation winner.[12] The Diné (Navajo) word for a Black person is *Nakai ʔizhinii,* which like previous terms listed here, basically just translates to "black." Radmilla has often discussed how this name was used to tease her when she was growing up.[13] She sought out a fluent speaker to find a name for Black people that would be more respectful. That speaker used the word *Naahilii/Nahilii,* and its meaning is broken down like this: "Na(a) – Those who have come across; hil – dark, calm, have overcome, persevered, and we have come to like; ii – oneness."[14]

Some might question why another word is needed, if one already exists. As Jihan Gearon puts it:

> Think about this: A young Black and Navajo girl or boy has been teased with the word *Nakai ʔizhini.* It makes them feel bad when they hear it. Still, when they introduce themselves in Navajo, they have to use that very word to describe themselves. I don't think its a stretch to worry about that little girl or boy's self image. Furthermore, while our other clans have histories and stories and songs and characteristics and responsibilities associated with them, this word identifies us as a color only.[15]

In contrast, every Indigenous person has a name, and sometimes a few different names, for settlers. After all, contact with European-descended peoples is something we have all experienced. These names tend to be descriptive of some trait or characteristic witnessed by Indigenous peoples back around contact. Sometimes, people can't really remember the actual etymology of the word, or have created a folk etymology that makes sense now and is widely understood as its origin, but may not be. Sometimes, an already existing word from a language used by Europeans has been Creecized or Anishinaabecized.

I recently did a roundup on Twitter asking for Indigenous names for settlers. Many of these words I had heard before, but hadn't heard all their understood meanings before. Any misunderstanding of what was shared with me is my own; I apologize if I have made any mistakes with spelling or translation. I obviously do not speak all of these languages, and this is all anecdotal.

I'll start with one of my traditional languages, which is Plains Cree (nêhiyawêwin). On the Plains, we often call settlers "môniyaw." The origin of this term is hotly contested. Some believe it is a Creecization of the French pronunciation of Montreal, where so many Europeans were travelling from. Others believe it is a way of saying "not me" or "not Cree" in our language. These are not the only theories. I am not going to pretend to have the authority to claim any theory above another.

The Cree on the Plains also use the word *wêmistikosiw* to refer to French people specifically, and it describes the big wooden boats they came on. The Cree farther east often use this term for all settlers – French or not.

Where I'm from, people from the United States are generally called "kihci-môhkomân," which means "great knives" and refers to the sabres that soldiers used to wear. It probably would have been a name for the British originally, and some Cree might still use it that way.

Our cousins, the Anishinaabe, have a language very related to Cree and have words similar to the ones above. One of the most common terms I've seen them use though is *Zhaaganaash*. It has been explained to me that this word refers to people of dubious character, while another explanation I've seen is that it has the same root as an Anishinaabemowin word meaning "to put something outside"; so it means "outsider," without any negative shading.

Interestingly enough, some Cree people use the word *sâkênâs,* which, despite the different spelling, sounds very similar to *Zhaaganaash* when spoken. It also does not have the nicest connotation. A number of times I have heard people say that this word originally comes from *sassenach* in Gaelic (possibly Scottish Gaelic brought over by Orcadians). It is said that this word may have been a name for the Saxon, and was later applied to the English, developing an unsavoury connotation.

Jumping to the West Coast, I was told the Nl'kapamux, who are part of the Interior Salish, say "sheme," which is the colour of a drowned person. The Halq'eméylem (Stó:lō) say "xwelitem," which means "hungry people," while the Sechelt use a similar word, *xwa'lat'en,* to refer to White people. Again, I cannot be sure of the true etymology of these words, only what people believe them to mean.

The Mohawk say "ose'ronni," which I've seen translated as just "other people" who are non-Indigenous, but also as "delicate white flower people."

I was told that among the Inuit of Ikaluktutiak (Cambridge Bay) *kapluunak* or *kabloonak* is used to mean "bushy eyebrows," but I am very uncertain of the correct spelling. In Nunavut and Nunavik (northern Quebec), the word *qallunaat* is generally used to refer to non-Inuit. Sheila Watt-Cloutier explains that this term is derived from *qallunaq*, and that it "describes the bones on which the eyebrows sit, which protrude more on white people than on Inuit."[16]

In Nimiipuutimpt (Nez Pierce), settlers are called "soyapos," which was translated to mean "the crowned ones" because of the hats they wore.

The Blackfoot have a trickster character named "Napi," and I was told that because he was a bit wild and unpredictable, settlers became known as "napikwan."

The Lakota called cavalry soldiers "míla hanska," which means "long knives." This seems like a pretty common description among Indigenous peoples! Another term is *wašicu*, often translated as "takes all the fat" or greedy, and has variations of use among the Lakota/Dakota/Nakota.

Of course, this is only a *tiny* slice of the many terms for Black, non-Black POC, and settlers, both neutral and not-so-neutral, that exist in our languages. If none of the English terms I listed above are suitable to you, I would certainly invite you to find out whose Indigenous territory you live in, in order to identify a word in their language that feels more appropriate. As well, it is always good to remember our languages are not frozen in time, and new terms can be created.

Although this entire section is focused on terminology, I have no desire to get overly hung up on specific words, because there are much more interesting topics to explore. So, let's get to it!

NOTES

1. To reiterate what I said in chapter 1, when I use the term *non-Indigenous* in this book, I mean people who are not Indigenous to what is now called Canada. I think it is incredibly important to recognize that many people currently living in Canada are Indigenous to other areas.

2. Many Indigenous peoples do not consider themselves Canadians for reasons that will be described in fuller detail later on in this book. While some have no problem with the term, it is best not to assume that *Canadian* can apply to every person living in this country.

3. Government of Canada. Census (2006), http://www23.statcan.gc.ca/imdb-bmdi/pub/instrument/3901_Q2_V3-eng.pdf. The 2006 long-form census, for example, allowed participants to identify as: White, Chinese, South Asian, Black, Filipino, Latin American, Southeast Asian, Arab, West Asian, Korean, Japanese, Aboriginal, or other.

4. If you are interested in exploring academic discussions of settler colonialism, you should check out the journal *Settler Colonial Studies*: http://www.tandfonline.com/loi/rset20.

5. Eve Tuck, and K. Wayne Yang, "Decolonization Is Not a Metaphor," *Decolonization: Indigeneity, Education and Society* 1, no. 1 (2012): 4–7, http://decolonization.org/index.php/des/article/view/18630.

6. Tiffany Jeannette King, "In the Clearing: Black Female Bodies, Space and Settler Colonialism" (PhD diss., University of Maryland, 2013), http://drum.lib.umd.edu/bitstream/handle/

1903/14525/King_umd_0117E_14499.pdf;jsessionid=F60781D31F860A28832010DD5D
67A9D3?sequence=1. I freely admit I did not understand this distinction until fairly
recently, though it now seems obvious. For more in-depth exploration of the relationship
between slavery and colonialism, and the way in which Black people are impacted by settler
colonialism, consult the source above.

7. What it means for the Americas to be the home of the descendants of enslaved Africans is
not something that has been very well articulated within Native Studies yet. It is something
that will hopefully receive more attention academically, as well as on the ground, through
strengthening Black and Indigenous relationships. Here is a piece that addresses this:
Eve Tuck, Allison Guess, and Hannah Sultan, "Not Nowhere: Collaborating on Selfsame
Land," *Decolonization: Indigeneity, Education and Society* (2014): https://decolonization.files.
wordpress.com/2014/06/notnowhere-pdf.pdf.

For more information on Black Indians, chattel slavery among some Native American peoples,
as well as successful Indigenous/Black resistance to slavery: Arica L. Coleman, *That the Blood
Stay Pure: African Americans, Native Americans and the Predicament of Race and Identity in
Virginia* (Bloomington: Indiana University Press, 2013); William Loren Katz, *Black Indians:
A Hidden Heritage* (New York: Atheneum, 1986); Barbara Krauthamer, *Black Slaves, Indian
Masters: Slavery, Emancipation and Citizenship in the Native American South* (Chapel Hill:
University of North Carolina Press, 2013); Clifford A. Weslager, *Delaware's Forgotten Folk:
The Story of the Moors and Nanticokes* (Philadelphia: University of Pennsylvania Press, 2006);
J. B. Bird, "Rebellion: John Horse and Black Seminoles, the First Black Rebels to Beat
American Slavery," http://johnhorse.com/; Paul Gilory, *The Black Atlantic: Modernity and
Double-Consciousness* (Cambridge: Harvard University Press, 1995).

8. Frank Wilderson III, *Red, White and Black: Cinema and Structures of US Antagonisms*
(Durhman: Duke University Press, 2010).

9. This translation was shared with me by Johnnie Jae, cofounder of A Tribe Called Geek,
described as "Indigenerdity for the Geeks at the Powwow." You should check out their work!
http://atribecalledgeek.com/.

10. Kenn Harper, "Portagee: The Inuktitut Word for Black Person," http://www.nunatsiaqonline.
ca/stories/article/65674taissumani_feb._1.

11. "Chinese-Canadians and First Nations: 150 Years of Shared Experiences," http://www.chinese-
firstnations-relations.ca/bibliography.html. Here, you will find an excellent bibliography of
resources on Chinese-First Nations relationships, particularly in British Columbia.

12. "Black, Red and Proud," http://www.theroot.com/articles/culture/2011/02/black_and_native_
american_an_interview_with_radmilla_cody.1.html. This is an interview with Radmilla Cody
describing the backlash she experienced as a Black and Indigenous person, when she ran for
Miss Navajo Nation.

13. "Offerings to the Holy People: Former Miss Navajo Radmilla Cody takes speaking tour to
Berkeley," http://navajotimes.com/entertainment/2012/0312/032312rad.php.

14. "Radmilla Cody: biography," http://radmillacody.net/biography.html.

15. "Black History Month in Indian Country," http://lastrealindians.com/black-history-month-
in-indian-country/.

16. Sheila Watt-Cloutier, *The Right to Be Cold: One Woman's Story of Protecting Her Culture, the
Arctic and the Whole Planet* (Toronto: Penguin, 2015), 4.

PART 2
Culture and Identity

3

Got Status?

Indian Status in Canada

If, like most people in Canada, you have no idea how Indian status works, don't feel too bad. The system of deciding who does and who does not have status is as deliberately convoluted and confusing as any system out there. To hear some tell the tale, a status card is a magical relic bestowing upon the bearer: tax exemptions, free gas,[1] new trucks, houses, and pretty much anything else under the sun dreamed up during a particular flight of fancy. Many people believe anyone identifying or identified as Aboriginal automatically receives a status card. As status is linked to supposed benefits received by Indigenous peoples, it is important to clarify what it actually is.

To begin, let's define what status *isn't*. Indian status is not a system created or enforced by Indigenous peoples themselves. Indian status is *not* the same as Indigenous identity. It is an administrative category created and applied by the federal government of Canada. Indigenous peoples have no control over how Indian status is defined legally. At best, Indigenous peoples have been able to battle the federal government in Canadian courts to force small changes to the way status is defined.

There are some terms that need exploring in order to untangle what status is, and what it is not, as well as clarifying other categories you may come across. Some of these were looked at in the first section on terminology, but some will be new. These are the terms you'll find in this chapter:

- Indigenous
- Aboriginal
- status Indian
- registered Indian
- non-status Indian
- Métis

- Inuit
- First Nations
- Bill C-31 Indians
- Bill C-3 Indians
- band membership
- treaty Indians

Obviously, I want to focus specifically on the Canadian context. Since I'm trying to clarify the terms used, in this chapter I'm going to avoid using them interchangeably even though I tend to do this elsewhere. When speaking generally, I will use the term *Indigenous* or *Native*. When referring to specific legal definitions, I will use the legislated terms. This chapter focuses mainly on status, and does not delve into definitions of Inuit or Métis.

Status versus membership

Status is a legal definition used to refer to First Nations who are under federal jurisdiction and the *Indian Act*. Federal jurisdiction over "Indians, and Lands reserved for the Indians" was set up in our first Constitution, the *Constitution Act, 1867*, in section 91(24).[2] This division of powers between federal and provincial/territorial governments is a hugely important detail that will be a constant refrain throughout this book; I'd like you to always keep it in mind in these discussions.

The particular piece of federal legislation that defines status is the *Indian Act*,[3] which was created in 1876 and has been updated many times since then. Status can be held only by those Indigenous peoples who fit the definition laid out in the *Indian Act*.

Membership is a much more complex issue. It can refer to a set of rules (traditional or not) created by an Indigenous community that defines who is a member of that community. It can refer to rules under the *Indian Act* that define who is a member of a community to which the *Indian Act* applies. It can also refer to those who are considered members of certain regional or national Indigenous organizations. It can also be used in a much less formal and subjective sense, such as being part of an urban or rural Native group. So, unlike status, membership can refer to any number of things.

Obviously, these definitions will overlap at times. The most important thing to note is that having membership is not the same as having status. For example, I am a member of the Métis Nation of Alberta. I am not a status Indian.

Who is Aboriginal?

The term *Aboriginal* came into legal existence in 1982 when it was defined in section 35 of the *Constitution Act, 1982*.[4] Section 35(2) defines Aboriginal peoples as including "the Indian, Inuit and Métis peoples of Canada." It is a general, catchall term that has gained legal status in Canada and, therefore, is particular to the Canadian context.

The *Constitution Act, 1982*, does not *define* Indian, Inuit, or Métis. The definitions have been fleshed out in other pieces of legislation, in court decisions, and in policy manuals, and have changed significantly over the years. Thus, you will see these terms used in different ways depending on how old your sources are, or what period of time is being discussed, and so on, adding to the general confusion about the meaning of these categories.

The first thing to understand is that being an Aboriginal person does not mean one has legal status; status is held only by Indians as defined in the *Indian Act*.

Status Indians and registered Indians

Status Indians are persons who, under the *Indian Act,* are registered or are entitled to be registered as Indians. For this reason, status Indians are also sometimes referred to as "registered Indians," and these terms are interchangeable. It may seem a bit redundant that an Indian is someone who is entitled to be an Indian, but let this highlight the artificial nature of the category itself. The Canadian government basically takes the position that, "you're an Indian if we *say* you're an Indian." If this seems like a vague definition, I'd like to stress that it is not. In fact, the definition of who is a status Indian is incredibly detailed, which tends to make understanding it even more difficult.[5] Adding to the confusion, the definitions have been changed many times over the years.[6]

Not all status Indians are actually Indigenous (more on that in a bit), and there are many Indigenous peoples who do not have status. Status Indians are not the *only* Indians (First Nations) that exist. Non-status Indians are those who, through various pieces of legislation, lost their status, or were never eligible for status because their parents or grandparents lost status. Non-status Indians are still Indigenous; lack of status does not change this.

All registered Indians have their names on the Indian roll, which is administered by Indian Affairs.[7] Yes, the Indian roll is an actual list of names, less reminiscent of Santa Claus and more evocative of a legion of bored Indian Affairs clerks with quills. This department administers programs and services that apply only to status Indians.

Of the estimated 1.4 million Aboriginal peoples in Canada in 2011, roughly 637 660 are status Indians, which represents 1.9 percent of the total population of Canada. Non-status Indians account for 25 percent of all First Nations peoples, and status Indians represent only about 45 percent of all Aboriginal peoples in Canada.[8]

It is important to clarify again that the *Indian Act* does not apply to Indigenous peoples who are not status Indians. Despite a 1939 Supreme Court ruling that Inuit are "Indians," this only meant the Inuit are a federal concern under s. 91(24) of the *Constitution Act, 1867,* not that they are considered status Indians.[9] In 2016, in *Daniels v. Canada,* the Supreme Court found that Métis and non-status Indians are *also* Indians as per section 91(24).[10] This is an issue of determining whether responsibility for Métis and non-status Indians falls to the federal or provincial/territorial governments. The Daniels decision does not create more status Indians, and it is unclear yet how such a ruling will impact Métis and non-status Indians.

Bill C-31 and status

There were various federal policies over the years that caused status Indians to be removed from the Indian roll. Some lost status when they earned a university degree, joined the armed forces or the priesthood, gained fee-simple title of land, or married a non-Indian (this last one applied only to women). One minute you were legally an Indian, and the next you weren't. Magic! This process was rather cruelly labelled "enfranchisement," a term usually positive in nature. For non-Indigenous peoples, enfranchisement was often viewed as victory over exclusion, the recognition of full rights of citizenship, including the ability to vote. For Indigenous peoples, enfranchisement was the often nonconsensual process through which federal recognition of Indians was withdrawn. With that withdrawal of recognition came an end to constitutional responsibility. Enfranchisement was a concrete way to assimilate Indigenous peoples out of legislative existence, extinguish their rights, and solidify colonial control over lands and resources.

Bill C-31[11] was passed in 1985 as an amendment to the *Indian Act* and was intended to bring the *Indian Act* into line with gender-equality provisions under the Charter of Rights and Freedoms, as well as end the process of enfranchisement.[12] In particular, the Bill was supposed to reverse sexual discrimination that had caused Indian women who married non-Indians to lose their status, while men who married non-Indian women not only kept their status but also passed status on to their non-Indian wives.

Read that over if you need to. For 116 years, under the old provisions of the *Indian Act,* Indigenous women and their children were specifically targeted for loss of status while non-Native women could become registered Indians! All based on who they married. Today, there are over 26 000 non-Native women who have status gained through marriage to a status Indian man before 1985.[13] They did not lose this legal status with the *Indian Act* amendment, but the ability to "become Indian" via marriage ended.

Bill C-31 added new categories to the *Indian Act,* defining who is a status Indian, and who will be a status Indian in the future. Enfranchisement was traded in for a process that continues to legislate Indians out of legal existence.

The current legislation does not specifically refer to any sort of blood quantum; therefore, there is no official policy that would take into account half or quarter Indian ancestry. Nonetheless, ancestry continues to be a determining factor in who is a status Indian.

Section 6 of the *Indian Act* identifies two categories of status Indians, called 6(1) and 6(2) Indians. Both categories provide full status; there is no such thing as half status – it's all or nothing. The categories determine whether the children of a status Indian will have status or not.

This might be a good time to get a coffee, because this next bit is always confusing for people.

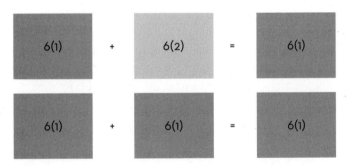

FIGURE 3.1. A 6(1) Indian who marries a 6(1) or a 6(2) Indian will have 6(1) children. Everyone in this equation is a full-status Indian.

FIGURE 3.2. If two 6(2) Indians marry, their children will have 6(1) status.

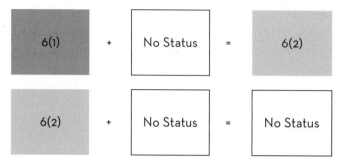

FIGURE 3.3. A 6(1) Indian who marries anyone without status (whether that person is Aboriginal or not) will have children who have 6(2) status. A 6(2) Indian who marries anyone without status (whether that person is Aboriginal or not) will have children with no legal Indian status.

Look at this again. Two generations of out-marriage. That is all it takes to completely lose status. It does not matter if you raise your grandchildren in your Native culture. It does not matter if they speak your language and know your customs. If you married someone without status, and your grandchildren have a non-status parent, your grandchildren are no longer considered Indian; not legally.

To be honest, it is amazing there are any status Indians left in this country.

Bill C-31: Way to not fix sexism!

One of the most criticized aspects of Bill C-31 was that it did not actually reverse the sexism inherent in denying women status if they married a non-status man.

Women who had their Indian status reinstated under Bill C-31 had 6(1) status, but their children were given 6(2) status. They would not pass status onto their children unless they married another status Indian. That makes sense according to the charts above, right?

The problem is that Indian men who married non-Indian women actually passed on Indian status to their previously non-status wives. Thus, the children of those unions have 6(1) status, and can pass status onto *their* children. The children of Bill C-31 children were still being penalized based on the gender of their parent who had status stripped and then reinstated.

Sharon McIvor and Bill C-3: Gender equity in *Indian Registration Act*

Sharon McIvor launched an epic court battle to address the problems with Bill C-31 and the *Indian Act*.[14] In response, a Bill was introduced to Parliament for First Reading in March 2010. The full title of this Bill is: *An Act to promote gender equity in Indian registration by responding to the Court of Appeal for British Columbia decision in McIvor v. Canada (Registrar of Indian and Northern Affairs).*[15]

Bill C-3 was given Royal Assent on 15 December 2010 and came into force (became law) on 31 January 2011. A great many grandchildren of women who regained status under Bill C-31 (but who passed on only 6(2) status to their children) can now regain their 6(2) status if they choose to, and are willing to, go through the confusing process of applying for it.

Band membership

There are a number of sub-categories that can apply to status Indians. One of these categories is band membership. No, not *that* kind of band.[16] In anthropology, a band is:

> …a small group of related people, who are primarily organized through family bonds. Foraging typifies the subsistence technology. A respected and older person may be looked to for leadership, but the person has no formalized authority.[17]

It is impossible to ignore the anthropological (and patronizing) connotations to the use of this term for First Nations communities, but we'll get to that later on. Suffice it to say, the anthropological definition isn't that helpful.

Legally, in Canada, a band is defined as a group of Indians for whom land has been set aside (a reserve), or who have been declared a band by the Governor General (no reserve).[18] A band might have a number of reserves, but can also have no land reserved at all.[19] Think of a band as the people themselves.

Some status Indians have membership in a band, and some do not. Again, it is important to note this is an administrative category created by the federal government, not traditional groupings of Indigenous peoples. The colonial government did not just come in and document what already existed. In fact, in some cases, bands were created with no thought to traditional groupings at all, and people from different First Nations were thrown together and renamed homogeneously with no regard for how this impacted kinship ties.

Before Bill C-31, having Indian status automatically gave you band membership entitling you to the rights and benefits as a member. Bill C-31 gave bands the ability to stay under the *Indian Act* band membership rules (which conferred automatic membership along with status), or bands could choose to make their own rules regarding membership. The latter included deciding who would be entitled to rights and benefits as members.

With one hand, the federal government was offering the reinstatement of status to women (and their children) who had been denied it due to the sexist provisions of the *Indian Act*. With the other hand, bands were being offered the ability to create new membership rules, denying membership to those who had their status reinstated, or restricting what rights and benefits they would receive if they did become members. In some cases, women who finally had their status restored, and who wished to return to their home communities, were turned away by newly minted membership codes that kept them out.

This was not an easy choice for First Nations communities. There was no guarantee from the federal government that funding would be increased to account for reinstated members who wanted to return to the community. Already, communities were grappling with shortages of resources, land, housing, infrastructure, and services. The idea of dozens, even hundreds, of people returning to dip into the depleted funding pot was daunting. Whether the federal government intended to create this conflict or not through uncertainty, the conflict existed and had immediate impacts.

Thus, you can have status Indians who have no band membership, just as you can have non-status Indians who do have band membership. Being a status Indian is no longer a guarantee you will be a member of a band.

Bill C-3 Indians face the same problems as Bill C-31 Indians did. Having status does not necessarily mean they will be able to live on-reserve or get band membership. The pros and cons of this are hotly debated, so I'm going to back away slowly and not touch that, except to point out there were no and are no adequate plans to make federal funding responsive to the influx of those with newly acquired status under either Bill.

Reserves

Related to band membership, another subcategory is between reserve and non-reserve Indians. This does not refer to whether one actually *lives* on the reserve, but rather describes whether an Indian is affiliated with a reserve. These are people who have access to a reserve and the right to live there if they choose.

To confuse the matter (as usual), this is not always the way on- and off-reserve Indians are counted. Sometimes the count only factors in where someone actually lives, rather than whether they are affiliated with a reserve or not. So, keep that in mind when looking at statistics. Depending on how those statistics address this issue, the numbers will vary.

Even though no historic treaties were signed in British Columbia, there are many reserves, while in the Northwest Territories, which is covered by a Numbered Treaty, there are no reserves. I also pointed out above that you can have membership in a band that doesn't have a reserve at all.

As in other situations, being a status Indian does not guarantee you access to a reserve, and there are non-status and non-Indigenous peoples who live on-reserve, as well.

Treaty Indians

Another subcategory you should know about has to do with whether or not someone is a treaty Indian.

Treaties, in this context, refer to formal agreements between legal Indians or their ancestors and the reigning monarch of Canada, on behalf of the Canadian government. The so-called Numbered Treaties were signed between 1871 and 1921 and cover most of western and northern Canada.[20] British Columbia, with the exception of Vancouver Island, is not covered by any historic treaty.

A treaty Indian belongs to a band that was party to one of these eleven Numbered Treaties. The term *treaty Indian* is often used interchangeably with *status Indian,* although one is not always the same as the other.[21]

Other treaties were signed in eastern Canada, but there are vast areas in the east that are still not covered by any treaty. A number of modern (since 1975) treaties have been signed in British Columbia and in other areas of the country (such as the James Bay and Northern Quebec Agreement), and negotiations are still underway to create more treaties. Some treaties provided for reserves, and others did not.

Confused yet?

To sum up, status is held only by Indians who are defined as such under the *Indian Act.* Inuit and Métis do not have status, nor do non-status Indians.

Status Indians account for less than half of all Aboriginal peoples in Canada. Status Indians can be Indigenous or not, have band membership or not, can live on-reserve or not, and can be treaty Indians or not. What you should take away from this is to not make assumptions about status, what status entails, and what rights and benefits are associated with status.

If an Indigenous person is not a status Indian, this does not mean he or she is not legally Aboriginal; in other words, someone without status can still legally be Aboriginal. More important, not having status does not mean someone is not Indigenous. Native peoples will continue to exist and flourish whether or not we are recognized legally, and you can bet on the fact that terms and definitions will continue to evolve.

NOTES

1. "Justin Bieber Chided by Aboriginal Group for Free Gas Comment." *CBC News,* August 3, 2012, http://www.cbc.ca/news/canada/justin-bieber-chided-by-aboriginal-group-for-free-gas-comment-1.1193233.

2. *Constitution Act, 1867,* 30 & 31 Victoria, c 3, http://laws-lois.justice.gc.ca/eng/const/page-1.html. Originally enacted as the *British North America Act, 1867*; sometimes referred to as the *BNA Act.* This is just one part of Canada's Constitution.

3. *Indian Act,* RSC 1985, c I-5, http://laws-lois.justice.gc.ca/eng/acts/i-5/.

4. *The Constitution Act, 1982,* Schedule B *Canada Act, 1982* (UK) c 11, http://canlii.ca/t/ldsx.

5. Check sections 5–7 of the *Indian Act* on the "Definition and Registration of Indians" if you are into bureaucratic gobbledygook: http://laws.justice.gc.ca/eng/acts/I-5/page-3.html.

6. If you want to read more about how the definitions have changed, this webpage is a great overview of pre- and post-1867 definitions and explains some of the more shocking aspects of the *Indian Act* over time: http://www.mapleleafweb.com/features/the-indian-act-historical-overview.

7. The name of the ministry that administers the *Indian Act* has changed many times over the years, so I am simply going to continue to call it "Indian Affairs." It is now Indigenous Affairs and Northern Canada (INAC), and was Aboriginal Affairs and Northern Development Canada (AANDC) under former Prime Minister Stephen Harper. For more of my life, it was Indian and Northern Affairs Canada (INAC) or the Department of Indian Affairs and Northern Development (DIAND). Many people continue to refer to it simply as "INAC" or "Indian Affairs." A list of all the departments that have been responsible for the portfolios of Indian and Northern Affairs since 1864 is available online, along with annual reports from 1864–1990: http://www.bac-lac.gc.ca/eng/discover/aboriginal-heritage/first-nations/indian-affairs-annual-reports/Pages/introduction.aspx.

8. "Aboriginal Peoples in Canada: First Nations People, Métis and Inuit," *Statistics Canada,* last modified March 28, 2014, http://www12.statcan.gc.ca/nhs-enm/2011/as-sa/99-011-x/99-011-X2011001-eng.cfm.

9. *Re: Eskimos, 1939,* SCR, 104.

10. *Daniels v. Canada (Indian Affairs and Northern Development), 2016,* SCC 12. This decision is explained in further detail in chapter 4.

11. *Bill C-31: An Act to Amend the Indian Act, 1985,* SC 1985, c 27.

12. *Canadian Charter of Rights and Freedoms,* s 15, part I, *Constitution Act, 1982.*

13. Statistics Canada, "Aboriginal Population Profile, Canada 2011," National Household Survey, https://www12.statcan.gc.ca/nhs-enm/2011/dp-pd/aprof/details/page.cfm?Lang=E&Geo1= PR&Code1=01&Data=Count&SearchText=Canada&SearchType=Begins&SearchPR=01&A1 =All&B1=All&Custom&TABID=1. Footnote 30 states: "'Aboriginal identities not included elsewhere' includes persons who did not report being First Nations (North American Indian), Métis or Inuk (Inuit) but who did report Registered or Treaty Indian status and/or membership in a First Nation or Indian band."

14. *McIvor v. Canada, 2009,* BCCA 153. CanLII.

15. Parliament of Canada, LEGISinfo. "House Government Bill C-3 (40-3)," http://www.parl.gc.ca/ legisinfo/BillDetails.aspx?billId=4336828&Language=E&Mode=1.

16. Indigenous musical bands *are* quite awesome; some of my favourites are: CerAmony, Buffy Sainte-Marie, Kashtin, Tanya Tagaq, Samian, and Digging Roots; you get the picture.

17. "Definitions of Anthropological Terms," *Oregonstate.edu,* last modified December 26, 2012, http://oregonstate.edu/instruct/anth370/gloss.html#B.

18. *Reserve* is the legal term in Canada, while in the United States, the term is *reservation.*

19. Examples of landless bands are the Papaschase and Michel Bands near Edmonton, Alberta.

20. "Aboriginal People and the Growing Nation of Canada," *Social Studies/Manitoba Education,* 2015, http://www.edu.gov.mb.ca/k12/cur/socstud/foundation_gr6/blms/6-1-4f.pdf.

21. As one can be a non-status Indian with band membership, thus a treaty Indian; or, a non-status Indian whose ancestors were members of a band who were party to a Numbered Treaty, etc.

4

You're Métis? Which of Your Parents Is an Indian?

Métis Identity

As I write this in January of 2016, I am in my seventh year living in Quebec, where I've come to realize *Métis* still means "half-breed" to most. If you identify as Métis here, people will ask which of your parents is an Indian.

I am used to Alberta, where there is very little confusion about the Métis, at least among Indigenous peoples. I didn't have to explain myself often back home because more people know who we are. Oh, Alberta, where I always thought we were pronouncing it the French way, saying "may-TEA," though the French way is actually "may-TISS." This is funny because we *severely* anglicize every other French surname and place name out west. (You should hear how we pronounce Rivière Qui Barre!)[1] In French, the word *métis/métisse* literally translates as "mixed."

When I moved to Montreal, I considered it a homecoming of sorts – a return to the lands of some of my Mohawk ancestors before they picked up and dragged their relations to the shores of our sacred lake, Lac St. Anne, in what is now called Alberta. Instead, I had to face the fact that the Métis weren't born in Quebec; we became a people elsewhere.

When I first started getting that question – "Which of your parents is an Indian?" – I used to go into this long explanation about how the founders of my community were Mohawk from Kahnawake, which is just outside of Montreal. I would tell people how these Mohawk had intermarried with Europeans, and then with Cree women when they arrived at Lac Ste. Anne and the surrounding areas. I'd explain that we are Métis, not Mohawk or Cree. I'd tell them a little about Louis Riel and Gabriel Dumont and the Battle of Seven Oaks and how we are connected to the Red River Métis through intermarriage and shared history. I'd explain how the 19th-century capriciousness of "taking Treaty" or "taking Scrip"[2] meant that some people who are First Nations are now considered Métis, while others from the same family are on a band roll.

Still, after all of this, I'd invariably be asked, "So, is it your mom or your dad who is an Indian?"

To which I'd say, a little challengingly, "Neither. My mom is Métis." That is the moment bored, drifting eyes would snap back with skepticism written large all over my interrogator's face.

"Oh," they'd say, sounding disappointed and perhaps a little triumphant to have found a fake. "So, you're like a quarter Indian?"

As impressed as I am with the mathematical skills of all the people who have asked me this question since I moved to Quebec, my answer is: no; I am full Métis. I rarely bother with the long explanation anymore, because I am tired of repeating myself. At some point, it's up to other folks to put in a little effort to learn more about us on their own. They could, for example, buy this book!

Is there Métis status?

There is no real legislative context I can focus on when discussing who we are as Métis. There is no *Métis Act* equivalent to the *Indian Act* to provide an administrative context we can be shovelled into. Hopefully, by now, you have realized that even if there were, the boundaries would be anything but neat and would not necessarily reflect how we see ourselves. So, no. There is no such thing as Métis status. If you know someone with a Métis card, this is typically a membership card for a provincial Métis organization, not a status card.

The discussion we are about to have, as with many pieces in this book, is going to leave you with more questions than answers. Nonetheless, I'd rather have you asking those questions than believing you already know the answers. That alone would be incredible progress in this country!

Since there is no administrative context akin to status to explore, the question, "Who are the Métis?" will not be so (deceptively) cut and dry. This is me warning you about the mess we are about to delve into, because questions of identity are always fraught with strong emotions. Some may disagree with the way I frame discussions of Métis identity, and others are going to get downright angry once I make my particular biases clear. That is because, as with all questions of identity, definitions include certain people and exclude others.

To any academic readers, I apologize in advance for bringing up debates or issues that some think are settled, or should be moved past. Whether or not I agree

(I do, wholeheartedly), the fact is that the majority of Canadians have not been part of these mostly internal discussions. In this context, I feel it necessary to rehash supposedly old territory with the little *m* versus big *M* identity arguments.

Okay, I think I've covered my butt enough. Let's do this!

Little *m* and big *M* arguments

If you were to consider common approaches to Métis identity, you generally end up with two categories, sometimes overlapping, sometimes entirely separate, and sometimes with all sorts of anomalies left over and scattered about. When a Métis person is asked, "Which of your parents is an Indian?" the little *m* definition is in play.

Little *m* métis is essentially a racial category. This is the category I've encountered most in Quebec. As a racial category, one is little *m* métis when one is neither fully First Nations nor fully non-Indigenous. Métis was not the only term that was used historically; other terms included: *half-bloods, half-breeds, michif, bois brûlé, chicot, country-born, mixed bloods,* and so on. The name I blog under reflects that history, as *âpihtawikosisân* literally means "half-son" in Cree.

On one extreme of little *m* métis identity, one must literally be half First Nations and half not. On the other extreme, one can be Métis with a minimal amount of First Nations blood, something I will explore in more detail shortly. You can just imagine the range of arguments involved in deciding where Métis identity is supposedly legitimate along the spectrum of "blood quantum." There are also little *m* discussions that include connection to culture as a Métis, so it is not always focused on blood. However, the cultural connection referred to is generally a First Nations culture, such as Anishinaabe, Cree, or Mi'kmaq, rather than a distinct Métis culture.

This leads us into the big *M* discussion. Big *M* Métis tends to be a sociopolitical definition, one that still often relies on the core concept of "mixture." The belief is that mixing between European men and Indigenous women happened, and the Métis were born as a people (a process known as "ethnogenesis") when they began to share a common experience that eventually crystallized into a national identity during a specific period of time in the history of Canada.[3] There is *less* focus on race, although kinship ties are very much present.

One end of this spectrum considers only the Red River Métis and their descendants (including far-flung relations who may have never been to the Red River area) as legitimately Métis.[4] Others consider any community to be Métis if it included people of mixed First Nations and European ancestry, who developed their own culture and shared a history. On this extreme end, you could imagine contemporary emerging Métis communities, not just historical ones.

So, who really is Métis?

You mean, what is the definition I use for myself and, thus, present as the definition all others should live by? Oh, come on. Are any identity issues that easily navigated, even on an individual level?

I will get personal because it's important you know where I come from so that you understand why I have the opinions I have, and why others from different backgrounds may agree with me or not.

My understanding of my Métis identity has shifted considerably over the years. You see, I was only about five years old when the term *Métis* was recognized officially in section 35(2) of the *Constitution Act, 1982*.[5] Although the term *Métis* predates that official recognition, it was not necessarily the most common term in use. Often we were referred to on the Prairies as the "Road Allowance People."[6] The term *half-breed* still got tossed around a lot when I was growing up and was pretty ubiquitous in my parents' and grandparents' time.[7] Using, and being known by, many different names are experiences shared by almost all Indigenous peoples.

At that time, what I knew (but did not really understand the history of) was that we were related to pretty much every Indigenous person in Alberta, lots of folks in Saskatchewan and Manitoba, and many people in northern British Columbia. I have since also found kin in the Northwest Territories, in the upper Great Lakes area, and in the northern United States. Some of our relations lived on Stoney reserves, others lived on Cree reserves, still others had farms near places like Keephills, Smokey Lake, Rivière Qui Barre, and so on. Names like L'Hirondelle, Loyer, Callihoo (spelled a million different ways), Gladu, and Belcourt were a dead giveaway that someone was somehow related to me. Aside from the odd family story – that didn't interest me as a child (but fascinates me as an adult) – I knew very little about our regional history.

When I started paying attention and began to feel part of something bigger, I turned toward the concept of a Métis national identity. That is when I started learning about our connections to the Red River, and what led to the Red River diaspora.

At first, I focused on the most visible symbols of a national culture: our language (Michif), our own style of music and dance, our own flag, our unique decorative style, the sash, and the Red River cart.

I still consider all those things important, and I appreciate the fact that the name Louis Riel no longer refers just to some French guy whom the English killed.[8]

FIGURE 4.1. Angelique Callihoo and Louis Divertissant Loyer.

However, the history of my region, the history so many Alberta Métis share, is equally as amazing and rich and worth learning about. The Red River diaspora is much more than a handful of symbols. We are many communities speckled throughout the Métis Homeland.

Take the photo (left), for example. Angelique Callihoo was the daughter of Louis Kwarakwante Callihoo, a Mohawk fur trader, and his second wife, Marie Patenaude.[9] Almost every Alberta Métis can tie him- or herself to Louis Kwarakwante somehow through family lines![10] Louis Divertissant Loyer was the son of Louis Loyer (heads up: naming your kid after yourself confuses things) and Louise Genevieve Jasper.

Families linked to the Red River moved west into Alberta, founding communities and forming strong relationships with First Nations there. The history of these families is a major part of the history of Alberta, yet I never learned about it in school. In fact, I'm still learning about it, and it becomes more fascinating and interesting with each new detail. My identity as a Métis person is linked to my family history and the history of the community of Lac Ste. Anne in particular.

The point of all of this is to give you a better sense of how kinship and history play a much more important role in my identity as a Métis person than quantifying my "mixedness." This has absolutely impacted my views on who is Métis.

Dude, I still don't get it; just how Indian are you?

Sigh. I have no idea. That's not the point. I am not First Nations, and I am not Métis by virtue of being "mixed." At this point, all Indigenous peoples are mixed and are not defined by the fact of being mixed; so, why should Métis accept such a definition? My Métis ancestors intermarried with one another over generations linking me to so many different Métis families that I tend to greet most Alberta Métis as "cousin." Many of us Métis interact like this, which never ceases to make my husband laugh. You are Métis when you have Métis ancestors.

Some of us look very "Indian." Some of us have blonde hair and dark skin with green eyes. Some, like myself, are very pale and are seen and treated as White (with all of the privilege that entails). Some of us look nearly "pureblooded" (if you insist on blood quantum definitions), and others look more stereotypically mixed. What links us is our history, and our present sense of kinship and community.

We are Lac Ste. Anne Métis, Settlement Métis, Smokey Lake Métis, St. Albert Métis, and so on – a history of settlement, movement, intermarriage, cultural growth, and roots dug deep. Some of us are closer to our Cree and Stoney relations than others. We all have our own ideas about what it means to be Métis based on our lived experiences.

This isn't helpful at all; surely there is some definition you can explain?

Sure, but you might not like it.

You should be asking yourself why it even matters that there is a definition for us. As pointed out in this editorial:

> The questions of who is Métis, how do you become one, and where are their ancestral lands are not idle historical problems. If the Métis can claim resources and the right to hunt, fish and gather food all year without a license, then they might also have a right to negotiate with the private sector and governments on how those resources are used.[11]

The idea that the Métis have some (as yet ill-defined, amorphous) rights is a big motivator for wanting to pigeonhole Métis into a knowable category, even as it encourages some to try creating new categories of Métis in order to gain benefits.

It wasn't until 2003 that the question, "Who really is Métis?" got some serious attention.[12] The Supreme Court of Canada heard a case involving a father and son who shot a moose out of season and without a licence. Exciting stuff, no? No?! Well, it turned out to be exciting. It got a lot of people talking about a legal definition for the Métis besides "half-Indian, half-European."

The Powley Test, as it is known, set out basic criteria for determining who is accepted as Métis by the Canadian state. Here, I am using the Métis Nation of Alberta's summary of those criteria, which is pretty similar to what other regional Métis organizations have adopted and use to determine regional membership: "Métis means a person who self-identifies as a Métis, is distinct from other aboriginal peoples, is of historic Métis Nation ancestry, and is accepted by the Métis Nation."[13]

Egads! There is so much in there to unpack and debate! So many more questions than answers! A little bit of "calling yourself Métis is good enough," with some "have to have at least some First Nations blood," and a whole lot of "other people have to agree that you're Métis."

Then, there is that whole "distinct from other aboriginal peoples" part that so baffles the many Cree-Métis and other First Nations-Métis mixtures out there. You can legally be Métis or First Nations, but not both! That would be double-dipping… or something.[14]

The Powley definition is still fairly vague, though, and the issue of Métis identity continues to be hotly contested.

Okay, so where do you stand?

For many years, I was comfortable with a pretty expansive definition of Métis, particularly little *m* categories because, whether or not I believed everyone identifying was actually Métis, I didn't see how it affected me or my community in any way. I felt if people were misidentifying, it was usually as a way to assert their legitimate indigeneity in one of the three ways "familiar" to Canada: as First Nations, as Inuit, or (when those categories were unavailable) as Métis. Most of these people were non-status Indians, so it wasn't a situation of non-Indigenous peoples claiming to be Indigenous. More important, this was happening at the individual level. I did not see organizations claiming to represent "Métis" communities that did not exist.

I saw a few instances in Alberta of non-Indigenous peoples claiming to be Métis, right around the time Premier Ralph Klein signed an Interim Métis Harvesting Agreement with the Métis Nation of Alberta (MNA) in 2004. That *did* bother me. I actually heard people discussing how to get a "Métis card," and how it was going to get them cheap smokes and tax breaks. Of course, Métis cards don't allow any of those things; but there is a huge lack of awareness about this in Canada, so I wasn't surprised.

However, when the Harvesting Agreement expired two years later, and when there was no longer much "benefit" to being Métis, most of these claims evaporated. Many of those folks had been unsuccessful in getting MNA membership anyway, because they had no ties to actual Métis communities in the first place (the Harvesting Agreement required valid MNA identification). The MNA had revamped its entire membership process after Powley, re-vetting all current MNA members to ensure genealogical documentation existed. This is not to say the only legitimate way to identify as Métis is by obtaining membership in a provincial organization; however, in this case, the Agreement was made with that organization, so its membership policies mattered to the exercise of hunting rights in Alberta at the time.[15]

When the furor died down, I thought this was a one-off and that non-Indigenous peoples identifying as Métis was not a problem worth worrying about. As it turns out, that was only the beginning.

Rejecting the myth of Métissage

So, my own views on this have been influenced by the way in which many people attempt to claim a Métis identity, and by the sheer volume of these claims over the past decade. I also think our relative silence on the issue of Métis identity has allowed some very strange ideas to bubble into the minds of settler intellectuals.

For example, in 2009, John Ralston Saul tried to whip together a cohesive Canadian identity in *A Fair Country: Telling Truths about Canada,* using the Métis as a synecdoche for "a unique people" (i.e., Canadians). He argued Canadian culture was less a result of English and French Enlightenment values, and more a result of interactions between English and French newcomers and First Nations.[16] To call this a rosy reading of history is an understatement as vast as the Prairie sky. The goal of this approach is to encourage Canadians to "learn who they truly are" via reconnecting with their Indigenous roots – real or very much imagined.

Saul's choice to discuss Canada as a "Métis Nation" was even more perplexing to those of us who actually are Métis.[17] Why us? Why the Métis, as opposed to the Cree, or the Mohawk, or the Inuit? Why is our nation so attractive to those seeking an Indigenous identity? I think it basically boils down to the fact that, for many people, Métis = mixed. After all, that's what the French word means, and that is almost exclusively how we are discussed in the mainstream: as a hybrid people formed from the unions between European men and First Nations women. Apparently, we're the only ones who married out, interbred, mixed. According to this logic, anyone with a single Indigenous ancestor 300 years ago is mixed, and, therefore, Métis.

I hope it is obvious that this claim is ridiculous.[18] It also needs to be said that we are not the only post-contact Indigenous people. The Lumbee, Oji-Cree, Comanche, and Seminole are other examples of Indigenous peoples who formed a unique identity after contact with European settlers.

Extending Métis to mean "anyone with even the most tenuous claim to a First Nations ancestor" is precisely the kind of mythology discussed by E. Tuck and K.W. Yang as a "move to innocence."

In this move to innocence, settlers locate or invent a long-lost ancestor who is rumored to have had "Indian blood," and they use this claim to mark themselves as blameless in the attempted eradications of Indigenous peoples....

[It] is a settler move to innocence because it is an attempt to deflect a settler identity, while continuing to enjoy settler privilege and occupying stolen land.[19]

While there are certainly people claiming a First Nations identity based on blood myths (long-lost or imagined ancestors), it tends to be a less common phenomenon in Canada than in the United States. Part of that, at least where I come from, is a deep-rooted racism against Indigenous peoples that makes being Indigenous in no way an enviable or sought-out identity.

Since moving to eastern Canada, however, I have seen that deep-rooted racism expressed in forms that encourage stereotypes of noble savagery; claiming Indigenous identity here is much more hip and edgy. In any case, it is still difficult to claim one is Mohawk, or Mi'kmaq, or Cree without a person from one of those First Nations asking pointed questions about relatives and community. It is much easier to avoid a fuss and simply claim that any tiny scrap of Indigenous blood (again real or imagined) makes one Métis. In this way, our nation becomes a bin for all those who are not otherwise defined.

Of course, the problem with this is the fact that many of the people claiming us are not claimed *by* us. Self-identification is not enough. As an Indigenous people, the Métis have the right to define our own kinships rather than having anyone who wishes come along and claim kinship with us. Again, if this seems extreme, consider whether it would make sense to lecture the Mohawk on why they should allow anyone with an Indigenous ancestor to claim to *be* Mohawk.

Recently, the mythology of Métissage has reared its head in a very aggressive way in Quebec. While the flavour is different from Saul's claims (more maple syrup, obviously), the story is roughly the same. Some people, merely by *feeling* more Indigenous than French, want to identify as Métis. Unique; not French (European), not even Québécois. Something else. Something that belongs here, does not engender guilt, and washes away Quebec's history of colonialism while reinforcing Quebec's own experiences as a colonized people.

In fact, Roy Dupuis, Carole Poliquin, and Yvan Dubuc have an entire film about the Québécois-as-Métis called *L'Empreinte*.[20] In interviews, Dupuis has stressed that the French did not come to Quebec as conquerors and that they were charmed by the "sexual liberation of *les sauvagesses*" (Indigenous women).[21] Much like Ralston Saul, Dubuc and Poliquin claim Quebec's tolerance for differences (Islamophobia and a penchant for continuing to champion the use of blackface aside), consensus-seeking, and love of nature all come from the mixture of European and First Nations cultures.[22] Folks, this is some hardcore myth-making.

All of that would be lovely to acknowledge, true or false, if it weren't for the way in which such claims are used to identify the Québécois as Indigenous. Please stop viewing Indigenous peoples as "the other," but do not replace that with "we are all Indigenous" (I'm looking at you, too, John Ralston Saul).

> "Si les Français sont nos cousins, les Amérindiens sont nos frères," says Dupuis. ("If the French are our cousins, the Indians are our brothers.")
>
> "Quels seraient les avantages de cette redéfinition? Énormes, croient-ils. Comme le dit Denys Delâge dans le film, reconnaître cet héritage voudrait dire que notre histoire n'a pas commencé avec l'arrivée de Champlain, mais il y a 12 000 ans," dit Roy Dupuis. ("What would advantages of such a redefinition be? They believe them to be enormous. As Denys Delâge said in the film, recognizing this heritage means our history did not begin with the arrival of Champlain, but rather is 12,000 years old!" says Roy Dupuis.)[23]

Others are not so quick to jump on the bandwagon of imagined Québécois indigeneity. Gérard Bouchard points out the obvious: Indigenous communities in Quebec are in general far removed from where the Québécois live(d), the Roman Catholic Church always discouraged mixed unions with First Nations, and First Nations genes represent a mere one percent of the Quebec genetic makeup.[24]

And yet, the myth of Métissage holds a powerful sway. As Dupuis says in this trailer:

> When I arrived in America, I was French, but before long, I no longer lived nor thought like a Frenchman. I was Canadian from the Iroquois name Kanata. My tribe has given itself other names since: French Canadian, then Québécois....[25]

In another interview, Dupuis was asked, "Are you more French or Indian?" To which he replied, "Indian."[26]

Don't get me wrong; Dupuis is just another manifestation of a burning desire to claim indigeneity and is hardly the only person involved in furthering such claims. He does not even explicitly claim to be Métis, except in the sense that *métis* means "mixed." Others *are* identifying themselves as being Métis, however, via genealogical links to communities that ceased to exist hundreds of years ago and which were arguably never Métis communities to begin with. These claims are not harmless; they are being actively used to gain recognition from the Canadian state (a process already fraught with contradictions) in order to claim Constitutional rights. Their lack of success so far shouldn't detract from the racist logics through which these attempts are made.

A great deal of time, effort, and research is being put into claiming indigeneity via very strained genealogical ties. (Another example is claiming a Mi'kmaq Métis ancestor from 1684 as the sole basis for identifying as Métis.) That effort could much better be extended in developing healthy relationships with existing Indigenous communities, both in Quebec and throughout Canada. Sometimes I want to shake people and say, "Being non-Indigenous is *okay*."

"Becoming the Native" furthers colonial erasure of Indigenous peoples; the fact that this is being done more and more through the lens of *métissage* is of particular concern to Métis people. We are being used as a wedge to undermine Indigenous rights and existence (including our own!). This is no longer the action of isolated individuals. There are now organizations that claim to represent historic Métis communities of dubious existence – in other words, communities with absolutely no connection to the historical core of the Red River region. Many of these small *m* communities, characterized by at least some mixed unions between First Nations women and European men, ceased to exist hundreds of years ago or were not truly cohesive communities in the first place.[27] Furthermore, some argue that any participation in the fur trade is de facto proof of individuals or communities being properly identified today as Métis. (Since when does a profession grant indigeneity?)

Many of these "communities" rely on the narrative of having "hidden in plain sight" for generations, rather than being part of wider Métis kinship systems. The idea is that entire communities "hid" mixed unions between First Nations and Europeans (by passing as White) out of fear of colonial repression, and have only now, in the 21st century, been able to claim their indigeneity. This narrative requires acceptance of the notion that cultural knowledge is passed through the generations via blood, a problematic metaphor at best.[28]

Ironically, while these organizations rail against "Red River fundamentalism"[29] and argue Métis communities could and did arise outside of any connection to the Red River, they consistently use *our* symbols and history as proof of *their* Métis-ness. Beware "Métis" organizations that offer "status cards" for Métis, or that offer membership based on having one Indigenous ancestor as far back as 200 years.

At first, these organizations may have just been a way to connect people who share genealogical interests. Now, it is becoming more common for these groups to advance claims to rights based on section 35 of the *Constitution*, and to insist on a right to be included in things like resource extraction negotiations. Rarely, if ever, do these organizations acknowledge the territories of First Nations in the area.

The stakes are high. If enough people attain "Métishood" in these ways, the state-recognized category of Métis could contain a population that outnumbers First Nations and Inuit combined, making Métis *the* driving political force when it comes to Indigenous issues. As Indigenous Métis become outnumbered by those who self-identify as Métis (without any real connection to the Métis homeland), the agenda would be driven by settler, rather than Indigenous, needs.

Further, the claiming of indigeneity by settler populations means circumventing any need to engage in decolonization. Once we are all Métis (and Indigenous), none of us are. The categories of "settler" and "Indigenous" collapse into each other, allowing settlers to claim an unearned legitimacy in perhaps the most bizarre of ways. Rather than denying Indigenous peoples' right to the land and resources, this move to innocence affirms that right and then strips it of all meaning by "Indigenizing" the settler.

The pressure of settlers claiming indigeneity through the Métis identity triggers an obligation, on the part of Métis, to ensure we maintain our treaty relationships with First Nations by not avoiding unpleasant discussions about identity or about who claim us.[30]

Expect this issue to keep coming up as time goes by, because one thing is clear: Canadian (or Quebec) myth-making is far from over.[31]

For all of these reasons, I agree with the following definition provided by Chris Andersen:

> I use *Métis* to refer to the history, events, leaders, territories, language, and culture associated with the growth of the buffalo hunting and trading Métis of the northern Plains, in particular during the period between the beginning of the Métis buffalo brigades in the early nineteenth century and the 1885 North West Uprising.[32]

This is the big *M* definition, with the further requirement that the people and community in question have a connection to the historic Red River region.

Sounds confusing; doesn't this exclude a lot of people?

It does, yeah, but what identity issues are simple? To reiterate, this is not a universally accepted definition, but I don't want to be coy about where I stand.

Chris Andersen addresses some of the concerns about a narrower definition of Métis:

> When I argue for the drawing of boundaries around Métis identity to reflect a commitment to recognizing our nationhood, however, colleagues often object, as many of you might, in one of two ways. The first objection usually takes the form

of a challenge rooted firmly in racialization: "If someone wants to self-identify as Métis, who are you to suggest they can't? Why do you think you own the term *Métis*?" I ask them to imagine raising a similar challenge to, say, a Blackfoot person about the right of someone born and raised, and with ancestors born and raised, in Nova Scotia or Labrador, to declare a Blackfoot identity because they could not gain recognition as Mi'kmaq or Inuit. Second, I am sometimes asked, "What of those Indigenous people who have, due to their mixed ancestry and the discriminatory provisions of the *Indian Act,* been dispossessed from their First Nations community? What happens to them if we prevent the possibility of their declaring a Métis identity (some of whom, due to complex historical kinship relations, might legitimately claim one)?" Such disquiet is often buoyed by a broader question of fundamental justice: What obligation, do any of us – Métis included – owe dispossessed Indigenous individuals, and even communities, who forward claims using a Métis identity based not on a connection to Métis national roots but because it seems like the only possible option? Whatever we imagine a fair response to look like, it must account for the fact that "Métis" refers to a nation with membership codes that deserve to be respected. We are not a soup kitchen for those disenfranchised by past and present Canadian Indian policy and, as such, although we should sympathize with those who bear the brunt of this particular form of dispossession, we cannot do so at expense of eviscerating our identity.[33]

I've taken to boiling it down in this way when people ask who the Métis are: we are an Indigenous people. Fin.

The *Daniels* decision

In April 2016, the Supreme Court of Canada released the *Daniels* decision,[34] and the media has been almost universal in getting the judgment completely wrong. The court was asked to decide whether Métis and non-status Indians should be included in section 91(24) of the *Constitution Act, 1867*.[35] The court answered in the affirmative. So, what does this mean?

Section 91 of the *Constitution* defines the legislative authority of the federal government. Section 92 defines the legislative authority of the provinces. This is basic division of powers stuff.

The provinces have power over things like the solemnization of marriage, property and civil rights in the province, setting up municipalities, and so on. The federal government has power over things like the armed forces, banking, criminal law, and so on.

Responsibility and funding for systems of education, health care, social services, provincial infrastructure (water and waste management, roads, and so on) are generally a provincial power. There is an important exception, though, in section 91(24) of the *Constitution*, which states the federal government is responsible for "Indians, and Land Reserved for Indians." The federal government must provide to "Indians" the services normally provided by the provinces (education, health care, social services, and so on).

So, you have provincial systems, which tend to be available to everyone living off-reserve, and you have federal systems, which are focused on reserve populations. Lots to say about how inadequate those federal systems are, but let's move on.

The federal government has a long history of trying to interpret section 91(24) to mean they have responsibility only over Indians on Indian lands. The Court keeps insisting these are two separate things, Indians *and* Land Reserved for Indians.

"Who is an Indian?" then becomes important, because if you are an Indian, the federal government, not the provinces, is responsible for you.

The first group to clearly be "Indians" to come under the *Indian Act* is status Indians.

The second group to be defined as Indians under section 91(24) of the *Constitution* was the Inuit in 1939.[36] This obviously did not turn Inuit people into First Nations peoples, and Inuit peoples did not become Indians under the *Indian Act*. It was just about assigning responsibility, in this case the federal government, not the provinces, for Inuit.

Non-status Indians are those who are not considered Indians under the *Indian Act* but are still obviously Aboriginal peoples. The Métis are another group of Aboriginal peoples. For years and years and years and years, both groups have been tossed back and forth like a hot potato between the provinces and the federal government, each one saying, "They're your problem, not ours!" This has left non-status Indians and Métis in a sort of legal limbo.

The *Daniels* decision clarifies that both groups are a constitutional responsibility of the federal government and not the provinces. "Indians" now basically just means what "Aboriginal" does in section 35 of the *Constitution Act, 1982*.[37] It includes: Indians (status and non-status alike), Inuit, and Métis.

Here are important things to keep in mind:

- Non-status Indians and Métis are still not governed by the *Indian Act*.
- Non-status Indians and Métis did not just become status Indians.
- The federal government will still attempt to limit its responsibility to status Indians living on-reserve, which is where most of the (inadequate) federal funding goes.

- Non-status Indians and Métis do not suddenly have the right to live on-reserve (if they do not already have that right); this decision does not ensure that non-status Indians and Métis will have new federal funding opportunities, that is going to have to be negotiated for, or fought with, the federal government.

In addition to the confusion about what it means to be "Indians" under section 91(24) of the *Constitution*, there are a lot of claims being made that the definition of "Métis" has been changed.

The court basically said that for the purposes of deciding jurisdiction, it is not important to decide which people are Métis and which people are non-status. The federal government has legislative authority over all of these groups.

A lot of people are focusing in on a quote in the judgment however, which itself comes from a book discussing Métis identity:

> There is no one exclusive Métis people in Canada, anymore than there is no one exclusive Indian people in Canada. The Métis of eastern Canada and northern Canada are as distinct from Red River Métis as any two peoples can be....As early as 1650, a distinct Métis community developed in LeHeve [sic], Nova Scotia, separate from Acadians and Micmac Indians. All Métis are aboriginal people. All have Indian ancestry."[38]

This is not a finding of fact; this is merely what is referred to as *obiter dictum,* a thing "said in passing," which is not legally binding. The context of this quote in the decision is an extremely brief discussion of what this chapter has been about: there is more than one definition of what "Métis" means, and there is not a universally accepted definition. The court did not just acknowledge the existence of Métis communities in Nova Scotia or anywhere else.

The decision states: "Determining whether **particular individuals or communities** are non-status Indians or Métis and therefore 'Indians' under s. 91(24), is a fact-driven question to be decided on a case-by-case basis in the future" (bolding mine). There has been no blanket acceptance, and the burden of proof is still on the individual or community to prove they are Métis or non-status.

The decision also discussed whether the three-point Powley Test for defining who qualifies as Métis need not apply to section 91(24). The court determined the federal government has legislative authority over those who self-identify as Métis and have an ancestral connection to a historic Métis community. The third part of the test, acceptance by a contemporary Métis community, is not needed.

While this is a less stringent test for the purposes of deciding who can legislate with respect to the Métis, it is by no means a slam dunk for individuals or communities identifying as Métis! It is easy to self-identity, but not so easy to prove the existence of a historic Métis community!

There have been many cases brought before the courts that have attempted to prove the presence of a historic Métis community east of Ontario, but, in every single instance, the courts have found the evidence was lacking. Judicially, there are no Métis communities in Quebec or farther east. That has not changed with this decision.

Further, the three-point Powley Test remains intact for the purposes of the Aboriginal rights protected by section 35 of the *Constitution Act, 1982*. The court had this to say:

> The criteria in Powley were developed specifically for purposes of applying s. 35, which is about protecting historic community-held rights. That is why acceptance by the community was found to be, for purposes of who is included as Métis under s. 35, a prerequisite to holding those rights.[39]

What this will mean in terms of actual services and legislation, no one yet knows. What we do know after *Daniels* is when it comes time to ask for these things, we can go straight to the federal government rather than vacillate uncertainly between the provinces and the feds; and, most likely, they will make us fight tooth and nail every step of the way.

NOTES

1. A hamlet in central Alberta.
2. "Our Legacy," *University of Saskatchewan Archives*, accessed December 29, 2015, http://scaa.sk.ca/ourlegacy/exhibit_scrip. Scrip was a method of extinguishing Aboriginal title to open up lands for settlement in the West. Scrip was an individual extinguishment rather than a collective one. (Canada sees the numbered or historic treaties as collective extinguishment.)
3. By national identity, I do not mean in the nation-state sense. Indigenous peoples are not trying to claim or prove we are nation states, necessarily. Rather, it refers to national identity in the sense of being a connected people with our own sociopolitical orders, shared culture, territory, and history.
4. For a history of the Red River Métis (who settled along the Red and Assiniboine rivers in what is now known as Manitoba) within the wider context of the Plains Métis, try: Michel Hogue, *Metis and the Medicine Line: Creating a Border and Dividing a People* (Regina: University of Regina Press, 2015). This book also looks at how notions of race helped Canada and the U.S. gain access to Indigenous lands, and the subsequent settlement of the West.
5. Which reads: "In this Act, 'aboriginal peoples of Canada' includes the Indian, Inuit and Métis peoples of Canada."

6. Maria Campbell, *Stories of the Road Allowance People* (Penticton: Theytus Books, 1995). As Métis became increasingly dispossessed of land, many of them squatted on Crown land set aside for future use; hence, the term *road allowances*. Campbell's lovely book of poetry shares stories of the experiences of these families.

7. For more stories of life as a "halfbreed" on the Prairies, see: Maria Campbell, *Halfbreed* (Lincoln: University of Nebraska Press, 1973).

8. Probably the most accessible and entertaining biography of Louis Riel is Chester Brown's graphic novel. I highly recommend it. Chester Brown, *Louis Riel: A Comic-Strip Biography* (Montreal: Drawn and Quarterly, 2003).

9. Photo from family collection, provided by Crystal Hayes, my mother's cousin (my aunt via Métis kinship).

10. "Term/name searched," *Dictionary Title*, accessed October 12, 2015, http://biographi.ca/en/bio.php?id_nbr=3287.

11. "Métis Identity Matters," *Winnipeg Free Press*, September 2, 2011, accessed October 13, 2015, http://www.winnipegfreepress.com/opinion/editorials/metis-identity-matters-115625309.html.

12. *R. v. Powley, 2003*, SCC 43, [2003] 2 SCR 207, http://www.canlii.org/en/ca/scc/doc/2003/2003scc43/2003scc43.html.

13. Métis Nation of Alberta webpage, http://www.albertametis.com/MNAHome/Home.aspx.

14. *Alberta (Aboriginal Affairs and Northern Development) v. Cunningham, 2011* SCC 37. This case makes it clear that one cannot legally identify as both Métis and First Nations and continue to be a member of the Métis Settlements in northern Alberta. First Nations peoples are excluded from this membership and can be removed.

15. To clarify further, the *Interim Métis Harvesting Agreement,* which was not extended, did not grant any sort of Aboriginal rights. The province simply does not have the power to recognize, or not recognize, Aboriginal rights. Rather, the province agreed not to charge Métis hunters as long as those hunters had a valid MNA membership. This was a contractual agreement only and in no way impacts any inherent hunting rights the Métis may have.

16. Some have said this is an unfair reading of Saul's work. I understand his use of Métis here is intended to reflect a mixing of cultures, a hybridization that created a uniquely Canadian context, which is far more influenced by Indigenous cultures than is often acknowledged. It is precisely this use of the term I am objecting to. Stop using Métis to mean "mixed culture," particularly when the mixing of cultures referred to occurred within an incredibly oppressive context.

17. Adam Gaudry, "The Métis-ization of Canada: The process of claiming Louis Riel, Métissage, and the Métis people as Canada's mythical origin," *Aboriginal Policy Studies,* Vol. 2, No. 2 (2013): accessed April 3, 2016, https://ejournals.library.ualberta.ca/index.php/aps/article/view/17889/pdf. This piece nicely outlines and deconstructs the ways in which the Métis identity is sometimes claimed on behalf of Canada.

18. Adam Gaudry, "Respecting Métis Nationhood and Self-Determination in Matters of Métis Identity," pp. 152–163 in *Aboriginal History: A Reader,* Geoff Read and Kristin Burnett, ed. (Toronto: Oxford University Press, 2015). If it isn't obviously ridiculous, then please read this spot-on piece by Adam Gaudry, which helps to clarify the origin of the Métis identity.

19. Eve Tuck, and Wayne Yang, "Decolonization Is Not a Metaphor," *Decolonization: Indigeneity, Education and Society* 1, no. 1 (2012): accessed December 27, 2015, http://decolonization.org/index.php/des/article/view/18630/15554, pages 10–11.

20. *L'Empreinte*, directed by Carole Poliquin and Yvan Dubuc (QC: Isca Productions, 2015), http://www.cinoche.com/films/l-empreinte/index.html.

21. Isabelle Hontebeyrie, "Lever the Voile sur le 'Grand Tabou de L'Histoire du Quebec,'" March 6, 2015, accessed December 27, 2015, http://www.journaldemontreal.com/2015/03/06/lever-le-voile-sur-le-grand-tabou-de-lhistoire-du-quebec.

22. "Quebec Muslim Women 'Scared to Walk Alone,'" *CBC News*, November 6, 2013, accessed December 27, 2015, http://www.cbc.ca/news/canada/montreal/quebec-muslim-women-scared-to-walk-alone-1.2416443; Rachel Zellers, "Troubling Question of Blackface in Quebec," *The Star*, February 16, 2015, accessed December 17, 2015, http://www.thestar.com/opinion/commentary/2015/02/16/troubling-question-of-blackface-in-quebec.html.

23. Chantal Guy, "L'Indien Pilier Manquent de L'Identité Québéquoise," *La Presse*, March 9, 2015, accessed December 27, 2015, http://plus.lapresse.ca/screens/0f959929-7aac-4322-b560-b90d562316e7%7C_0.html.

24. Gérard Bouchard, "Le Faux 'Sang Indien' des Québéquois," February 7, 2015, accessed December 27, 2015, http://www.lapresse.ca/debats/nos-collaborateurs/gerard-bouchard/201502/06/01-4841971-le-faux-sang-indien-des-quebecois.php. Of course, Bouchard is a bit of a character; he was attempting to prove the "purity" of the Quebecois.

25. "L'Empreinte Bande-Annonce," Les Productions Isca, YouTube video, October 21, 2014, accessed December 27, 2015, https://www.youtube.com/watch?v=pRYg7cP1RQM.

26. Steve Martel, "Nos Origines," YouTube video, February 22, 2015, accessed December 27, 2015, https://www.youtube.com/watch?v=vo7bmkQZ7bg.

27. Robert Michael Morrissey, "Kaskaskia Social Network: Kinship and Assimilation in the French-Illinois Borderlands, 1695–1735," *The William and Mary Quarterly* 70, no. 1 (2013): 103–146, http://www.jstor.org/stable/10.5309/willmaryquar.70.1.0103?seq=1#page_scan_tab_contents; Cecile Vidal, "Africains et Européens au Pays des Illinois Durant la Periode Français (1699–1765)," *French Colonial History* 3 (2003): 51–68.

Kaskaskia ceased to exist as a community in the mid-1700s. Morrissey points out that, despite there being a number of mixed-marriage families between French and First Nations peoples, Kaskaskia was unique in the way in which First Nations women were assimilated into French culture rather than the other way around. A mostly agrarian society, with some fur-trading links, Kaskaskia and other French communities in the area relied heavily on the labour of enslaved Africans.

Despite this, a number of people use genealogical ties to Kaskaskia as the basis for identifying as Métis now, merely on the basis that mixed-race (White and First Nations) couples did exist there. Vidal further asserts White women arrived in the community as early as 1720 and were preferred for marriage.

28. Kim Tallbear, *Native American DNA: Tribal Belonging and the False Promise of Genetic Science* (Minneapolis: University of Minnesota Press, 2013). Here, you will find a more complete discussion of how blood, DNA, and genealogy are used to undermine (and claim) indigeneity.

29. Framing the exercise of asserting a Métis identity as "fundamentalism" is one way in which a number of groups not linked to the Red River in any way attempt to argue for a more expansive definition of Métis identity. The basis for this is the notion that enforcing definitions is inherently colonial (or fundamentalism). This ignores the fact that First Nations also enforce definitions of membership, as is the right of all Indigenous peoples, including the Métis.

30. Nicholas Vrooman, "Cree, Assiniboine, Ojibwa, and Michif: The Nêhiyaw Pwat Confederacy/Iron Alliance in Montana, https://www.academia.edu/8968491/Cree_Assiniboine_Ojibwa_and_Michif_The_Nehiyaw_Pwat_Confederacy_Iron_Alliance_in_Montana.

31. Darryl Leroux unpacks this myth-making very clearly here: https://soundcloud.com/indigenousstudiesusask/native-studies-speakers-series-darryl-leroux-now-i-am-metis-how-white-people-become-indigenous.

    I also put together a *storify* of my live tweets as I listened to the above talk: https://storify.com/apihtawikosisan/now-i-am-metis-how-white-people-become-indigenous.

32. Chris Andersen, *Métis: Race, Recognition, and the Struggle for Indigenous Peoplehood* (Vancouver: UBC Press, 2014), 24. In my opinion, this book is the most complete exploration of Métis identity that exists. If you still have questions after this chapter, Andersen's book is an essential read.

33. Chris Andersen, "'I'm Métis, What's Your Excuse?' On the Optics and the Ethics of the Misrecognition of Métis in Canada," *Aboriginal Policy Studies* 1, no. 2 (2011): 164.

34. *Daniels v. Canada (Indian Affairs and Northern Development)*, 2016, SCC 12. Available online: https://scc-csc.lexum.com/scc-csc/scc-csc/en/item/15858/index.do.

35. *Constitution Act, 1867,* 30 & 31 Victoria, c.3 (UK)

36. *Re: Eskimo,* [1939] SCR. 104.

37. *Constitution Act, 1982,* Schedule B to the *Canada Act, 1982* (UK), 1982, c 11.

38. supra note 34 at para 17.

39. Ibid, para 49.

5

Feel the Inukness

Inuit Identity

If your understanding of the Inuit and Inuit culture came from films like *Nanook of the North,* it's time to update your references.[1] You might want to start with Becky Qilavvaq's 2012 short film starring Anguti Johnson called *Feel the Inukness.*[2] The video features Anguti flipping through various songs on his iPod before settling on a rousing jig, which has him dancing all around Iqaluit in a whole-body jigging style very specific to the North. The video went viral and, among my Inuit students in particular, it got heavy play for many months. While the video is sure to have you giggling, Qilavvaq pointed out in an interview that the video is more than just something to make you laugh. "It's about being ourselves and embracing who we are," she said.[3]

Now, wait a minute, isn't jigging an Irish thing? Or, a Métis thing? Since when is it an Inuit thing?

There are lots of "Inuit things" that aren't widely known to people outside of the North. That seems to be changing, however, as people like Becky Qilavvaq and others bring authentic portrayals of Inuit life to a global audience. Who are the Inuit? As is so often the case, the best people to ask, and listen to, are the Inuit themselves.

Eleven years before Qilavvaq's toe-tapping ode to Inuit jigging, Zacharias Kunuk brought an ancient Inuit story to life on the big screen in *Atanarjuat: The Fast Runner.*[4] The actors are all from Kunuk's home community of Igloolik, and the entire movie is in Inuktitut. This film, rooted in Inuit language and culture, provides a compelling portrayal of precontact Inuit life without spoon-feeding it to the non-Inuit audience. To give just one example, there are aspects to the film that will be a bit confusing if you are unaware of Inuit naming practices.[5] Nonetheless, it is a universal story of love, ambition, and revenge that unfolds gorgeously against the backdrop of the Arctic tundra.

Kunuk went on to work on two more films, which form the Fast Runner trilogy. In *The Journals of Knud Rasmussen,* Kunuk depicts the way in which Christianity replaced traditional Inuit spirituality in a very short period of time during the 1920s.[6] In the final film of the trilogy, *Before Tomorrow,* written and directed by the Arnait Video Productions Women's Collective, the transmission of smallpox from non-Inuit traders creates a truly Inuit post-apocalyptic setting for a story about the sole survivors, a grandmother and her grandson.[7]

To date (and in my opinion), no other Indigenous peoples in Canada have so successfully seized hold of modern technology to tell authentic, Indigenously rooted stories as the Inuit. I am a bit biased, though, because I am an Indigenous-language fanatic. The fact that so much of what the Inuit produce is in their own language, rather than translated into English or French, makes me extremely happy and provides me with a concrete example of something to strive for.

Through Inuit-language films, to websites, to social media, Inuit presence is becoming much harder to ignore in Canada. I know that when I first saw *Atanarjuat,* I was filled with an exhilaration unlike anything I've felt since. Here is how we revitalize our languages and traditions! Here is how we combat the stereotypes and invisibility we experience! So much of the information about Inuit peoples, territories, and experiences are being transmitted by Inuit people themselves. This is becoming more common all across Canada as other Indigenous peoples find or create the tools needed to accomplish the same.

Okay, but maybe list some digestible facts about the Inuit

Three quarters of Inuit people live in Inuit Nunangat, often translated as "the Inuit homeland." The term *Inuit Nunangat* includes land, water, and ice.[8]

In 2011, the census pegs the total population of Inuit in Canada at almost 60 000, which is 4.2 percent of the total Aboriginal population, and 0.2 percent of the total population in Canada.[9]

Inuit Nunangat is comprised of four regions: the Inuvialuit Settlement Region of the Western Arctic, the territory of Nunavut, Nunavik in northern Quebec, and Nunatsiavut in northern Labrador.[10] Within Inuit Nunangat, Inuit are the majority population, which is a unique situation among Indigenous peoples in Canada. The Inuit also have strong ties to other Inuit peoples in Alaska (United States), Greenland (Denmark), and Chukotka (Russia) through the international Inuit Circumpolar Council.[11]

As explained in chapter 3, the Inuit are considered Indians only in the sense that, according to constitutional division of powers, the federal government is responsible

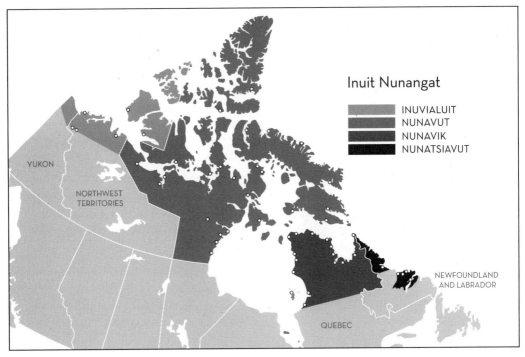

FIGURE 5.1. The four regions of Inuit Nunangat.

for Inuit peoples.[12] Inuit are not subject to the *Indian Act* and, in fact, are specifically excluded from it.[13] However, in *Baker Lake v. Canada,* Justice Mahoney stated:

> [T]he term *Indians*, in Canadian constitutional law, includes the Inuit…in the absence of their exclusion from that term, either expressly or by compelling inference, decisions relevant to the aboriginal rights of Indians in Canada apply to the Inuit.[14]

Therefore, when laws are passed, or court decisions made, and the Aboriginal rights of First Nations are addressed, these laws and court decisions also affect the Inuit. The only way to make sure not to include the Inuit is to say, "This does not include the Inuit."

There is also no such thing as Inuit status and, unlike the Métis, there is not a lot of discussion about who is and who isn't Inuit. In fact, finding any reference to definitions of who the Inuit are (administratively speaking) is difficult. In 1978, federal Northwest Territories Fishing Regulations included a blood-quantum definition of the Inuit (and the term *Eskimos*) that required at least one-quarter Inuk blood. This was changed in 2010 to the following definition: "Inuk means a person who is a direct descendant of a person of the race of aborigines commonly known as Inuit."[15]

Although there is no such thing as an Inuit status card, from 1941 to 1978 Inuit were forced to wear "Eskimo" identification discs similar to dog tags. This was for ease of colonial administration, as bureaucrats had difficulty pronouncing Inuit names, and the Inuit, at this time, did not have surnames. For a while, Inuit were officially defined as "one to whom an identification disc has been issued."[16]

The discs were circular, about 2.5 centimetres in diameter, and made of pressed fibre, or leather, or, sometimes, copper. Each disc was stamped with one letter, representing whether the wearer lived east or west of Gjoa Haven, followed by a series of numbers. Official government correspondence often used only these disc numbers to refer to individual Inuit. The discs were phased out after Operation Surname, undertaken by Inuk Abe Okpik. He visited *every Inuit home* and asked each family to choose a surname.[17]

The administrative category Inuit is not as tightly controlled as status Indians, not as ignored as non-status Indians, and not as fraught with competing definitions as the Métis; however, certain terms get used with respect to all Aboriginal peoples in Canada that have the potential to impact how identity is defined in legislation and court decisions. I thought this would be a great time to switch gears a bit and discuss some of those terms in the Inuit and First Nations context.

NOTES

1. Robert J. Flaherty. *Nanook of the North,* directed by Robert J. Flaherty (1922; Pathé Exchange), Theatrical Film, http://www.imdb.com/title/tt0013427/. The film was directed by Robert Flaherty who left his half-Inuk son, Joseph Flaherty, behind when the film was completed. Joseph Flaherty was one of the three dozen Inuit who were forcibly relocated to the high Arctic and abandoned in the harshest conditions imaginable. To read more about this story: Melanie McGrath, *The Long Exile: A Tale of Inuit Betrayal and Survival in the High Arctic* (New York: Vintage, 2008).

   Inuk throat singer and complete badass Tanya Tagaq was commissioned to create a new soundscape for the film: http://www.cbc.ca/news/aboriginal/inuk-throat-singer-tanya-tagaq-on-reclaiming-nanook-of-the-north-1.2508581.

2. Becky Qilavvaq, *Feel the Inukness.* YouTube video. Released 2012, https://www.youtube.com/watch?v=iawDXQGQsro.

3. Sarah Rogers, "Feel the Inukness on Iqaluit Filmmakers Short Film," accessed October 13, 2015, http://www.nunatsiaqonline.ca/stories/article/65674feel_the_inukness_on_iqaluit_filmmakers_short_film/.

4. Available for viewing on IsumaTV: https://www.isuma.tv/atanarjuat. While the film can be viewed for free, please consider donating whatever you can afford to support the work of IsumaTV, "a collaborative multimedia platform for Indigenous filmmakers and media organizations." They have amazing content.

5. Pelagie Owlijoot, and Louise Flaherty, eds., *Inuit Kinship and Naming Customs: Inuit ilagiigusinggit amma attiqtuijjusinggit,* trans. Pelagie Owlijoot (Iqaluit: Inhabit Media, 2014).

6. *The Journals of Knud Rasmussen* are available to view for free (or preferably for a reasonable donation) at IsumaTV/Arnait Productions: https://www.isuma.tv/isuma-productions/journals-knud-rasmussen.

7. Zacharias Kunuk, *Before Tomorrow,* IsumaTV/ Arnait Productions, https://www.isuma.tv/isuma-productions/before-tomorrow.

8. "Maps of Inuit Nunangat," *Inuit Tapirit Kanatami,* accessed October 14, 2015, https://www.itk.ca/publication/maps-inuit-nunangat-inuit-regions-canada.

9. "Stats Canada: Aboriginal Peoples in Canada," *Statistics Canada,* accessed October 14, 2015, http://www12.statcan.gc.ca/nhs-enm/2011/as-sa/99-011-x/99-011-x2011001-eng.cfm#a1.

10. An interactive map, showing the four Inuit regions and all communities, can be accessed from Aboriginal Affairs and Northern Development Canada: http://www.aadnc-aandc.gc.ca/Map/irs/mp/index-en.html.

11. "Inuit Circumpolar Council Canada," ICC *International,* accessed October 14, 2015, http://www.inuitcircumpolar.com/icc-international.html.

12. Crommunist, "Black History Month: Re Eskimos (1939)," *freethoughtblogs.com,* last modified February 4, 2013, http://freethoughtblogs.com/crommunist/2013/02/04/black-history-month-re-eskimos-1939/. This blogger offers a very clear and well laid-out summary of Constance Backhouse's book, *Colour Coded: A Legal History of Racism in Canada, 1900–1950,* as it pertains to the context of Inuit peoples becoming "Indians."

13. Section 4(1) of the *Indian Act* states: "A reference in this Act to an Indian does not include any person of the race of aborigines commonly referred to as Inuit."

14. *Baker Lake (Hamlet) v. Canada, 1997,* 107 DLR (3d) 514 (1979, FCC, Trial Division).

15. Northwest Territories Fishing Regulations, CRC 1978, c 847, §2.

16. Natasha MacDonald-Dupuis, "The Little-Known History of How the Canadian Government Made Inuit Wear 'Eskimo Tags,'" (blog), last modified December 16, 2015, http://www.vice.com/en_ca/read/the-little-known-history-of-how-the-canadian-government-made-inuit-wear-eskimo-tags.

17. Ann Meekitjuk Hanson, "What's In a Name?" accessed December 30, 2015, http://www.nunavut.com/nunavut99/english/name.html.

6

Hunter-Gatherers
or Trapper-Harvesters?
Why Some Terms Matter

The Inuit make no bones about it. Theirs is still very much a hunting culture. But what does that mean?

Most Inuit still eat a solid diet of country food, which is just like it sounds – traditional foods such as caribou, whale, seal, fish, and so on.[1] Hunting remains a central practice in Inuit communities. So, is that all it takes to be a hunting culture?

Actually going out and hunting is a pretty important part of a hunting culture, but the act itself is not everything. The focus on hunting informs the language, the traditions, the stories, the music, and the art. According to the Inuit Art Foundation:

> The hunting theme can be found in every aspect of Inuit culture, especially art. Many of the tools and weapons used in the past were decorated with hunting images, as were objects used by shamans. Many stories revolve around hunting. Alootook Ipellie, formerly of Iqaluit, Nunavut (now deceased), wrote that so many Inuit are good carvers because "...they come from a very visual culture. Their very livelihood depended solely on dealing with the landscape every day during hunting or gathering expeditions. They were always visualizing animals in their thoughts as they searched the land, waters, and skies for game."[2]

Culture informs our interactions with the world around and inside us. It informs our pedagogy. When you look at some of the principles of Inuit Qaujimajatuqangit (IQ),[3] which is traditional Inuit knowledge (I avoid the term *epistemology* because, holy cats, that's an annoying word), it is not difficult to see how these principles have been shaped by hunting. Also, it should not be so difficult to see how these traditional ways of knowing are absolutely applicable to the modern era:

- **Inuuqatigiitsiarniq:** concept of respecting others, relationships, and caring for people
- **Tunnganarniq:** concept of fostering good spirit by being open, welcoming, and inclusive
- **Pijitsirarniq:** concept of serving and providing for family/community
- **Aajiiqatigiingniq:** concept of decision-making through discussion and consensus
- **Pilimmaksarniq:** concept of skills and knowledge acquisition
- **Qanuqtuurungnarniq:** concept of being resourceful to solve problems
- **Piliriqatigiingniq:** concept of collaborative relationship or working together for a common purpose
- **Avatimik Kamattiarniq:** concept of environmental stewardship

As with other Indigenous peoples, these hunting principles were eroded by the introduction of fur trapping. As noted on the Inuit Art Alive website, when discussing the changing nature of work among Inuit:

> Previously, work and profit had been shared among community members, but with the advent of trapping, hunters worked alone for a private income. In the early 1900s, posts were commonplace in most areas of the Arctic, as were guns and traplines. Their widespread use greatly changed northern practices as the trapping way of life was in direct conflict with the old way of hunting, which was done in groups with proceeds being shared.[4]

New principles were introduced and had a profound effect on Inuit relationships with one another, and with the land. Nonetheless, when modern Inuit articulate foundational cultural principles and apply them to present-day issues of governance, law, pedagogy, and so on, they do so within the framework of the "Inuit Way," which continues to be rooted in a hunting culture, not a trapping culture.[5]

Is the difference between hunting and trapping at all important?

Yes and no. Yes, in that trapping is an activity focused on the individual, commercial aspect of one particular form of hunting. As discussed above, trapping tends to be an activity that is more individual, rather than collective. The values of a hunting culture are not necessarily the same as the values of a trapping culture.

That is not to say that trapping must be incompatible with values such as those expressed through Inuit Qaujimajatuqangit or other Indigenous peoples' principles. The ethnogenesis of the Métis, for example, is linked to the fur trade, yet our collective values are not so widely divergent from those of our First Nations relations. Commercial transactions between Indigenous nations were happening long before contact with Europeans, so the commercial nature of trapping does not automatically render it untraditional.

An estimated 25 000 Indigenous peoples and 35 000 Canadians continue to participate in the fur trade through trapping, though antifur campaigns have put a serious dent in the industry.[6]

However, if trapping is just one activity within the broader category of harvesting, then the difference may not be important at all. Indigenous peoples trapped fur-bearing animals before the fur trade, though never as an end in itself. It can be viewed as just another hunting practice.

The way in which the Canadian state treats hunting versus trapping is important to examine. In Treaty 8 territory,[7] for example, Alberta treats trapping as a purely commercial right and "regulates it accordingly."[8] Blanket trapping regulations are applied to Indigenous trappers on the basis that commercial rights under Treaty 8 were extinguished by the Natural Resource Transfer Agreement.[9] Licensing, fees, quotas, regulations about the building of cabins for trapping, and so on are all applied to Indigenous trappers. In addition, trapping is often seen as a "weak right" to land in comparison to hunting.

Worse, Peter Hutchins points out that "the very existence of traplines has been used to deny the survival of aboriginal rights or titles" based on the notion that traplines are a form of individual tenure extinguishing collective Aboriginal or treaty rights.[10]

So, what is going on here?

In essence, there are two views of what trapping is. Canada tends to take the view that trapping is an imported, specific activity. It is different from Aboriginal hunting in that it is individual and commercial in nature, not rooted in indigeneity. Most Indigenous peoples see trapping as a subset of hunting, which is, itself, integral to our cultures.

This "subset of hunting" approach can be seen in practice by neighbours of the Inuit of Nunavik, the Eastern James Bay Cree of Eeyou Istchee.[11] Under the James Bay and Northern Quebec Agreement (JBNQA), of which the Cree and Inuit are both signatories, provision was made for the creation of a Cree Trapper Association (CTA).[12]

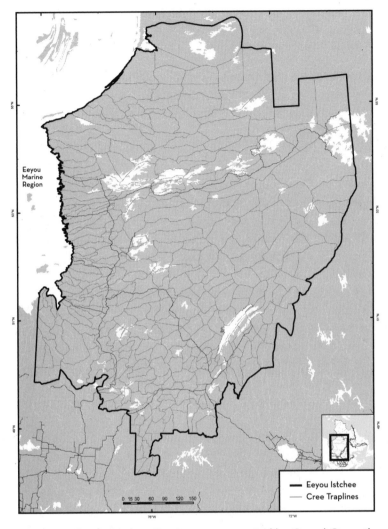

FIGURE 6.1. Eeyou Istchee Territory, represented by Grand Council of the Crees on the east shore of James Bay. The region (above) is divided into family territories.

The name and focus would seem to be on trapping alone: "One of the many goals of the CTA is to promote sales and assist in the orderly collection and marketing of wild furs by its 5000 members."[13] It is very clear, however, that as envisioned by the CTA, trapping is an integral part of the collective culture of the Crees of Eeyou Istchee:

The role of the Cree Trappers' Association is an important one, it is to protect and maintain a way of life that completely identifies who we really are as Eeouch who depend and continue to depend on the land for survival.[14]

More fundamentally, the CTA and its members are guided by the Eeyou Indoh-hoh Weeshou-Wehwun, the traditional Cree hunting law.[15] The trapping of fur-bearing animals is treated as a subset of this wider Cree hunting law, all of it part of Indoh-hoh (hunting activities).

What is most interesting to me is the difference between the Cree and the English in this situation. Eeyou Istchee is divided into many irregularly shaped trapping territories. According to customary law, each trapping territory has a tallyman who is in charge of managing the resources within his or her territory. The name *tallyman* is defined in various pieces of legislation applying to the Eastern James Bay Cree as "a Cree person recognized by a Cree community as responsible for the supervision of the activities related to the exercising of the right to harvest on a Cree trapline."[16]

Originally, of course, the tallymen tallied up furs for the fur trader. The informal Cree word for this person is *ouchimaw* (in my dialect, it's *okimâw*), often translated as "chief," or "boss" – someone put in a position of authority over something; in this case, the management of the land. The job of the ouchimaw is not just to keep an eye on trapping in his or her territory, but also to ensure the health of the territory as a *whole*. The formal title for a tallyman is *Kaanoowapmaakin*, which can be translated as "hunting leader," and in English is defined as being "the steward, guardian and custodian of the territory."[17]

In Cree, the whole of Eeyou Istchee is the Indoh-hoh Istchee, the traditional hunting territories as defined by Cree traditional law. Indoh-hoh wun are all the animals within one of these territories, not just the fur-bearing ones. The responsibilities of a Kaanoowapmaakin, in his or her traditional Indoh-hoh Istchee, goes far beyond what you might envision a head trapper doing.[18] The responsibility is not just extended to individual trappers, but to all Cree people, and all living things within Cree territory. The Kaanoowapmaakin must monitor, manage, and share resources within his or her territory. His or her authority extends to resolving territorial disputes, inviting guests into the territory, and so on.

So, while the English terms focused on trapping as an imported, individual economic activity, the Cree terms (translated into English through a Cree world-view) make it clear that trapping is part of a wider hunting culture governed by traditional laws and central to the Cree culture.

All very cool, but where is this going?

I am not drawing you toward some stunning conclusion; I am merely drawing you toward the question itself. Does it matter whether the Canadian government calls Indigenous peoples "hunters and gatherers" or "trappers and harvesters?"

I am of the opinion that it does. When the terms used are English ones, defined in English, and seen through the colonial lens, much is lost. If some Indigenous hunting activities are being defined as trapping, and this definition results in the erosion of Indigenous rights, which has indeed been the case, then it is important for us to challenge these terms.

Rather than seeking better English or French translations for Indigenous concepts, I feel it is important to return to our languages for the proper terms. The Inuit and the Cree of Eeeyou Istchee are already doing this. In this way, we centre ourselves in our traditional laws and our traditional understandings of the reciprocal obligations we have to our territories and to one another. Far from being feel-good, back-to-nature yearning for precontact mumbo jumbo, our legal principles are foundational and applicable to the modern era.

Most of the Eastern James Bay Cree communities in Quebec have shed their English and French names in favour of Cree names, and all of the Inuit communities of Nunavik have been renamed in Inuktitut. Chaos did not ensue. I think Indigenous resurgence is very much rooted in the use of Indigenous languages. Canadians in general, individually and collectively, must become more accustomed to forgoing facile translations in favour of delving into the complexities of our Indigenous principles. To be honest, we could all benefit from doing this more often.

To take this back to administrative categories and issues of identity, language has been used as a vehicle for the erosion of inherent Indigenous rights, including the right to determine who we are as peoples. I like to think language can also be a vehicle for the assertion of rights, and this is a topic I will come back to many times.

NOTES

1. "What Is Country Food?" *Inuit Cultural Online Resource,* accessed October 13, 2015, http://icor.ottawainuitchildrens.com/node/19.

2. Alootook Ipellie, "Land, Spirituality, and Mythology in Inuit Art," in *The 1998 Nunavut Handbook,* ed. Marion Soublière (Iqaluit: Nortext Multimedia Inc., 1998), quoted in Inuit Art Foundation, "Hunting," *Inuit Art Alive,* accessed October 13, 2015, http://inuitartalive.ca/index_e.php?p=115.

3. Government of Nunavut, "Hivunikhaliurutikhat," *Department of Executive and Intergovernmental Affairs,* accessed October 13, 2015, http://www.eia.gov.nu.ca/PDF/IQ_Principles_2010.pdf.

4. Inuit Art Foundation, "Hunting," *Inuit Art Alive,* accessed October 13, 2015, http://inuitartalive.ca/index_e.php?p=115.

5. "The Inuit Way," *uqar.ca,* accessed October 13, 2015, http://www.uqar.ca/files/boreas/inuitway_e.pdf. This is an amazing resource on Inuit culture that should be read by everyone who works with Inuit people, or who intends to visit Inuit territories.

6. Fur Institution of Canada, accessed October 17, 2015, http://www.fur.ca/files/fur_trade_at_a_glance.pdfhttp://fur.ca/fur-trade/canadas-fur-trade-fact-figures/accessed.

7. Treaty 8 covers areas of northern Saskatchewan, most of northern Alberta, about half of northern British Columbia, and extends a little into the Northwest Territories.

8. Monique M. Passelac-Ross, "The Trapping Rights of Aboriginal Peoples in Northern Alberta," (Occasional Paper 15, Canadian Institute of Resources Law, University of Calgary, 2005), accessed October 13, 2015, http://dspace.ucalgary.ca/bitstream/1880/47194/1/OP15Trapping.pdf.

9. *Alberta Natural Resources Act, 1930,* SC 1930, c 3.

10. See note 8. This is an amazing document exploring the treatment of Aboriginal trapping rights in Alberta (specifically in Treaty 8 territory), including how oil and gas exploration has impacted these rights, as well as offering some suggestions for a more generous interpretation and redefinition of the treaty right to trap. Peter Hutchin's quote is on page 65.

11. *Eeyou Istchee* is the Eastern James Bay Cree term for their homeland.

12. Grand Council of the Crees, "James Bay and Northern Quebec Agreement," last modified October 23, 2015, http://www.gcc.ca/pdf/LEG000000006.pdf.

13. Cree Trapper Association, *creetrappers.ca,* last modified October, 2012, accessed October 16, 2015, https://web.archive.org/web/20140517052150/http://creetrappers.ca/. These quotes are by Isaac Masty when he was President of the Cree Trapper's Association. Using the *Wayback Machine,* you can read his full welcome above. To see the current welcome, at any given time, visit: http://creetrappers.ca.

14. Ibid.

15. Ibid., http://creetrappers.ca/wp-content/uploads/2014/02/CTA_EEYOU_HUNTING_LAW.PDF. The original Cree language document can be found here: http://creetrappers.ca/wp-content/uploads/2014/02/EEYOU_HUNTING_CREE_VER.pdf.

16. *An Act Respecting Hunting and Fishing Rights in the James Bay and New Quebec Territories,* CQLR c D-13.1 s 1(n).

17. See note 15, page 16, 5.2.

18. See note 15, page 17.

7

Allowably Indigenous:
To Ptarmigan or Not
to Ptarmigan[1]

When Indigeneity Is Transgressive

For thousands of generations before contact, diversity of culture was a fact in what is now known as Canada. Despite today's official policy of multiculturalism, Canada has nonetheless collapsed cultural diversity into, essentially, four categories: White anglophone settlers, White francophone settlers, Aboriginal people,[2] and Newcomers (which is basically Everyone Else and is, in my opinion, the more honest term).

None of these categories is neat, or even particularly coherent when examined at all closely. For example, Black families who have lived in Canada as long as any of their White counterparts are still often categorized as Newcomers, and the existence of slavery as a reason for Black presence in Canada is thoroughly denied. The incredible diversity of Aboriginal peoples is ignored in favour of a one-size-fits-all federal policy. The meaning of White has shifted and changed over time as European-descended settlers expanded the category through official immigration policies, and so has meant very different things at different times in Canadian history.[3]

Despite the flaws inherent in these categories, there is still a strong sense that Aboriginal culture was supplanted by White settler culture, and Newcomer-Everyone Else cultures are welcomed only to the extent that they enrich the Canadian experience; in other words, as long as they are expressed via costumes, food, and music.

Obviously, I am simplifying what are a very complex series of relationships and social phenomena, all to state what is fairly obvious: Canada has a set of (relatively new) cultural norms that are settler-based, and these cultural norms constitute "the mainstream." In Canada, there are strong ideas about "how to act," which do not always mirror Indigenous expectations.

Cultural expressions that can be commodified are part of that mainstream, providing a very narrow outlet for Indigenous and Everyone Else (particularly Black and non-Black POC) cultural expression. Cultural expressions that can be purchased in the form of goods and services, or entertainment, are acceptable. Cultural expressions that cannot be so easily commodified can be seen as threatening, transgressive, or simply not Canadian.

What does it mean to be "allowably Indigenous"?

Indigenous peoples who visit or live in areas where they are not the majority of the population must navigate a series of cultural expectations that are still very foreign to many of us, no matter how many generations of interactions there may have been in our families/communities.

Often, the biggest shift is moving from an isolated/rural environment to an urban one. Rarely is this a one-way relocation; it tends to be cyclical, at least among the first generation to make the move. Though these experiences can be described to others, I do not believe it is something you can fully prepare for. Thus, there is almost always an element of culture shock for those Indigenous peoples leaving their nonurban community for an urban centre.

On the other side, there is no expectation within Canadian (non-Indigenous) culture that Indigenous cultures must be accounted for, learned about, or even really accommodated. Knowing nothing about the Inuit, for example, is not considered a fault. Yet, when Nunavummiut (Inuit of Nunavut) or Nunavimmiut (Inuit of Nunavik) go south, their lack of knowledge about city culture/living is considered to stem from small-mindedness, a lack of education, or ignorance.

Thus, you can have a situation as there is in Quebec, where very few Canadians know anything at all about Nunavik and Inuit people other than they are located in the very northern parts of the province. You have a situation where Canadians are accustomed to seeing Indigenous peoples only within very narrow circumstances: as urban homeless, struggling with addictions/mental illness, or within the context of cultural celebrations (costumes, food, or music). Any other show or embodiment of culture is not socially acceptable, because Canadians have no way of categorizing them according to settler norms. This is what it means to be allowably Indigenous when you step outside an Indigenous community.[4]

Indigenous transgression: Connection to the land is weird.

Although commodified culture (costumes, food, or music) is an accepted and encouraged part of Canadian multiculturalism, there is an unspoken rule that none of these things should be too weird; at least, not in public. Settler mainstream cultural norms still hold sway over how these things can be expressed. For example, when Indigenous peoples began holding round dances in shopping malls in the winter of 2012, this aspect of entertainment/music and unrequested hypervisibility was seen as transgressive by many.

So, when a video began circulating in 2014, and news articles ran headlines like "Woman plucks, eats raw bird on Montreal subway," I definitely wondered if this was an Indigenous person doing something that was being misinterpreted through a lens of settler mainstream culture. Sure enough, Inuk Christina David, who grew up in Kangiqsujuaq and Kuujjuaq, took credit for the action and quickly began setting the story straight.

I cannot help but feel there is a delicious irony in the fact that Christina David became (in)famous for an action that took place on Canada Day. Christina did a bunch of really fantastic interviews about what was actually happening. She clearly detailed the bird in question was a ptarmigan brought to her by an aunt, she was very excited to get it home and cook it, and she was removing its feathers inside a plastic bag – not eating it raw.[5]

During one of the interviews she gave, Christina was asked if ptarmigan is expensive and, thus, a delicacy.[6] There was a pause, and a startled "what?" from Christina. She then explained, "As Inuit, we don't buy that. We hunt it up north, and we share it with our people!"

Later, she was asked where people who want to eat ptarmigan can go and buy one. I was struck by the leap to commodification here, as in, if a settler wants something, it must be available for purchase, or at least defined by its monetary value. Christina had to once again explain this is not how things work when you're discussing country food.

I wonder if this made the interviewers a bit angry, like they were possibly being denied something that, whether they wanted it or not, they felt they should at least be able to have if the desire came a-knocking. It's probably mean of me to even wonder, so I'll cut it out. The funny thing is, as Christina explains, if they really wanted ptarmigan, they could probably get it for free if they were willing to put in the work to build a relationship with Inuit folks. But picking it up at the local supermarket? Hahahaha – now *that's* weird.

For me, watching this as someone who gets more excited over smoked fish and caribou meat than I do over Christmas morning, I felt there was a huge cultural divide here that a lot of Indigenous peoples can relate to. Where I'm from, hunters are expected to share their catch, and getting fresh country food is pretty much the best thing ever – especially when it's a care package sent to you in the city. Bringing price into it and wanting to know which supermarkets sell ptarmigan make no earthly sense.

I think the underlying fascination with what Christina did is based on the feeling that, in mainstream Canadian culture, continuing to have a connection to the land, and therefore with the food you eat, is weird – especially if you're living in a city. For Indigenous folks who have relocated to the city, on the other hand, getting some wild meat is a little slice of home.

A lot of non-Indigenous peoples commenting on the story, when it came out, focused on how plucking a bird in public is unsanitary. They are forgetting (nonurban) wild animals are much less prone to disease and contamination than domesticated animals, and a Metro car is already much more unsanitary than a ptarmigan could ever possibly be. The real issue is that the act was transgressive. It broke rules about how people are supposed to behave within mainstream Canadian culture. *Regular* Canadians don't get that close to their food, and definitely *not* in public. Food preparation happens in specific places set aside for that purpose. Who says so? Mainstream settler values say so.

As soon as the story broke, the Montreal police were talking about the possibility of laying charges. Was it transgressive or rude enough to merit a fine or criminal charge? Is having a connection with the land, and with country food, something that has to be restricted like this? Is it something we can only be allowed to do in our communities or in the privacy of our homes?

She should become a superstar!

Another aspect to Christina's story that just fascinated the heck out of me was the many questions she received about what she wanted to do now that she was "famous." I was told there were even suggestions about reality television! That immediate jump to commodification, of her entertainment value as an Inuk, blows my mind. It makes me think about the perceived performative value of "doing Indigenous stuff" because it is supposedly strange and exotic, instead of the *original normal*. Commodification of Indigenous cultures as a tourist attraction (and enticement to settlement) has a long and sordid history in Canada and continues unabated.[7]

I imagine the reaction to an Inuit picnic in some Montreal park. Cardboard put down, nikku,[8] mattaq,[9] and misiraq[10] spread out on top of it. Or, slicing off pieces of frozen raw caribou…. Is this a performance piece, perhaps? People don't *really* eat like that, do they?

The point is, even though Canadian multiculturalism is supposedly open to other cultures' food, the reality is, if this food does not conform to Canadian norms, then preparing or eating it is transgressive unless it is done for entertainment value. Perhaps an "eww gross, can you eat that?" challenge on some game show. *That* is a place for an Inuk, even a place she can make some money! Plucking ptarmigan in a Metro car because she's too excited to wait? Having a country-food picnic? These are possibly criminal acts.

We're not the weird ones; true Inuk pride

There has been a lot of political talk over the years about reconciliation and respecting Indigenous peoples, and blah, blah, blah. The reality is we seem outlandish (how ironic) and maybe even a little scary when we present as Indigenous outside of spaces where this is expected. People immediately speculated Christina was mentally ill, perhaps homeless, and desperate enough to eat a pigeon. Christina was not even recognized by most as being Inuit. Her actions were pathologized because they were so incredibly foreign in the context she found herself.

Yet, Montreal is home to hundreds of Inuit; the estimate from 2011 was at least 900.[11] Many more travel there to visit family members, to receive medical care, or just to do some city shopping from time to time. Maybe that's a drop in the bucket for a city that boasts over a million people, but hearing Inuktitut spoken around Atwater is a pretty common thing. Seeing women in beautiful sealskin kamiks[12] and babies in amautiit[13] is not at all unusual. Despite this, there does not appear to be any space made for Inuit. Routinely harassed by the police, followed around stores, and too often treated like second-class citizens, urban Inuit do not have an easy time of it in Montreal.

So, when Christina asserted her pride in being a "true Inuk," I thought this was important. It felt like she was quite humbly acknowledging who she is and where she comes from, and refusing to be ashamed about it. It is a reminder that Inuit people have been here for a very, very long time.

That's not to say what she did is, or needs to be, representative of the values of all Inuit people. I know some Inuit found her actions to be out of place, and I am not going to try to step in and say otherwise. However, I do not think what she did should be something subject to any criminal or bylaw charges. Montreal is not Inuit territory, but it is Indigenous territory. All of Canada is Indigenous territory and, whether Canadians wish to acknowledge it or not, all of us living in Canada rely on the land. Valuing cultures that have not lost connection to the land needs to become a priority; that cannot happen if space is not made in Canadian culture to expand the notion of *allowably Indigenous.*

NOTES

1. The original version of this piece was published in *Ilinniapaa*, a collaborative northern magazine available online: Chelsea Vowel, "Allowably Indigenous: to Ptarmigan or Not to Ptarmigan," *Ilinniapaa*, last modified August 14, 2014, http://www.ilinniapaa.com/blog/2014/8/14/allowably-indigenous-to-ptarmigan-or-not-to-ptarmigan#_ftn2.

2. I deliberately use the singular here to highlight the perceived homogeneity of Indigenous cultures.

3. Noel Ignatiev, *How the Irish Became White* (New York: Rutledge, 1995); David R. Roediger, *Working Toward Whiteness: How America's Immigrants Became White: The Strange Journey from Ellis Island to the Suburbs* (New York: Basic Books, 2005).

4. The rules governing what is "allowably Indigenous" inside our communities are less clear, since settlers are often not there to provide guidance.

5. "Christina David, Former Nunavik Resident, Takes Credit for Picking Bird on Montreal Metro," *CBC News*, last modified July 28, 2014, http://www.cbc.ca/news/canada/montreal/christina-david-former-nunavik-resident-takes-credit-for-plucking-bird-on-montreal-metro-1.2719136; "Stop Freaking Out About the Woman Who 'Ate' a Raw Bird on the Montreal Metro," *vice.com,* last modified July 29, 2014, http://www.vice.com/en_ca/read/stop-freaking-out-about-the-woman-who-ate-a-raw-bird-on-the-montreal-metro-653.

6. Davidson Video, BQWSC – 100 Jobs: "Exclusive Interview with the Montreal Metro 'Bird Plucker,'" YouTube video, 1:01, July 27, 2014, https://www.youtube.com/watch?v=Oisxo6u1UUs.

7. Jennifer Adese, "Aboriginal: Constructing the Aboriginal and Imagineering the Canadian National Brand" (Hamilton: McMasters University, 2012), https://macsphere.mcmaster.ca/bitstream/11375/15246/1/fulltext.pdf. Here, you will find an in-depth analysis of historic and contemporary commodification of Indigenous peoples, lands, art, and culture.

8. Dry meat.

9. Beluga skin; an Inuit delicacy.

10. Aged seal fat used as a condiment.

11. Statistics Canada, *Inuit*, last modified March 28, 2014, http://www12.statcan.gc.ca/nhs-enm/2011/as-sa/99-011-x/99-011-x2011001-eng.cfm#a5.

12. Sealskin boots.

13. Parkas with hoods large enough to put babies and toddlers in, yet still draw the hood up over the head of the parent carrying the infant.

8

Caught in the Crossfire of Blood-Quantum Reasoning

Popular Notions of Indigenous Purity

I read voraciously. While, for a time, my love of reading was suppressed (thanks, law school), I'm happy to report it's come back with a vengeance! (There is light at the end of the tunnel, law students! Your literary libido is not lost! It's just dampened for a few years after graduation.)

I particularly enjoy science fiction, and I'm always on the lookout for new authors. New to *me*, I mean. I decided to delve into the world of eReaders and purchased a Kindle – though, on some undefined level, I was philosophically opposed to deviating from the printed form. Any vague objections I had were quickly overcome by the fact I no longer had to lug around huge Neal Stephenson novels in my shoulder bag, which is nothing to scoff at when your commute on public transit takes two hours one way. Even better than this, however, is that oft-maligned experience of instant gratification an eReader can provide. When I've exhausted my current store of novels, I run a quick search online for top sci-fi novels in any given year, and then I flip over to my Kindle and download them. Some have been flops, but many have been a window into a body of work I'd never have known about otherwise.

And so it is that I came across the author Nancy Kress. I burned through her short stories and novels, completely taken with that "old-school aliens-are-neat, let's-imagine-just-how-neat" approach to even the current post-apocalyptic fad.

Of course, I wouldn't be writing this just to mention I'd found some excellent reading material. In chapter 18, I discuss Robert J. Sawyer's portrayal of Indigenous peoples in his Neanderthal Parallax trilogy. In some ways, he does an excellent job of questioning certain assumptions, while in another area his writing fits in with mainstream views. Overall, I think he does a good job of avoiding stereotypes and delving a bit deeper than is often done when Indigenous peoples are brought in as characters in novels, film,[1] or video games.[2]

I've found a much more problematic approach in the Nancy Kress novel, *Crossfire*, which was published in 2003.[3]

The starting premise of this novel is that a bunch of extremely wealthy groups are travelling together off-earth to colonize a distant planet. You've got a large extended family of scientists, a Chinese contingent, deposed Arab royalty, Quakers, assorted others, and – about a thousand Cheyenne.

(As a quick aside, another bonus of the Kindle is that when I want to pull up quotes for you, all I have to do is search the term *Cheyenne* and boom. One drawback is the location in the book is not expressed by page number, but rather by location; so, if you have a copy of this book sitting on your shelf, it might be harder for you to find the same quote.)

The Cheyenne are a Plains culture. The Northern Cheyenne live in what is now Montana, while the Southern Cheyenne live in Oklahoma after being forced there onto a Cheyenne-Arapaho reservation. Like a great many First Nations, the Cheyenne have experienced many cultural changes over the centuries. From farming settlements to a horse-based, buffalo-hunting culture, the Cheyenne were never frozen in time and have adapted to new technologies and circumstances while maintaining kinship relationships and cultural cohesion.

First, some background from the book. The story takes place in the far future, so the year is undefined. I'll just quote from the book for this:

> Once they [Native American reservations] were terrible places, the dregs of arable land, full of poverty and alcoholism. Since the natives figured out that as a separate nation they could legally offer services that places part of the Unites States could not, they flourished. First gambling, then genemod and pet-cloning clinics, and –"
>
> "I'm aware that reservations are great scientific centers," Gail said dryly, "And greenly rich."[4]

All right! Kress has the reserves crawling out of poverty and into scientific innovation and wealth, an approach somewhat similar to that taken by Charles de Lint in his futuristic yet fetishistic novel, *Svaha*.[5] (The *noble savage* trope appears often in *Svaha*.) However, unlike de Lint's novel, the characters in *Crossfire* do so in morally questionable ways by providing seedy, legal-limbo services not available elsewhere, which certainly fits into contemporary notions about Indian tribal sovereignty in the United States being mostly used for gambling, cigarettes, and so on.[6] I sort of prefer de Lint's approach of riches being accumulated by the explosive popularity of a mixture of traditional Indigenous music with pop tunes for the masses. Of course, I am casting A Tribe Called Red in the updated version of this![7] However, emerging out of crushing poverty is a somewhat positive future prediction, I guess – even if the root causes of that poverty (colonialism) are never addressed.

The "no true technology" fallacy[8]

But wait, that quote isn't over! Here's more necessary background:

> That's why I don't understand why this lot wants to dump it all and go back to living as if the last two or three centuries hadn't ever happened. But with genetic labs in tow, of course.[9]

One of the themes related to the Cheyenne in this novel is their occasional use of, and reliance on, technology. Of course, technology, as it's generally used, and specifically in this novel, is not any human-made tool; it is "the application of scientific knowledge for practical purposes."

By definition, this means no Indigenous peoples can ever invent technology, because doing so would require the use of scientific principles, which were not known among Native peoples before contact *because settlers invented science* – at least, science as it is defined in relation to technology.

However, this is not a universally applied principle. After all, in science fiction, aliens can have technology even if they have nothing comprehensibly equivalent to the scientific method. Maybe we can even retrofit the concept of science to include peoples like the Maya with their complex and precise astrological observations, but probably not. Clearly, I do not agree this is the correct definition of technology, but when the word comes up, I'm fairly certain this is the way people are thinking of it.

Throughout Kress's novel, the "desire to leave all technology behind" that has been attributed to this fictional group is described in derogatory terms – "Quixotic, ridiculous mission" and other similar sentiments.[10] These Cheyenne have been set up as foolish Luddites and are mocked throughout.

In chapter 19, I address the frozen-in-time approach to Indigenous peoples and why I believe it is a ridiculous and arbitrary standard. Nonetheless, it is an enduring belief, and one that comes out loud and clear in this novel. In this story, the Cheyenne are trying to rid themselves of all "Volcano Man" (settler) technology, because they are suspicious of it; but the big irony in the book is they can't seem to live without it. Once again, the desire to return to traditional Indigenous principles somehow gets conflated with the notion that doing so requires Indigenous peoples to eschew all forms of technology and revert to exactly how they lived precontact.

I would *really* appreciate it if authors and individuals stopped pushing precontact conditions as a goal or a desire on our part. Having to constantly explain there isn't a large movement to get rid of indoor plumbing (assuming we have it in the first place, which, given contemporary living conditions in Indigenous communities, should not be taken for granted), vaccinations, and so forth, is frustrating and draining. Integrating settler technology into traditional Indigenous practices does not require us to accept settler philosophies, and it certainly does not erase our indigeneity. Unless you're talking about settler notions of what it means to be Indigenous. And do I need to point out how flawed those Hollywood stereotypes are to begin with? (If so, check the resources listed at the end of this chapter.)

Kress has deliberately set up this splinter group as a minority Indigenous view against a backdrop of Indigenous peoples who have embraced and benefited from technology; but, this is a tired meme and no new ground is being broken by rehashing it. This is the first time I've seen Indians go into space in a sci-fi novel, and I expected more than this.

"Fake" Indians: The blood-quantum mess

The technology issue is not even the reason I'm writing this. It's a pretty standard issue I can ignore for the sake of my sanity and an otherwise good read. So let me get to the real point. Here are some quotes describing the space-faring Cheyenne:

- "Larry Smith's dubious tribe of 'Cheyenne.'"[11]
- "Saying good-bye to nine hundred sixty-seven Cheyenne Native Americans, almost none of whom possessed actual Native American ancestors."[12]
- "On Earth, he [Larry Smith] had been a cattle breeder. Now he was a Cheyenne chief."[13]
- "Oh for God's sake, Gail didn't say aloud. She'd read the personnel records. Larry Smith was one thirty-second Cheyenne. The 'tribe' included Irish, German, Spanish, Swedish, and French blood, and it was in the majority. One brave was three-quarters Chinese, with features no seventeenth-century Native American had so much as ever set eyes on."[14]

Almost every time the name *Cheyenne* is written in this novel, it is done in scare quotes: they are the "Cheyenne." As is made clear in that last quote, these are not full-bloods. They are fakes; not really Indians – just people playing Indian.

Oh, blood quantum; what a strange concept.[15]

In chapter 3, I explain the system used in Canada to determine who is a legally recognized (status) Indian and who is not. Essentially, you are no longer an Indian once an Indian parent and an Indian grandparent have married out. That amounts to extermination of your identity in two generations.

The situation in the United States is somewhat more complicated. The Bureau of Indian Affairs (BIA) can issue a Certificate of Degree of Indian Blood (CDIB) with the blood quantum of the bearer and his or her tribal affiliation. Each tribe in the United States has its own enrollment requirements, some require half or a quarter blood quantum, others less, and still others have no minimum blood-quantum requirements and determine membership by lineal descent (descent from an original enrollee of the tribe).

In Canada, blood quantum is relevant to those Indigenous peoples born in Canada who want to enter the United States to live or work without a green card or work permit. The United States requires First Nations peoples to have at least 50 percent blood quantum to do this, and this must be proven through a letter from a First Nation or from Indian Affairs.[16]

The widespread imposition and acceptance of blood-quantum definitions by settlers and their governments means that culture and community acceptance doesn't matter. You are a *real* Indian only if you haven't intermarried with non-Indigenous people. Nancy Kress buys into this notion completely in her portrayal of the "dubious Cheyenne."

Leaving aside the fact not all "out-breeding" was voluntary and sexual violence was (and continues to be) an issue faced by Indigenous women, the concept of blood quantum puts enormous pressure on Indigenous peoples not to marry non-Indigenous people. Imagine someone telling you that you can't be Canadian because your father and your grandmother came from a different country. Oh, I'm sorry, am I conflating citizenship with ethnicity? Well, we never agreed to be defined by blood in the first place, so I'm going to give myself permission to discuss identity in the various forms it is defined.

Blood-quantum rules have been called a "slow genocide," and I think this is an apt description. Not mass murder, but extinction via definition. Every time a non-Indigenous person enters the "Indian gene pool," fewer people in the next generation are counted as Indians. I'm sorry, but what are we? A breed? Or peoples with distinct languages, customs, and beliefs?

I can understand the reluctance on the part of settlers and settler governments to consider Indigenous culture as a defining aspect of Indigenous identity, given how intensely our cultures were repressed and deliberately interfered with. A lot of effort was put in to erasing our languages, kinship ties, territorial relationships, and so forth. How can any of that possibly matter now, if it's basically all gone?

The answer is, of course, it isn't all gone. Indigenous peoples have tenaciously resisted colonization and the destruction of our cultures – not without cost, setbacks, and battles, which continue to be fought. But our demise is greatly exaggerated.

Also, the blood-quantum approach freezes us in time. No genetic mixing was allowed after contact. The unstated belief is that genetic mixing was fine before contact, when it only involved Indigenous nations and did nothing because it did nothing to dilute identity as an Indigenous person; but, for some reason, non-Native blood erases indigeneity?

The idea that Indian blood has some sort of magic quality that imbues one with legitimate Indigenous culture is as ridiculous a notion as I can think of, and so is the idea that "outside" blood can dilute or destroy Indigenous culture. That kind of thinking is 19th-century pseudo-science, and I don't want it in my 20th- and 21st-century-produced science fiction, thanks.

I don't care if Larry Smith's Cheyenne are all 100 percent ethnically Chinese – which is somehow presented by Kress as being even less legitimate than being a mixture of European stock. Unpack that if you will. This novel takes place *centuries* in the future, in a time when it is conceivable, given current policies, there will be no more "pure-breed" Indians in existence. If Nancy Kress can imagine such a future, yet still make space for there to be a continuation of an Indigenous land base (unfortunately still restricted) where Indigenous culture is still legitimately practiced, then surely she can reboot the entire notion of blood quantum!

What this novel did for me was to highlight some of the more problematic stereotypes out there about Indigenous peoples. I cannot avoid confronting these portrayals when they are presented to me, and I'm hoping the next time you come across an Indigenous character in a book you're reading, you give more than a cursory thought to the image the author creates.[17]

NOTES

1. Catherine Bainbridge, Neil Diamond, and Jeremiah Hayes, *Reel Injun* (National Film Board of Canada, film, 2009), https://www.nfb.ca/film/reel_injun/. Here, you will find an invaluable breakdown of the portrayal of North American Indians in cinema; this film is on my list of resources teachers should absolutely be using with their students.

2. Elizabeth LaPensée, *Native Representations in Video Games* (video, 2011), https://vimeo.com/25991603. This is a short film on Indigenous representations in video games by the incomparable Elizabeth LaPensée. Elizabeth is passionate about Indigenous futurisms, and

designs Indigenous video games, comics, and art. You should definitely check her out: http://www.elizabethlapensee.com/.

3. Nancy Kress, *Crossfire* (New York: Tor, 2003).

4. Kress, *Crossfire* (Location 591, Kindle version).

5. Charles de Lint, *Svaha* (New York: Ace Books, 1989).

6. *Tribal sovereignty,* a term specifically used in the United States but not in Canada, refers to tribes' right to govern themselves as domestically dependent nations. Although they have power over certain matters, First Nations in the United States are still subjects of the United States government. This is simply another type of colonial regime; one that differs significantly from what exists in Canada – though the standard of living for Indigenous peoples in Canada and the United States remains abysmally poor regardless of which regime is in place.

7. A Tribe Called Red is an Indigenous electronic music group that blends traditional and contemporary powwow music with other music samples. They describe their music as "powwow-step."

8. This is a trope often applied to Indigenous peoples. If you are interested in the way in which science fiction depicts indigeneity, you might want to check out the *Métis In Space* podcast, cohosted by myself and Molly Swain. Here is the show description: "In otipêyimisiw-iskwêwak kihci-kîsikohk (Métis In Space), Molly and Chelsea drink a bottle of (red) wine and, from a tipsy, decolonial perspective, review a sci-fi movie or television show featuring Indigenous peoples, tropes, and themes." You can find us on the Indian and Cowboy Media Network (http://www.indianandcowboy.com/) at: metisinspace.com.

9. See note 4.

10. Kress, *Crossfire* (Location 3953, Kindle version).

11. Ibid., location 52.

12. Ibid., location 558.

13. Ibid., location 562.

14. Ibid. location 1518.

15. Kim Tallbear, *Native American DNA: Tribal Belonging and the False Promise of Genetic Science* (Minneapolis: University of Minnesota Press, 2013). This is a fantastic read on the way blood quantum has been modernized through DNA testing.

16. http://www.aadnc-aandc.gc.ca/eng/1100100032383/1100100032385, accessed April 30, 2016.

17. Debbie Reese, "About," *American Indians in Children's Literature blog,* last modified October 19, 2014, http://americanindiansinchildrensliterature.blogspot.ca/p/about.html. As a parent or an educator, if you are interested in avoiding such stereotypes in your children's literature, here you will find a stellar resource courtesy of Debbie Reese. Debbie is enrolled at Nambe Pueblo, and does close readings of children's literature that feature Indigenous peoples or themes. She publishes her reviews on her website.

9

What Is Cultural Appropriation?

Respecting Cultural Boundaries

Cultural appropriation is a seriously hot-button topic. It ranges from the aggressively entitled stance of "I can do whatever I want!" to the perpetually angry approach of "everything is cultural appropriation!" Of course, the former is a much larger portion of the debate, and the latter is almost always a huge strawman argument few people actually make, but it serves to bolster the idea that anyone who takes issue with cultural appropriation is a hysterical hater. That might not be clear when you first start looking into the issue, however.

I bring this topic up precisely because it does scare and confuse and inflame. Except I want to avoid all that negative stuff as best I can. I won't be completely successful, but that is because there are no set-in-stone rules here. There is no common sense, because our viewpoints on the subject can and will diverge radically, and we lack a common understanding.

It shouldn't need stating that I am not presenting myself as an authority on this, but I've found I do need to include this disclaimer. Much like in the chapter on what to call us, I present you with my thoughts on the matter, recognizing there are legitimate arguments for and against my various positions. In short, nitôtêmitik, this issue isn't easy for anyone – not for me, not for you. If easy answers are what you seek, I shall leave you disappointed. I promise.

Because so much has been said on this topic about colonialism and racism and marginalization, and so forth, I want to add in a few points from a related but slightly different perspective than I often see discussed. To cut down on verbiage (too late), consider this entire chapter an add-on to the larger discussion, rather than a complete encapsulation of it.[1]

Knee-jerk arguments to avoid (if you give two craps)

Whenever the topic of cultural appropriation comes up (usually in the context of someone engaging in it), there are a series of knee-jerk arguments that almost always occur. If you are facing the issue of cultural appropriation for the very first time – perhaps even being told you've done something cultural appropriative – then this debate will be new to you.

If, on the other hand, you have been trying to address cultural appropriation for any length of time, these arguments are predictable, and extremely frustrating. It can feel Promethean having to experience your intellectual liver being consumed over and over by the same tired talking points, with no progress to show, and no chance of escaping your punishment for "bringing it up."

I thought I would start with some of the standards to show you that, yes, we've heard it before, and, no, none of these arguments is a get-out-of-jail-free card. If you really care about the issue, you'll move beyond these points and have an honest discussion. If you *don't* care about the issue, why are you reading this, anyway? Just admit you don't care if what you do offends someone, and move on!

Consider the following:

- I'm just showing my appreciation for the culture!
- There are much more serious issues to worry about; you must not care about those things if this is all you focus on.
- I don't find this offensive/I'm part (insert claim to the culture), and I think this is okay/my friend who is (insert culture) thinks this is fine.
- You should be happy people care about your culture and want to celebrate it!
- Nothing is sacred/no one has a right to tell anyone what to do. Freedom of speeeeeeech!
- All cultures borrow from one another.
- If you are wearing jeans and typing on a computer, you're appropriating Western culture.
- I'm an *artist*, and I draw inspiration from everything around me. Artistic freeeeeeedom!
- I don't mind if you use things from my culture.
- What about the Irish?!!²

I don't want to engage these arguments anymore. They are like a hydra; you explain why one argument does not excuse cultural appropriation, and three more arguments get thrown at you. Having to address each one of these points again and again and again and again and again and.... Well, you get the picture. It's boring, it's frustrating, and it gets us nowhere. Let's start this from somewhere else this time.

A guy walks into a bar and asks...

What do the Victoria Cross,[3] the Order of Canada,[4] a framed bachelor's degree, the Giller Prize,[5] and an eagle feather all have in common?

There is no punch line, actually. Each one of these things is a symbol, a visual recognition of a certain kind of achievement. I'm sure you can think of many more of these symbols of military, humanitarian, academic, literary, or what-have-you achievements.

The symbol is important but only because of what it represents. Without that deeper meaning, the Victoria Cross is gaudy jewellery, a bachelor's degree is just a piece of paper, the Giller Prize is abstract art, and an eagle feather is just an ornament.

These symbols are restricted to those who have fulfilled certain criteria. Yes, there are people out there who would mock the symbols and wear representations of them for kicks. They'd get some odd looks, though. I mean – how ironic can you claim to be lugging around a fake Giller Prize?

There are also people who would lie about their achievements and pretend to have earned what the symbols represent. You can imagine the reaction to someone pretending he'd earned the Victoria Cross or someone claiming she has a degree in medicine, when they have not. Sometimes, these kinds of claims are met with criminal sanction, so seriously do we take this sort of thing.

Restricted versus unrestricted

There is a category of symbols in Canadian culture that is restricted within that culture. Not everyone can use those restricted symbols. There are rules about how you can earn them, who can fashion the symbols for you, who can present you with these symbols, and even sometimes what you can do with the symbols. Always behind each material, physical symbol is the often intangible thing you achieved that is linked to the symbol itself. Obviously, other cultures also have restricted symbols linked to deeper, less obviously visible achievements.

Then, there are symbols in Canadian culture that are *not* restricted to those who have achieved specific things. Every Canadian is entitled to use the Canadian flag, for example, and the meaning behind the use of the flag will vary depending on what a person individually wishes to symbolize. A connection to the country? A call for unity? A protest against some action or policy? Questionable fashion?

The meaning varies though the symbol stays the same, and we can (and do) alter that meaning with how we use the symbol. We express different ideas with how we use the symbol, and we do not generally punish people for doing what they want with that symbol.

If someone unfamiliar with Canadian culture were to decorate herself with a string of fake Victoria Crosses, the reaction would be different than if the same person draped a Canadian flag over her non-Canadian shoulders.

In the case of the Victoria Cross, there is a possibility the person wants to make a statement about what the Victoria Cross represents. That would require understanding what the medal represents, of course. Simply choosing it because it looks nice and wanting to wear it to a party does not a statement make.

Since the Canadian flag does not have such a clear-cut meaning, there is not as much need to understand what it means. Its meaning can vary just as much outside Canadian culture as within it. Canadians might be offended with how someone outside the culture uses the flag, but they can also just as likely be offended by how someone within the culture uses it.

Cheapen the symbol, cheapen the achievement

In case it isn't extremely clear, eagle feathers are restricted symbols in the many Indigenous cultures found throughout Canada and the United States. They represent various achievements made by the person who is presented with the feather. Being presented with a feather is a great honour. Many Indigenous peoples will receive only one in their lifetime or perhaps never have that opportunity.

Because of the significance of the eagle feather, very few Indigenous peoples would display feathers they haven't earned. It would be like wearing that Victoria Cross I keep mentioning. Someone outside the culture might not realize what the symbol means and perhaps would not call that person out in disgust for wearing it, but those from within the culture probably would. It would be shameful.

It also cheapens the symbols earned by others. Oh, those who earned the symbol would still know what they did, and that would never go away, but part of the power of a symbol is what it says to others. These kinds of symbols are not solely for our own personal recognition of our achievements. They say, "Here is a visual representation of the honour bestowed upon this person for his or her achievement." When everyone is running around with a copy of that symbol, then it is easy to forget some people have to earn it and it means something. In fact, when many people run around with copies of restricted symbols, there may never be widespread understanding the symbol ever meant anything.

That is exactly where we are at with so many symbols from cultures other than our own: no understanding of everything they mean, and if they are restricted or not, and why.

The symbol most appropriated from Indigenous peoples of Canada and the United States is the okimâw-astotin, the headdress. For the most part, headdresses are restricted items. In particular, the headdress worn by most non-Indigenous peoples imitates those worn traditionally by only a handful of Plains nations. These headdresses are sometimes further restricted within some of those nations to *men* who have done certain things to earn them.

Now that you know these things, unless you are an Indigenous male from a Plains nation who has earned a headdress, an Indigenous female from one of those Plains nations that have women's headdresses, or you have been given permission to wear one (sort of like being presented with an honorary degree), then you will have a very difficult time making a case for how wearing one is anything other than disrespectful.[6] If you choose to be disrespectful, please do not be surprised when people are offended, regardless of why you think you are entitled to do this.

Even if you have "Native friends," or are part-Indigenous yourself, individual choices to "not be offended" do not trump our collective rights as peoples to define our symbols.

How do I know what's restricted and what isn't?

Ask.

Ha, okay, of course I have more to say on the subject, but it really can be as simple as asking sometimes, or even just doing a little research on ye olde interweb.

I find nothing wrong with someone wearing beaded Métis moccasins, for example. Moccasins are not restricted in my culture. They are often beautiful works of art, but they are not symbols of achievement beyond the amazing work put into them by the artisan.

I would not be okay with someone wearing a Métis sash if they are not Métis, however.[7] The sash has become a symbol of identity and achievement. Perhaps it was not always that way, because in the past it was a very utilitarian item used to carry all sorts of things (including infants), or to tie your coat together, or what have you. But it is a powerful symbol now and sometimes presented to Métis in the same way the eagle feather is presented.

Stop rolling your eyes at the term *sacred* and think *important* instead.

I do not care if you are religious, spiritual, or atheist. These are choices you make, and I respect them. However, because of the turbulent history of religion in Western settler philosophy, as well as in many other parts of the world, the translation of terms from our languages into the word *sacred* can sometimes cause confusion and trouble – being associated mostly with organized religion. Let's talk about that for a second.

I feel that when many other cultures discuss "sacred" things, some people feel obligated to reject or elevate those things because of how they feel about their own religious traditions or their atheism. The issue gets confused as being about religion, when that is not necessarily what is going on. Someone might argue, for example, that as an atheist, one has no obligation to respect any sacred object, because religion is bunk. Or, someone might try to compare the object in question to something sacred in their own faith and find the comparison lacking.

Usually when we say "sacred," there are more complex terms in our own language that apply, all of which basically mean the thing in question is important and meaningful in a specific way. When you see the term *sacred*, please remember that. Do not come at the concept through the lens of your own religion – or lack of religion.

Adapting to the interest

The Maori have sacred tattoos called "tā moko." As I note above, this is not just some religious mumbo-jumbo without further meaning. The tattoos are specific symbolic representations of relationships, often kinship relationships. In addition, they no doubt have all sorts of meanings I don't have a clue about, because I am not Maori. The point is, they aren't just pretty designs. They are designs with restricted, important meaning.

But they are nice. Like, really beautifully, wonderfully, gorgeously nice, and humans like nice things and want them for themselves. So when non-Maori started copying these tattoos, a decision was made to promote *kirituhi*. These are designs similar to tā-moko, but without the specific important meanings. The kirituhi are not restricted and are specifically designed to accommodate interest in the style of tattoo without violating the meaning of the tā-moko.

More important, the decision to create a nonsacred version of the tattoos was made *within* the culture. It is very likely that not every Maori person agreed this should be done at all, but you will never have complete agreement in any community.

It is extremely problematic when people from outside a culture decide a restricted symbol should be changed, or opened up, and made nonrestricted. Generally, the people from outside a culture who take this task upon themselves do not actually understand the symbol they are dealing with. Even in cases where they do have this understanding, the imposition of change on a group replicates colonial violence in a way no ally or supporter of a group should ever engage in. If a group does not wish to adapt to the interest of outsiders, that is their choice and their right.

Respectful access

I would be uncomfortable wearing a sari. For one thing, I have no idea how to put one on and would end up looking terrible, but they are truly beautiful, aren't they? Amazing fabrics I can drool over all day. Yet, my discomfort is not really about how to wear them, nor is it based on the sari being a restricted form of dress – because, as far as I know, it is not.

I would feel uncomfortable because I know very little about the cultures from whence the sari comes. I have not attended an Indian wedding or other occasions where wearing a sari makes sense for a person who is not South Asian. I do not believe I would be disrespecting South Asian cultures by wearing a sari – unless I chose the very unfortunate day of Halloween to put it on as a costume, in which case, please feel free to metaphorically slap me. Nonetheless, my lack of any real connection to South Asian cultures makes the entire thing awkward.

Other people who are not South Asian have experiences with and within the cultures that mean they can wear the sari and not feel strange. I think some people from outside a culture can have legitimate access to these things without it being cultural appropriation. The key, in my opinion, is respect. Not *declared* respect from the person wishing to access something, but rather respecting the cultural expectations of access as laid out within the culture itself. As in, when you are told "this is how you do this respectfully," you don't pooh-pooh the guidelines; you follow them.

It is a minefield, because thoughtless cultural appropriation of meaningful symbols is still very much the status quo in settler cultures. Mocking or prohibiting non-Western forms of dress, even creating overblown (and xenophobic) political controversies over them, is frighteningly common.[8] Indigenous people, Black people, and non-Black POC often have to fight to be allowed to wear traditional styles. For example, Baltej Singh Dhillon came up against an RCMP ban on turbans and, after a long fight, became, in 1999, the first RCMP officer allowed to wear one.[9] In 2009, in Thunder Bay, a young First Nations boy had his long hair cut off by a teacher's aide without his consent, leading to a human-rights complaint (that was settled in 2012). He had been growing it long in order to participate in traditional First Nations dancing.[10] Lettia McNickle, a Black woman in Montreal, had a complaint filed on her behalf with Quebec's Human Rights Commission when her employer sent her home for having neatly braided hair.[11]

It can be very frustrating to have people access certain styles and be praised for their creativity or worldliness, while people from within cultures where those styles originated are made fun of, or even punished, for doing the same. With this sort of dynamic at play, it is still more reasonable to assume someone has little real understanding of the culture from where the symbol or style originates than to assume they have a meaningful connection to that culture. This can be very discouraging for people who have learned a lot about another culture and who are even integrated into it. However, until things change and thoughtless (and even mean-spirited) appropriation is a fringe behaviour, this is something you may have to live with if you do not come from the culture you so admire.

Let me reiterate: feeling a deep appreciation for a culture not your own may require you to refrain from immersing yourself in the culture in the manner you wish. Remaining an outsider, in certain ways, might be the most respectful way you engage with another culture. If that is not enough for you, then you need to explore why that is. What access do you think you are owed? Why? How have you earned it? Who could appropriately give it to you? And, most important, *what would further access do for the people you claim to admire so much?*

That there are examples of people with legitimate access to the cultures of others does not mean you personally are not engaged in cultural appropriation if you do the same as they do.

If you admire a culture, learn about it.

It does not take long to find out certain modes of so-called geisha dress are restricted in Japanese culture, for example. The aesthetic commonly known as geisha among non-Japanese attempts to imitate the maiko. A maiko is an apprentice geisha, and there are many subtleties of makeup, dress, and behaviour as a maiko trains to become a geisha, and many rules about who can become a maiko or geisha. This aesthetic symbolizes certain training and achievements, and is not open to just anyone.

The bastardization of geisha culture is not a happy history, and these abuses do not mean the symbolism has lost meaning within Japanese culture *even if* some Japanese play into the stereotypes. To put it another way, just because many people before you have ignored the symbolism and importance of geisha styles of dress does not mean it is okay for you to do so. If people from within the culture do not respect the symbols, this does not give you licence to also disrespect them. We're trying to become better people, aren't we? There are many other beautiful, unrestricted Japanese styles you can access and integrate into your own personal style. Please do not claim you are honouring someone else's tradition or culture when you fail to learn even this much about it.

Combating misinformation

For many Indigenous peoples, it is a disheartening experience to search for other people from our culture online, only to discover every conceivable search term related to indigeneity is full of non-Indigenous peoples in really awful costumes. If you go on Tumblr or Twitter and search #NativeAmerican, you will be exposed to non-Indigenous peoples in various stages of being clothed and sober, wearing headdresses, showing off their dream catchers, repeating that damn "two wolves" story, and spouting racist stereotypes of Native Americans and First Nations peoples. The tags that ought to belong to us, and that ought to help us find each other, are often being used by others and slapped insensitively onto images and ideas that actively demean us.

The emergence of social media platforms has created amazing possibilities for Indigenous peoples to combat centuries-old stereotypes and misconceptions. However, we are up against the sheer volume of those stereotypes, and sometimes it can feel like a losing battle. Fighting cultural appropriation is not just a way of lashing out at people engaged in it. There is a real desire to get accurate information out there, for Indigenous and non-Indigenous peoples alike.

Many Indigenous peoples have been disconnected from their own cultures because of residential schools, the Sixties Scoop, and ongoing fostering-out into non-Indigenous families. When these people want to learn more about their own culture, they have to wade through so many inaccuracies that it can feel impossible at times to reconnect. Non-Indigenous peoples with a real interest in Indigenous cultures face this, as well.

For example, when artwork is mistakenly represented as Dene, Ojibway, *and* Cree, the viewer does not have an opportunity to see how the styles are different, contributing to an inaccurate pan-Indigenous view of our cultures. All the misinformation out there is a serious impediment to having Canadians understand who we are. It is a serious impediment to understanding ourselves.

Try celebration, instead of appropriation.

It's okay to love our stuff. You can even have a whole lot of it, legitimately and guilt-free! There are so many Indigenous-owned online boutiques now, full of gorgeous, high-quality, and unrestricted items. Notice that none of these places is going to sell you eagle feathers or war bonnets.

Still, there are a lot of knockoffs out there, and regardless of your views on pirated anything, the fact is that buying cheap imitation "Native stuff" hurts our communities and quite often perpetuates stereotypes and cultural confusion.

A lot of work and high-quality materials go into Indigenous stuff. Carvings, woven baskets, clothing: there are skills and training involved in producing these sorts of things that can be imitated but not matched. You can't afford $200 for beaded and fur-trimmed moose-hide moccasins? Perhaps you should consider going without until you can. Can't afford an original piece of Indigenous art? Buy a print. You can support Indigenous communities in a real, tangible way by supporting our artisans.

A lot of fakes are being produced both here in Canada and overseas. Yes, that shite is offensive. If you like our stuff enough to want it, then please buy the authentic stuff. Find out what nation it comes from – Cree? Dene? Inuvialuit? – and who the artisan is. If you're buying art, find out what it means. Does it represent a traditional story or a modern one? I mean, if you're buying this stuff, don't you want to know about it?

Sigh. I know that's expecting a little much when you're looking at a dream-catcher-print T-shirt from H&M, but, hopefully, this will at least help people avoid buying stupid, ugly, fake headdresses from online and retail stores.[12]

It's okay to make mistakes. Maybe you had no idea about any of this stuff. The best thing you can do is admit you didn't know, and maybe even apologize if you find you were doing something disrespectful. A simple acknowledgment of the situation is pure gold, in my opinion. It diffuses tension and makes people feel they have been heard, respected, and understood.

If you make this kind of acknowledgment conditional upon people informing you of these things *nicely,* however, that is problematic. The fact is this issue does get people very upset. It's okay to get heated about it, too, on your end, and maybe bad words fly back and forth. My hope is once you cool down, you will accept you are not being asked to do something unreasonable.

NOTES

1. For example, the blog *Native Appropriations* by Dr. Adrienne Keene is a great place to do some reading: http://nativeappropriations.com/ (accessed October 18, 2015). The post "But Why Can't I Wear a Hipster Headdress?" is excellent, and Keene includes links to further readings as well: http://nativeappropriations.com/2010/04/but-why-cant-i-wear-a-hipster-headdress. html (accessed October 17, 2015). You should also check out: Bell Hooks, *Black Looks: Race and Representation* (New York: Routledge, 2014) – particularly chapter 2: "Eating the Other: Desire and Resistance." This, as well as a fantastic YouTube video by Amanda Sternberg, helps explain the way Black styles are appropriated, and the impact of that appropriation: https://www.youtube.com/watch?v=O1KJRRSB_XA&feature=youtu.be.

2. The last few years have seen a near-viral proliferation of the Irish slavery myth, which essentially claims more Irish people were enslaved than Africans, and the Irish were treated even more horrifically. Liam Hogan is a librarian and historian based in Limerick. He has been following the growth of this myth on social media, and offers a number of resources to fight back. You can find his work here: https://medium.com/@Limerick1914. A great place to start would be his piece, "The Myth of 'Irish Slaves' in the Colonies," https://www.academia.edu/9475964/The_Myth_of_Irish_Slaves_in_the_Colonies.

3. The Victoria Cross is the highest military decoration awarded for valour in battle among the Commonwealth nations.

4. "Orders," *The Governor General of Canada: It's an Honour*, last modified January 24, 2014, http://www.gg.ca/document.aspx?id=72.

5. The Scotiabank Giller Prize is an annual English-language literary award.

6. This also applies to Indigenous peoples who are not from one of these nations. For example, the Cherokee do not wear Plains-style headdresses. Thus, if a Cherokee person wears a Plains-style headdress not gifted to him or her, this is still cultural appropriation.

7. Of course, *le ceinture fléchée* is also a traditional French-Canadian symbol, so they get to wear it, too.

8. For example, the Quebec Charter of Values, proposed in 2013 and defeated when the Parti Québécois lost to the Liberals in 2014, would have prohibited public-sector employees (everyone from public servants to bus drivers) from wearing "objects such as headgear, clothing, jewelry or other adornments which, by their conspicuous nature, overtly indicate a religious affiliation" – a ban that would have had the most impact on non-Christians. This debate was taken up again during the 2015 election when Stephen Harper made the niqab an election issue. Both public debates were surrounded by increased aggression against Muslim women in particular.

9. "Creating Change: Baltej Singh Dhillon," *Asia-canada.ca*, accessed October 24, 2015, http://asia-canada.ca/asia-pacific-reality/wisdom-diversity/creating-change-baltej-singh-dhillon.

10. Rick Garrick, "Haircutting Incident Heading to Human Rights Tribunal," *wawataynews.ca,* 2010, http://www.wawataynews.ca/wwt/story-archive/haircutting-incident-heading-human-rights-tribunal.

11. Anne Leclair, "Young Black Montrealer Claims She's Losing Work Over Her Hair," *Global News,* modified March 19, 2015, http://globalnews.ca/news/1888024/young-black-montrealer-claims-shes-losing-work-over-her-hair/.

12. Julia AKA Garconniere, "The Critical Fashion Lover's (Basic) Guide to Cultural Appropriation," *À L'Allure Garçonnière,* April 15, 2010, http://alagarconniere.blogspot.ca/2010/04/critical-fashion-lovers-basic-guide-to.html. This is a great article on approaching questions about fashion, by the way, if you're worried about feathered earrings and so on.

10

Check the Tag on That "Indian" Story
How to Find Authentic Indigenous Stories

Stories and sayings attributed to Indigenous peoples have been floating around probably since settlers stopped spending all of their time and energy on not dying in their new environs. I am not entirely certain why stories that never originated in any Indigenous nation are passed around as "Native American Legends," but listeners beware!

You've probably heard this one at least once:

An old Cherokee is teaching his grandson about life. "A fight is going on inside me," he said to the boy.

"It is a terrible fight and it is between two wolves. One is evil – he is anger, envy, sorrow, regret, greed, arrogance, self-pity, guilt, resentment, inferiority, lies, false pride, superiority, and ego." He continued, "The other is good – he is joy, peace, love, hope, serenity, humility, kindness, benevolence, empathy, generosity, truth, compassion, and faith. The same fight is going on inside you – and inside every other person, too."

The grandson thought about it for a minute and then asked his grandfather, "Which wolf will win?"

The old Cherokee simply replied, "The one you feed."

Wow, I'm just shivering with all that good Indian wisdom flowing through me now. Give me a moment.

Okay. I'm better now.

The specific nation the old, wise Indian comes from is not really important. We have all seen some version of this story passed around on social media, and while the details vary somewhat, the basic message and symbolism does not.

It was through the wonder of social media, Tumblr to be exact, that I saw someone had finally looked into the real origins of this particular story.[1] This story seems to have begun in 1978 when an early form of it was written by the evangelical Christian minister Billy Graham in his book *The Holy Spirit: Activating God's Power in Your Life.*[2]

So, wait…this is actually a Christian-style parable? Let's just quickly read the story as told by Minister Graham in a chapter called "The Christian's Inner Struggle":

> An Eskimo fisherman came to town every Saturday afternoon. He always brought his two dogs with him. One was white and the other was black. He had taught them to fight on command. Every Saturday afternoon in the town square the people would gather and these two dogs would fight and the fisherman would take bets. On one Saturday the black dog would win; another Saturday, the white dog would win – but the fisherman always won! His friends began to ask him how he did it. He said, "I starve one and feed the other. The one I feed always wins because he is stronger."[3]

Oh, oh, oh! I get it! Black is evil, and white is good! Traditional Indigenous wisdom galore! Well, okay, not really.

Graham goes on to explain the meaning of this story in great detail, linking it explicitly to allowing the Holy Spirit to dominate our lives versus feeding our sinful nature. The story is meant to highlight the universal nature of original sin and the universal need for the love of a specific version of the Christian god. Surely there is little harm in appealing to what is *universally true?*

Um…wait a second. Do Indigenous cultures also believe in black = evil, white = good? I mean, pre-Christianity? It's quite possible that some might, but given the diversity of Indigenous cultures in the Americas, it's safer to assume this is not universally true.

This kind of thing is harmful.

These misattributed stories aren't going to pick us up and throw us down a flight of stairs, but they do perpetuate ignorance about our cultures. Cultures. Plural. The fact that this story, like so many others, can be attributed to multiple nations without causing eyebrows to be raised merely highlights the practice of collapsing the incredible diversity of Indigenous nations into a homogenous and simplified whole.

Not only do these stories confuse non-Indigenous peoples about our beliefs and our actual oral traditions, they confuse some Indigenous peoples, too! There are many disconnected Indigenous peoples who, for a variety of reasons, have not been raised in their cultures.[4] It is not an easy task to reconnect, and a lot of people start by trying to find as much information as they can about the nation they come from.

It can be exciting and empowering at first to encounter a story like this, if it's supposedly from your (generalized) nation. Nonetheless, I could analyze this story all day to point out how Christian and Western influences run all the way through it, and how these principles contradict and overshadow Indigenous ways of knowing. Encountering these fake "Native American" stories during the arduous and painful process of reconnection, or in the process of just trying to learn more about Indigenous peoples, makes things very confusing. And, please. It does not matter if this sort of thing is done to or by other cultures, too. The "they did it first" argument doesn't get my kids anywhere, either.

Let's call the practice of fabricating "Native American" stories what it is: colonialism. This is one of the ways colonial governments acquire full political control over lands and people – by erasing pre-existing cultures and replacing them with the culture of settlers.

The replacement of real Indigenous stories with Christian-influenced, Western moral tales is an aspect of colonialism, no matter how you dress it up in feathers and moccasins. It silences the real voices of Indigenous peoples by presenting listeners and readers with something safe and familiar. And because of the wider access non-Indigenous peoples have to sources of media, these kinds of fake stories are literally drowning us out.

Start asking questions.

If you are at all interested in real Indigenous cultures, there are some easy steps you can take to determine authenticity. I guarantee you that three short questions will help you weed out 99.9 percent of the stories that are made up and attributed to an Indigenous people. Ready?

1. Which specific Indigenous nation is this story from? (Cherokee, Cree, Dene, Navajo?)

2. Which community is this story from? (for example, Saddle Lake Cree Nation. If you get an answer like the Hopis of New Brunswick you can stop here. The story is fake. It needs to be a community that actually exists or existed at the specific time a version of the story was told.)

3. Who from that community told this story?

You see, our stories have provenance; a source, an origin. That means you should be able to track down *where* the story was told, *when*, and *who* told it.

There are specific protocols (rules) involved in telling stories that lay this provenance out for those listening. The person telling the story describes how he or she came to know the story, often sharing the circumstances surrounding being gifted with this piece of entertainment and knowledge. This can be done orally, or in writing if the story is being printed. There are often protocols involved in what kinds of stories can be told to whom, and when. Every Indigenous nation is going to have its own rules about this, but all of them have ways of keeping track of which stories are theirs. These are the internal rules that apply.

External rules also dictate that where the story comes from matters.

There are all sorts of different citation styles out there developed to ensure people list their sources and acknowledge where they got their information from. Those citation methods can be easily adapted to ensure Indigenous stories are properly sourced and credited.

If you cannot determine where the story came from, then please do not pass it on as being from "X nation."

For example, once a friend picked up a book for me, called *Raven the Trickster*,[5] at a library sale. I immediately became uneasy when I read the inside covers. Here are some partial quotes that stood out for me:

- "This book contains nine stories about the wily Raven..."[6]
- No mention of where those stories originated other than from "the North West coast of the Pacific Ocean."[7]
- "The tales collected and retold here by Gail Robinson, a distinguished Canadian poet who has lived among the North American Indians and listened first-hand to the stories they tell...."[8]

No actual communities are listed. No actual Indigenous people are named. There is zero attribution here. I have no idea if these stories are made up, mistranslated, or ripped off wholesale and profited from without any recognition given to those who carry traditional stories from generation to generation.

The stories are interesting, just like the "Cherokee" Two Wolves parable is. But, I'm not presenting this to my children as authentic; nor should it be accepted as such without a heck of a lot more research into the origins of these tales.

Contrast that with the book *Unipkaaqtuat Arvianit: Traditional Stories From Arviat*.[9] The book description is as follows:

Well-loved and respected community member Mark Kalluak has collected stories from around Arviat since the 1970s, including stories he grew up hearing his mother tell. In this delightful book for audiences of all ages, Mr. Kalluak shares his favourite versions of traditional and personal tales, lovingly illustrating and translating them himself.[10]

Although it is not stated, we know these are Inuit stories (because Arviat is an Inuit community). We also know the specific community (again, Arviat). Further, we know who told these stories to Mr. Kalluak (his mother and other Inuit from Arviat). In addition, this particular book is a bilingual version, offered in both English and Inuktitut. The fact that this is in an Indigenous language, as well as in English, makes it a bit more likely that it is authentic.

Indigenous genres

Many people seem to think Indigenous stories are only authentic if they are myths or legends, but there are many Indigenous literary genres. Let me introduce you to two nêhiyaw (Plains Cree) genres: the âtayôhkêwina and âcimowina.[11]

The âtayôhkêwina are often described in English as sacred stories.[12] These are stories describing ancient times – the original creators or storytellers are long forgotten. Often classified as myths – for their descriptions of the creation and shaping of the world, as well as the creation of plants and animals – these stories are the ones many people seek out when looking to learn about nêhiyaw culture or integrate nêhiyaw culture into the classroom. Far from being stories anyone can fabricate, the âtayôhkêwina are very specific. Trying to produce a sham âtayôhkêwina would be as unsuccessful as a sham Greek myth. People would know.

The âtayôhkêwina continue to have social and cultural importance; they are not merely entertainment. They represent and express a nêhiyaw world-view and philosophy, as well as forming a body of nêhiyaw laws. In order for laws to be effective, they must be known. The telling of âtayôhkêwina ensures these laws continue to be passed down from generation to generation.

These are the stories that have the most restrictions surrounding their telling, so people hoping to access them or use them in educational settings need to be aware of some of these cultural expectations. For example, many âtayôhkêwina are supposed to be told only during the winter months. As part of this, the nêhiyaw cultural hero, wîsahkêcâhk, is generally only referred to as "nistês" (Elder Brother) outside of the winter season, rather than by name.

People who have learned how to tell the âtayôhkêwina have studied very hard to get the details right, and some of these stories in their full telling can last for days! Shortened versions or sections of longer stories are sometimes shared, and can be very confusing without knowing the fuller context. If you're struggling to make a connection with something familiar, think once again of Greek myths. The body of Greek mythology is extremely long and detailed, and makes cohesive sense if you know most of it. If you were merely exposed to a single story, however, you may be left scratching your head.

Although I've made this sound like super serious stuff, a great many of these stories are humorous despite the important lessons they contain. Others are scary, or downright disturbing.

You will not find many âtayôhkêwina in print – with the exception of anthropological texts; so if a book claims to contain sacred Cree stories, be wary.

The âcimowina, on the other hand, happen after the âtayôhkêwina and tend to be regarded as more factual than mythological – though within the âcimowina are many tales that are not always meant to be taken literally. Some âcimowina record historical events, and their retelling requires details be very specifically remembered and passed on. Others integrate some of the beings that are told of in the âtayôhkêwina. Because many of the âcimowina are specific to certain communities and families, they are not all necessarily as widely known as the âtayôhkêwina and may be passed down within just a family or community. These stories are not restricted in the same way as the âtayôhkêwina, but you can imagine that if a story belongs to a certain family, it would be extremely unbecoming to tell that story without permission. New âcimowina will be created as time passes, and experiences are chronicled in this fashion.

These are just two examples of Indigenous genres from a specific Indigenous nation. The idea here is to get you used to the idea that not all "Native American" stories are the same.

Then, there are contemporary stories told by Indigenous peoples that can be fiction or nonfiction and can rely on traditional stories or not. We exist as contemporary peoples, too, and our experiences in the 21st century are no less authentically Indigenous.

So, get the real stories! There are so many Indigenous publishing companies these days; there is really no excuse to buy sketchy stories bastardized from Billy Graham sermons. Most exciting, from my perspective, is how many of these resources are being offered in English (or French) *and* in the original language! You can absolutely build a solid library of authentic Indigenous literature that represents every single genre (both Western and Indigenous) from K–12. All it takes is asking the right questions and caring enough to bypass the fakes.

If you want a curated list of age-appropriate literary resources that accurately represent Indigenous peoples, Debbie Reese has put in an enormous amount of effort to provide exactly this on her blog, *American Indians in Children's Literature*. She does close readings of books and publishes reviews of books when authors get it right and when authors get it wrong. If you aren't sure about a resource, you can usually find it on Debbie's website and find out if it's worth reading or using as a teaching resource.[13]

Be okay with difference.

Before I leave you to spend your every last cent on books, I want to warn you: authentic Indigenous stories come from a different cultural context than you may be familiar with. While many of the books you find will be written with a non-Indigenous audience in mind, the more traditional stories will have been created before that audience was even possible. That should be obvious, but I think it bears noting.

If you go into these stories always expecting to have your cultural beliefs and norms reinforced, you're doing it wrong. Trite Western moral lessons are not necessarily going to be handed to you in our stories.

Listening to, or reading, authentic Indigenous stories means you are accessing different cultures. Please don't forget that. Sometimes, what you are reading simply will not make sense to you because you lack the cultural context. That does not mean you should avoid these stories. It just means you might have to put a bit more work into getting the full benefit of them than you would with stories that come from a context you are already completely familiar with.[14]

So, the next time someone tells you a "Native American" saying or story, ask yourself if it resonates with you because it's really "Indigenous wisdom" – or if it's just a Western story wrapped up in a cloak of indigeneity.

NOTES

1. The Tumblr user I first saw identify Billy Graham as the author of this parable was known as Pavor Nocturnus, but that Tumblr account is no longer active. In any case, I thank that person very much for making the post that brought it to people's attention. I am sure others have also looked into this story and found similar origins, and I hope people continue to dig and question, always!

2. Billy Graham, "The Christian's Inner Struggle," in *The Holy Spirit: Activating God's Power in Your Life* (Nashville: Thomas Nelson, 1978), accessed October 20, 2015,

3. Ibid. (my emphasis).

4. Reasons such as being forcibly removed by the state and placed in residential schools or forcibly removed by the state and adopted into non-Indigenous families. Reasons such as arbitrary state-controlled definitions of identity being used to strip people of their *legal status* as Indians. Reasons such as centuries of prolonged attacks on our cultures and selves.

5. Gail Robinson, *Raven the Trickster* (New York: Atheneum, 1982).

6. Ibid.

7. Ibid.

8. Ibid.

9. Mark Kalluak, *Unipkaaqtuat Arvianit: Traditional Stories From Arviat* (Iqaluit: Inhabit Media, 2009).

10. Ibid., last accessed October 20, 2015, http://inhabitmedia.com/2009/01/10/unipkaaqtuat-arvianit-2/.

11. Just as in chapter 3, I choose not to capitalize any nêhiyawêwin (Cree language) words out of respect for the Standard Roman Orthography (SRO), which does not use capital letters.

12. Robert Innes, *Elder Brother and the Law of the People: Contemporary Kinship and Cowessess First Nation* (Winnipeg: University of Manitoba Press, 2013), 23–42. For a longer and more detailed discussion of the importance of âtayôhkêwina and âcimowina, see this source.

13. Debbie Reese, *American Indians in Children's Literature*, http://americanindiansinchildrensliterature.blogspot.ca/.

14. Keavy Martin, *Stories in a New Skin: Approaches to Inuit Literature* (Winnipeg: University of Manitoba Press, 2012). This book might help you better access and understand Inuit literature.

11

Icewine, Roquefort Cheese, and the Navajo Nation

Indigenous Use of Intellectual Property Laws

I'd like to tell you a story about icewine.

Icewine is pressed from grapes that freeze on the vine, and it is an incredibly sweet and expensive dessert wine. Not everyone likes it, but I consider it a pretty decadent treat.

Canada is the largest producer of authentic icewine in the world because, unlike many other wine-producing areas, Canadian vineyards experience some pretty cold winters. It first started being produced here in the early 1980s, but really gained traction in the late 1990s and early oughts. A 375-mL bottle will cost you about $45 Canadian here, but the price can go up to a couple of hundred smackarooneys on markets in China.[1]

As you can imagine, counterfeit icewine started popping up fairly early, both here in Canada and abroad. To deal with the fakes, British Columbia, Ontario, and Nova Scotia set up special provincial legislation under the Vintners Quality Alliance (VQA) to regulate the production and quality of icewines produced from those regions.

The VQA is a wine appellation system, meaning that certain terms applied to wines can be used only if the product meets specific criteria.[2] These criteria include alcohol content, authorized grape varieties, testing and approval of the wine, and so forth. It is illegal to use names restricted under an appellation system unless the criteria are met. When you see VQA on the label of an icewine, you, as the consumer, should be assured that what is in that bottle is of the highest quality.

Fake "Canadian" icewine produced by China had become such a problem that Canada developed a national standard in 2014 to address this kind of fraud. It can't stop the fake production, but it can ensure that the reputation of Canadian icewine producers is backed up by quality assurances. The standard is quite simple: "Only wine that is made exclusively from grapes naturally frozen on the vine is 'icewine,' 'ice wine' or 'ice-wine.'"[3] This standard prevents anyone from doing something like taking a table wine, adding sugar, and claiming it is icewine – something that was technically possible before.

Appellation laws have existed in many countries for centuries. Champagne originally enjoyed legal appellation protection under the *Treaty of Madrid, 1891,* which stated only sparkling wines produced in a specific area of France could be called champagne.[4] This has been affirmed in various treaties and laws since.

Alcoholic beverages are not the only products to enjoy such legal protections. Cheeses are another fine example, using something called a Geographical Indication (GI) to describe where the product comes from, guaranteeing everything from quality to production methods.

In Europe, these kinds of labels are specifically linked to *where* the product is made. Europeans focus on the concept of *terroir,* which encompasses all the environmental factors of a distinct geographic area that can possibly affect a crop or animal – soil pH, quality of water, climate, and so on.[5] Copying the process of making a certain product is not sufficient to use a restricted appellation, because the product is defined by its terroir. Thus, when you buy Roquefort cheese, you know it comes from a precise region in France where unique conditions exist that make this cheese one of a kind. Roquefort cheese was the first to receive the AOC label (*Appelation d'Origine Contrôlée* or Protected Designation of Origin) in 1725, kicking off the GI model of cheese naming.

In the United States, appellation is more a form of intellectual property (specifically, trademark), and whoever owns the trademark can use it regardless of terroir. This is meant to protect the brand itself and the quality that has come to be associated with it – rather than to describe the terroir the product comes from. There is overlap between these two approaches, but the overall purpose is to ensure individual names guarantee special qualities by protecting the usage of names.

Why terms like *Navajo* and *Native American* matter

You may have heard of a litigation launched by the Navajo nation in 2012 against clothing giant Urban Outfitters:[6]

> Brian Lewis, an attorney with the Navajo Nation Department of Justice, says the group wants Urban Outfitters to stop misappropriating the "Navajo" name and trademark. "Although Urban Outfitters had said previously that it had stopped using 'Navajo' in connection with the sale of its products, it merely transitioned its

misappropriation of the Navajo name and trademark to lesser-known websites and print advertisement – those of its subsidiaries," Lewis said.[7]

That's right. The Navajo nation has trademark ownership of the name *Navajo*, and it has the legal right under United States trademark law to stop people from using it to describe products that have not been approved by the Navajo nation. Just like Urban Outfitters owns the trademark to its name. The lawsuit states:

> The fame or reputation of the Navajo name and marks is such that, when the defendant uses the "Navajo" and "Navaho" marks with its goods and services, a connection with the Navajo nation is falsely presumed.[8]

Urban Outfitters responded with this back in October of 2012:

> Like many other fashion brands, we interpret trends and will continue to do so for years to come. The Native American-inspired trend and specifically the term *Navajo* have been cycling thru fashion, fine art and design for the last few years.[9]

This is true, but it likely won't save Urban Outfitters from being held accountable for their trademark infringement – the case was still going strong as of 2015. "Everyone else does it" is not a legal defence – unless the Navajo nation fails to enforce its rights.

In trademark law, there is a concept called "genericization," whereby a trademark can expire if it becomes overused outside of the narrow confines of its legal usage. A famous example involves the Xerox company. Its trademark was threatened when people began to use the term *xerox* in place of *photocopy*.[10]

Only an aggressive ad campaign saved Xerox from joining the ranks of trademarks lost to colloquial use.[11] They essentially begged consumers to say "photocopy" instead of "xerox," citing an example of the zipper as an example. At one time, *zipper* had been a trademarked name but no longer is.

Although the specific legal principles involved here may differ, use of the terms *icewine*, *Roquefort*, and *Navajo* all have something in common: they tell you something about what you are buying. And, in this case, the Navajo nation wants to ensure consumers are not associating the term *Navajo* with random southwest-inspired hipster fashion.

Fakers are not always so blatant.

There are many ways around the multitude of appellation, geographic indicator, country of origin, and trademark laws – and fakers love to exploit them. While not exactly fodder for a television show featuring ridiculously good-looking lawyers dashing in to protect intellectual property, the struggle to protect the integrity of certain names is very high stakes. Counterfeit products and piggybacking off trademark names to entice consumers account for billions of dollars of profit loss every year. It is also very much up to consumers to be aware of the standards involved in order to avoid being ripped off.

There is a statute in the United States called the *Indian Arts and Crafts Act of 1990*.[12] (There is no such equivalent in Canada.) This law states that only a person who is an enrolled member of a federally or state recognized tribe can produce items labelled Native American or Indian. In addition, members of one tribe cannot pass their items off as coming from a different tribe, so if your goods are labelled Hopi, you'd better be a member or a certified artisan of the Hopi.

There are many criticisms of this Act, as it also forbids nonenrolled Indigenous peoples from marketing their goods as Indian or Native American. Were this statute to exist in a similar form in Canada, it is conceivable that only status Indians would be able to market their products as authentically Indigenous, as they are the only Indigenous peoples with such a strict administrative identity – though it is very likely the Inuit would be included, as well. This would leave out more than half a million non-status Indians and Métis who could not, by law, call their products Native American, Aboriginal, or Indigenous, or use the name of any First Nation to identify their product.

Nonetheless, Urban Outfitters may also be in violation of this Act. One popular way people in the United States get around these restrictions is to use terms like *Native-American inspired* or *Indian style*. Adding the qualifiers "inspired" and "style" are a disingenuous but often effective way to skirt the Act. If you have ever wondered at the prevalence of such terms, you now have additional context.

Another way these laws are skirted is to claim responsibility for violating them does not lay with you. As pointed out by Dr. Jessica Metcalfe on her website Beyond Buckskin, the popular handcrafting web store Etsy is a haven for cultural appropriation and possibly even trademark violation.[13] When Dr. Metcalfe contacted the site about their Navajo-labelled goods in 2012, this was the response:

> Each shop is run independently by the shop owner, and the shop owner is responsible for their content and use of our services. By agreeing to our Terms of Use all members assure us they will follow all applicable laws while using our site. Etsy cannot judge the legality of items or the seller's ability to legally sell an item....[14]

The site chose to lay the onus on the shop owners who use Etsy to sell their goods. Such an approach forces a rights holder (such as the Navajo) to pursue each vendor individually, which is a much more arduous task than if the website itself were responsible for the legality of its content. Is this actually how the law stands? Is a site like Etsy able to skirt responsibility in this fashion? Well, a lawsuit launched in 2015 on behalf of shareholders of Etsy argues otherwise, claiming that a failure to weed out possible trademark violations threatened investor returns.[15]

Trademark laws and appellation rules will continue to evolve in response to efforts made to profit from evading these restrictions. I emphasize how seriously these issues are taken in settler courts so you do not dismiss the efforts of the Navajo nation to protect its brand. Whether the concept of trademark has any equivalent in traditional Navajo law or culture is not important. The Navajo have seized upon a tool available to them in order to protect the integrity of their nation's name and to ensure that people who are not Navajo cannot simply claim to be associated with the Navajo nation. This is a route more Indigenous nations may begin to take to protect Indigenous intellectual property.

It is unfortunate traditional Indigenous laws are not respected enough to protect Indigenous intellectual property, and we are forced to use settler laws like this instead. However, when this case first emerged there was a firestorm of criticism from many settlers against the Navajo for pursuing Urban Outfitters. If you think this case is frivolous or interferes with freedom of expression, and so forth, please ensure you are not singling out Indigenous peoples with this criticism. If you take issue with intellectual property law, with appellation statutes, or with geographical indication laws, then your concerns are not limited to us and need not focus on this case only. If you support intellectual property laws, but hate that Indigenous peoples can use them, too, you might want to take a hard look in the mirror and ask yourself why you have such a double standard.

In chapter 10, I asked you to "check the tag on that Indian story." I think, in general, checking the tags and labels and understanding what they mean is part of taking responsibility as consumers – whether you're buying icewine, cheese, or Navajo products. There are many more opportunities now for consumers to ensure the products they purchase are legitimately Indigenous and actually benefit the artists; this should be a priority for those claiming to respect our cultures so much. If, however, you just want to be able to call your stuff "Native American" or "Navajo" without consequences, I'm afraid you've got some explaining to do.

Now, go forth, savvy consumers, and do your best!

NOTES

1. Ben O'Donnell, "China's Fake Ice Wine Epidemic," *Wine Spectator,* 2011, http://www.winespectator.com/webfeature/show/id/44430.

2. "Information for Future Wineries," *VQAOntario.ca,* last accessed November 3, 2015, http://www.vqaontario.ca/FutureWineries/Overview.

3. "Icewine Regulations," *Canada Gazette,* last modified December 2, 2014, http://laws-lois.justice.gc.ca/PDF/SOR-2014-10.pdf.

4. Madrid Agreement Concerning the International Registration of Marks of April 14, 1891.

5. Because I am a sci-fi addict, I'd like to point you toward the Southern Reach Trilogy by Jeff VanderMeer, which deals with the concept of terroir in a very interesting and creepy way.

6. *The Navajo Nation, et al. v. Urban Outfitters Inc. et al.,* 1:12-cv-00195, in the US District Court for the District of New Mexico.

7. Elizabeth Fiedler, "Navajo Nation Sues Urban Outfitters Over Use of Name," *newsworks.org,* 2012, http://www.newsworks.org/index.php/local/item/34760.

8. "Navajo Nation Sues Urban Outfitters for Trademark Infringement," *The Guardian,* 2012, http://www.theguardian.com/world/2012/mar/01/navajo-nation-sues-urban-outfitters.

9. See note 8.

10. Niamh Pollak, "Change You Can Xerox," *trademarkblog.ca,* 2008, http://trademarkblog.ca/change-you-can-xerox/.

11. John Dwight Ingram, "The Genericide of Trademarks," *Buffalo Intellectual Property Law Journal* 2 (2004): 154, http://wings.buffalo.edu/law/biplj/biplj223.pdf.

12. *The Indian Arts and Crafts Act, 1990,* PL 101-644, http://www.iacb.doi.gov/act.html.

13. The Beyond Buckskin Boutique is one source of authentic Native American products and was launched in 2012, as a direct response to the Navajo nation vs. Urban Outfitters case. Dr. Jessica Metcalfe wanted to support Native American designers and artists by providing access to authentic products not available to the average person: http://shop.beyondbuckskin.com/.

14. Jessica R. Metcalfe, "Does Easy Condone Trademark Violation?" *Beyond Buckskin* (blog), 2012, http://www.beyondbuckskin.com/2012/02/does-etsy-condone-trademark-violation.html.

15. *Altayyar v. Etsy Inc.,* 1:15-cv-02785, U.S. District Court, Eastern District of New York (Brooklyn). For more information: Christine Smythe, "Etsy Sued by Investors Alleging Firm Hid Products' Trademark Risks," *insurancejournal.com,* 2015, http://www.insurancejournal.com/news/national/2015/05/17/368456.htm.

12

All My Queer Relations
Language, Culture, and Two-Spirit Identity

I am a huge language geek. As in, I'm a little obsessed with language and how it relates to culture, to identity, and to understanding the world around me.

If you speak another language, or have even tried to learn another language, you realize pretty quickly that although you might be using a comparable term in one language as in another, the connotations involved can be radically different. When you translate a word, you don't usually unpack those connotations. Without careful thought, you may simply switch from one context to the other, and not notice you're no longer discussing the same things.

Not sure what I mean? Consider the English term *justice*. Let that word roll around in your head. I bet you can think of all sorts of variations on that term in English: *natural justice, vigilante justice, impartial justice, social justice*, and so on. Each variation is shaded by another layer of connotations, all rooted within a particular sociopolitical structure you have likely been raised slowly learning about (indirectly and directly).

The concept of what *justice* means varies depending on which sociopolitical context you're in. It seems obvious when you think about it, but we don't always consider it enough. When I say this word to you in English, I am pretty certain you'll have a somewhat comparable understanding of the term as I do (provided I'm thinking in English), though we may quibble on the details.

How I would choose to translate the word *justice* into another language would depend on what *aspect* of justice (in English) I was trying to convey. Unless there was an easy-peasy equivalent like *justicia* (Spanish) or *justice* (French). Of course, what *justice* means in different Spanish-speaking countries or in French-speaking jurisdictions may (and does) also vary widely; be careful about those supposed equivalents.

There is no easy equivalent I can think of in Cree, so I would have to be more specific. Would I mean *kwayaskwâtisiwin*? This word has connotations of straightness, of even-handed fairness. No connotations of a rigid procedure and notions of "innocent until proven guilty"; no images of a courtroom with a judge. Getting someone who is unfamiliar with English common-law procedural norms of justice to understand those norms would take some serious explaining, Lucy. It would necessitate translating cultural context. There is no single-word equivalent in Cree I could rely on; this makes it less likely I'll fall into the trap of using a word that seems the same but is not.

It does not take a person long to figure these things out once they spend a bit of time considering them. Yet, that moment when you first realize an equivalent or translated term means something very different from the term in English is pretty amazing. Recognizing that the way people who speak that language perceive the term is different from the way you perceive it, because of historical and cultural specificities, means you've been given a very important insight (even if you do not fully understand those differences).

Peace, baby!

The word *pêyâhtakêyimowin* (pay-yah-tu-kay-YI-moo-win) often gets translated into English as "peace." If you're hasty, you might start using it in the same way you use *peace* in English – to mean an end to hostilities, perhaps. Except that's not what it means.

pêyâhtakêyimowin refers to peace within yourself. I suppose the idea of inner peace might be an okay equivalent. Within the word *pêyâhtakêyimowin,* there are aspects of taking things slowly, being careful, being quiet, and not getting riled up. There are further cultural connotations involved in concepts like being careful, being quiet, and going slowly. At the very least, I have to provide you with four concepts in order to begin to give you a sense of what this word actually means.

You might argue *peace* can be used in that same way in English, and you're probably right. However, the reverse is not true. I cannot use pêyâhtakêyimowin to mean an end to hostilities. It simply does not make sense. I'd have to use the word *wîtaskîwin,* and even then we would not necessarily think of what this means in the same way. (Fun fact for Albertans, wîtaskîwin = Wetaskawin.)

If you and I are talking and I have to speak in English because you don't understand Cree, I'm probably going to default to the term *peace.* In my head, I have the idea of pêyâhtakêyimowin. In your head, you have *your* understanding of the term *peace.* Every time I use the word *peace* it is going to trigger English-language cultural connotations. You might start thinking of me as a flaky New-Age hippie if I say it too often. I might start forgetting that it makes you think of a specific thing, mistakenly believing you and I are on the same page in terms of its meaning.

This kind of thing happens all the time when you try to translate concepts into other languages. We use translation because it is necessary when dealing with people who do not speak our language; we are pretty aware that misunderstandings can occur and we need to be careful.

I came here to read about Two-Spirit identity; Why am I reading this language stuff?

Oh, right, sorry. I get carried away talking about language sometimes.

In my parents' and grandparents' time, the term *berdache* was used to refer to Indigenous transgender individuals. It was also used a fair amount to refer to Indigenous homosexual men.[1]

It wasn't the most positive term. In 1990, during an intertribal Native American/ First Nations gay and lesbian conference in Winnipeg, the term *Two-Spirit* was chosen to replace it.[2]

Some say the term was a translation from Anishinaabemowin (niizh manidoowag). The term was deliberately chosen to be an umbrella term; a specifically pan-Indigenous concept encompassing sexual, gender, and/or spiritual identity. I think it is a useful term because it is so broad, and the kind of terminology that acknowledges Indigenous beliefs and traditions is absolutely needed. However, like many pan-Indigenous concepts, it is sometimes overly broad. I also feel that because it is an English term, it becomes coloured by settler beliefs.[3]

Nation-specific terms

I have been trying to find Cree-specific terms for Two-Spirit identities for many years. Recently, it has become easier with groups like the Facebook group, Nêhiyawêwin (Cree) Word of the Day. Many of the terms have been forgotten, and few people know them. Still, sometimes when you ask, you receive.

Learning the words is not enough, however. Digging deeper and trying to understand the way Indigenous peoples viewed Two-Spirit individuals is also important. Without that, all we have are equivalents – words we cannot help but think of in the context of their English counterparts. Like it or not, most of us have been educated within the Canadian system, and European notions of homosexuality, gender, and sex have found their way into every nook and cranny of our minds. Decolonization involves becoming aware of this and consciously trying to reclaim what existed before. It also includes building new traditions if, within specific First Nations, Two-Spirit people were not accepted. This is no easy task.

Anyway, I want to highlight some of the terms used by Cree speakers, with many thanks to those who have shared what information they do have. Of course, there is going to be disagreement, especially regarding meaning and authenticity, on some of these terms. There have also been many cautions that these terms may simply be translations from English into Cree, as no one I spoke to expressed a strong familiarity with traditional roles for these people. Yet, I thought it was a good start.

I am not 100 percent certain of the pronunciation for these words. I may miss where a macron is needed to alter the sound of a vowel, but I'll give it a shot!

- **napêw iskwêwisêhot** (nu-PAYO ihs-gway-WIH-say-hoht): a man who dresses as a woman
- **iskwêw ka napêwayat** (ihs-GWAYO ga nu-PAY-wuh-yut): a woman who dresses as a man
- **ayahkwêw** (U-yuh-gwayo): a man dressed/living/accepted as a woman (I have seen this word used to refer to a castrated animal, so I'm not sure how respectful it is. Some have suggested this word can actually be used as a third gender of sorts, applied to women *and* men.)
- **înahpîkasoht** (ee-nuh-PEE-gu-soot): a woman dressed/living/accepted as a man (also translated as someone who fights everyone to prove they are the toughest. Interesting!)
- **iskwêhkân** (IS-gwayh-gahn): one who acts/lives as a woman
- **napêhkân** (NU-payh-gahn): one who acts/lives as a man

A number of people claim there *were* no terms in Cree, people were not labelled in such ways, and despite there being pan-Indigenous notions of special roles for those now called "Two-Spirit," this may not have been the case in Cree communities. Yet, in these discussions, one belief is very clearly shared by most: there *was* acceptance of fluid genders/sexual orientations and so on.

This does not mean Two-Spirit people are always accepted and honoured now; unfortunately, Two-Spirit people are most at risk for violence, and most excluded from ceremonies and community. Hence, there is the need to take a serious look at ensuring Two-Spirit people are centred, not merely paid lip service.

Love in the time of Indigenous resurgence

Reclaiming our traditions is more than learning our languages, but our languages *do* give us a way in, which should absolutely be explored.[4] Overcoming colonially imposed views of sex, sexuality, gender, and identity is no small matter, particularly since Indigenous peoples are still experiencing colonialism in a very real way. We are not living in post-colonial times, no matter what Canadian politicians claim.

Ideas about tradition-specific approaches to those now called "Two-Spirit" have been emerging for some time and are becoming the subjects of Indigenous scholarship.[5] More important, Indigenous women and Two-Spirit people are on the ground, leading a resurgence movement in iyiniwi-ministik, the People's Island.[6] They draw on their traditional roles as protectors of the land and water to inform their work in our communities, and to root themselves in their specific sociopolitical orders to counter colonialism and to revitalize language and culture. Rather than being defined as a struggle against patriarchal gender roles and the division of labour, Indigenous women and Two-Spirit people combat the imposition of colonial barriers. Gender equality is not the goal; rather, it is to restore Indigenous nationhood, which includes gender equality and respect for gender fluidity.

As I write this, I can hear Khelsilem (Skwxwú7mesh-Kwakwaka'wakw), a community organizer from Vancouver, pointing out that not all Indigenous peoples have the same traditions, and that we need to have honest discussions about the diversity of our traditions to avoid perpetuating pan-Indigenous stereotypes. This is an important point, indeed, as not all Indigenous nations have the same traditions with respect to the fluidity of gender roles. Romanticizing ourselves as a collective, unfortunately, plays into "noble savage" stereotypes and does damage in the long run. With so many Indigenous people disconnected from their specific traditions, even so-called positive stereotypes are a form of continuing erasure.

Even among nations with traditional binary gender roles or hierarchical sociopolitical orders, there is nothing that compares to colonial patriarchy that mainstream settler feminism opposes. Our internal struggles with traditional roles are not analogous to the issues that settler peoples have with their traditions; therefore, using Western liberal theory to deconstruct them is inherently incongruous.

Indigenous traditions are not frozen in time any more than other people's traditions are. Our peoples have been trading more than goods for thousands of years, passing along ceremonies, medicines, and ideas just as easily as copper and fish. We are capable of change and embrace it, as long as that change respects our reciprocal obligations to one another and to the territories in which we live. We do not need to look to Western liberal notions of individual equality that so often ignore our communal existence and insist land and resources must be thought of as property. Instead, we can look to the laws of our Indigenous neighbours if we need to review our traditions. It is precisely this approach that is being taken up by many women and

Two-Spirit individuals in Indigenous communities as they pursue sexual health, revitalization of language and culture, and renewal of relationships with the land.

A focus on trans and Two-Spirit people as central to decolonization is incredibly important. The groundbreaking work of the Native Youth Sexual Health Network (NYSHN) epitomizes this approach. NYSHN works with:

> Indigenous peoples across the United States and Canada to advocate for and build strong, comprehensive, and culturally safe sexuality and reproductive health, rights, and justice initiatives in their own communities.[7]

NYSHN provides pragmatic, honest, and clear information on sexual health, as well as engages in the renewal and revitalization of Indigenous traditions related to all aspects of Indigenous health.

The barriers currently facing Indigenous women and Two-Spirit people are severe and informed by the

FIGURE 12.1. One of a series of posters on Two-Spirit teachings from the Native Youth Sexual Health Network.

history of colonialism. These barriers include the ongoing removal of Indigenous children from their families in numbers that exceed those taken by the residential-school system and the Sixties Scoop combined. While this cataclysmic interference has taken a devastating toll on the health of all of our peoples, colonially imposed gender imbalances ensure Indigenous women and Two-Spirit people bear the brunt of the consequences. The added marginalization experienced by Two-Spirit people can sometimes be overlooked because the social outcomes for Indigenous peoples are already, in general, very grim. To look at any of this solely through the lens of Western feminism is to miss the larger picture.

The imposition of colonial patriarchy has marginalized Indigenous women and Two-Spirit people through *Indian Act* governance systems, and by the *Indian Act* itself. As discussed in chapter 4, until 1985, when amendments were made to the *Indian Act,* an Indigenous woman or female-presenting Two-Spirit person who married a non-Indigenous man lost her legal status as an Indian, and was unable to pass on status to her children. In this way, generations of women and their children were denied their identities, and even their homes. The impact of the loss of legal identity is still being felt among Indigenous peoples through the struggle to reconnect with their families and communities.

Until very recently, Two-Spirit people were not recognized at all by Canadian law or society. In the eyes of Canadians, they do not exist; they are concealed by the gender-essentialized structures of colonialism, which have abolished their traditional places in Indigenous societies. So effective were Church- and government-led erasures of Two-Spirit people that reconstructing traditional Two-Spirit roles and ceremonies is often seen as peripheral to wider movements of resurgence. The work of groups like NYSHN reminds us that we must decolonize even our priorities as Indigenous peoples.

Structural erasures of Indigenous women and Two-Spirit people have had a role in shaping their work as agents of resurgence. In a way, the overwhelming masculinization of *Indian Act* governance systems has ensured that Indigenous women and Two-Spirit people are less likely to be co-opted by colonial powers, and less invested in maintaining those colonial structures. Indigenous women have continued to exercise power through traditional (and often unpaid) ways, thereby maintaining traditional governance structures in many communities. Two-Spirit people have not necessarily experienced the same retention of traditional roles, however, and much work is needed to reconstruct and recentre our Two-Spirit relations within our communities. Acknowledging and honouring Two-Spirit people is vital to resisting resurgence based on gender essentialism that purports to "honour women" while simply recreating colonial patriarchal gender roles with a bit of Indian flair.

The deliberate exclusion of Indigenous women and Two-Spirit people from colonial structures of power has meant that, almost by default, the work of these people is highly politicized, as it must happen outside those colonial structures. This is not to say Indigenous women and Two-Spirit people have no access to colonial structures of power. In recent years, there has been more inclusion of women, though not necessarily of Two-Spirit people, in *Indian Act* governance systems. Yet, one has only to do a head count of male to female *Indian Act* chiefs to notice this recent inclusion shamefully mirrors the "inclusion" of women in Canadian politics, which is tokenism at best.

Indigenous women and Two-Spirit people experience all of the barriers faced by settler women and LGBT people, as well as the barriers experienced by Indigenous peoples in a state defined by settler colonialism. These barriers cannot be sifted out and separated from one another.

Indigenous women and Two-Spirit people must bear a heavy burden as they work to reestablish and revitalize Indigenous sociopolitical orders, exercise sovereignty, and live resurgence; indeed, it can be very dangerous and draining work. It should not be necessary to work so hard to overcome barriers imposed by people who were supposed to share these lands as guests and, eventually, as kin, not as rulers. Nonetheless, to exist as an Indigenous woman or Two-Spirit person is an inherently political act. Simply resisting erasure is part of the work.

NOTES

1. Wesley Thomas, and Sue-Ellen Jacobs, "And We Are Still Here: From Berdache to Two-Spirit People," *American Indian Culture and Research Journal* 23, no. 2 (1999): 91–107, http://www.socqrl.niu.edu/forest/SOCI454/Berdache.html.

2. "Two-Spirit Community," *Re:searching for LGBTQ Health,* accessed October 22, 2015, http://www.lgbtqhealth.ca/community/two-spirit.php.

3. Hamish Copley, "The Disappearance of the Two-Spirit Traditions in Canada," *The Drummers Revenge* (blog), August 11, 2009, https://thedrummersrevenge.wordpress.com/2009/08/11/the-disappearance-of-the-two-spirit-traditions-in-canada/. This piece is excellent.

4. Part of this chapter was originally published in Issue 2 of *Guts* magazine; Chelsea Vowel, "Indigenous Women and Two-Spirited People: Our Work Is Decolonization!" *Guts Canadian Feminist Magazine,* Spring 2014, http://gutsmagazine.ca/issue-two/indigenous-women-two-spirited-people-work-decolonization.

5. There are few resources available on Two-Spirit identities and experiences. I crowdsourced some suggestions for those of you who want more to read than just this chapter:

Fiction

Thomson Highway, *Kiss of the Fur Queen* (Toronto: Doubleday Canada, 1998).

Craig Womack, *Drowning in Fire* (Tucson: University of Arizona Press, 2001).

Nonfiction

Qwo-Li Driskill, et al., eds., *Queer Indigenous Studies: Critical Interventions in Theory, Politics and Literature* (Tucson: University of Arizona Press, 2011).

Qwo-Li Diskill, et al., eds., *Sovereign Erotics: A Collection of Two-Spirit Literature* (Tucson: University of Arizona Press, 2011).

Drew Hayden Taylor, ed., *Me Sexy: An Exploration of Native Sex and Sexuality* (Vancouver: Douglas & McIntyre, 2008).

Alex Wilson, "How We Find Ourselves: Identity Development and Two-Spirit People," *Harvard Educational Review* 44, no. 2 (1996).

Dana Wesley, "Reimagining Two-Spirit Community: Critically Centering Narratives of Urban Two-Spirit Youth" (master's thesis, Queen's University, 2015), https://qspace.library. queensu.ca/bitstream/1974/13024/1/Wesley_Dana_L_201504_MA.pdf.

Video

Kelly Malone, "VIDEO: Journey of Indigenous Gender Identity," *ckom.com,* November 8, 2014, http://ckom.com/story/video-journey-indigenous-gender-identity/447504.

Lydia Nibley, *Two Spirits,* Film, directed by Lydia Nibley (2011; Riding the Tiger), http://www.pbs.org/independentlens/films/two-spirits/. (**Trigger warning for transphobic violence.** The film deals with the murder of Fred Martinez, a 16-year-old Two-Spirit Navajo. It also discusses traditional/contemporary Two-Spirit experiences.)

6. Cree term for the Americas.
7. *Native Youth Sexual Health Network*, accessed October 22, 2015, http://www.nativeyouthsexualhealth.com/.

PART 3

Myth-Busting

13
The Myth of Progress

Since December 2012 and the rise of the Idle No More movement, there have been numerous teach-ins throughout the country. Some of them focus on the theme of reconciliation. Others provide necessary background to those unfamiliar with the causes of Indigenous discontent, while others attempt to provide possible visions for the future. Whether you agree with a focus on education versus a widespread series of actions, it is clear much work is needed to overcome some very pervasive and damaging stereotypes.

You never have to wait long for unambiguously racist opinions, depicting Indigenous peoples in an unflattering light, to be given a public platform. In fact, certain people in this country manage to make a living claiming to be experts on us while basically assuring Canadians that Indigenous peoples are inferior and broken in every possible way. I don't like to provide a platform for this kind of thing, but this one chapter requires us to take a look at these narratives for a brief moment; so, my apologies in advance.

In January of 2013, a community paper in Manitoba, the *Morris Mirror,* ran an editorial by its editor-in-chief, Reed Turcotte, that likened Indigenous peoples to terrorists and decried our "corruption and laziness."[1] Not to be outdone, octogenarian Nanaimo resident Don Olsen submitted a letter to the editor of the *Nanaimo Daily News* in March of 2013, titled, "Educate First Nations to Become Modern Citizens," detailing our supposed total lack of achievements and inability to survive in a modern world[2] – that's the really nice summary version; it's a pretty awful piece.

Rounding out this vituperative triumvirate in July of the same year was Karin Klassen, a *Calgary Herald* journalist. She wrote an article that, in essence, defended the Sixties Scoop and suggested that First Nations peoples are culturally unfit to parent.[3] Her entire defence of the wholesale removal of Indigenous children from their families was that adoptive and foster families meant well. This opinion piece was not offered by a random citizen, but was delivered by a seasoned, paid journalist. In her article, she ignored all of the research on the subject in favour of a kneejerk personal reaction supported by nothing more than her anecdotal experiences. At its very best, the article was an example of a gross lack of professionalism.

The *Morris Mirror* experienced significant backlash and, despite its claims to "represent the views of the local community," local residents were quick to voice their disgust with the views expressed. In response, some businesses withdrew their ads from the publication.

The *Nanaimo Daily* also experienced negative publicity and lost ad revenue for its choice to publish Olsen's letter. Unlike the *Morris Mirror,* the *Nanaimo Daily* offered a full apology and withdrew the article.[4] By then, a number of people had published rebuttals to the letter, including a very detailed one by Danica Denommé, in which she highlighted Indigenous achievements and innovation.[5] In contrast, the *Calgary Herald* did not apologize or withdraw Klassen's piece.

In April of 2013, a British Columbia New Democratic Party (NDP) candidate resigned after some of her online comments about First Nations peoples came to light.[6]

You might be saying to yourself, "Well, self, don't these examples show how there are now consequences for writing racist things? Now that papers know they can lose advertising, and people know they can lose their jobs or political positions, things must be getting better!"

If only that were true. Unfortunately, opinion pieces and articles like these continue unabated. Sometimes, they are presented somewhat more carefully, but generally still contain gems like this one from Conrad Black in June of 2015: "Despite everything, even the First Nations should be grateful that the Europeans came here"[7] – this, after a discussion about residential schools. Sometimes, these pieces are so dripping with sarcasm and contempt it is difficult to read through them fully, like in a book review by Réjean Morissette, also in June of 2015.[8] Morissette denies that Indigenous peoples lived in Quebec before the French arrived; but rather, were pushed there to escape the "belliqueux [warlike] Mohawks," or under pressure from United States colonists, as well as coming to participate in the fur trade. This, of course, leaves Quebec's hands clean – no colonialism there, since there were no Indigenous peoples to colonize!

To provide a more recent example of a politician losing their position for racist comments, a Conservative riding association director lost her position in 2015 for her social media comments about Indigenous peoples, including one targeting the recently crowned Mrs. Universe, Ashley Callingbull (nêhiyaw), whom she described as "a monster."[9] So, no, I wouldn't exactly say things have gotten better.

The fact that people are able to outright dismiss literally centuries of oppression as though this could have no possible impact on events today, or claim that we somehow deserved to be colonized, or even flat out deny prior Indigenous presence (like Morissette) never ceases to astound me. How is this even possible? Clearly the first step, as exemplified by Klassen, is to claim good intentions negate oppression. Another tactic is to say, "Those were different times."[10]

When dealing with these kinds of opinions, one tends to have to weigh the pros and cons of ignoring them, or providing an often emotionally exhausting rebuttal. Indigenous peoples and allies are often faced with putting in extreme effort to refute and educate, but it can feel like little progress is being made.

Media portrayals of Indigenous peoples in Canada

That feeling is unfortunately supported by extensive research. Anderson and Robertson's *Seeing Red: A History of Natives in Canadian Newspapers* provides exhaustive evidence of how little the narrative has changed in the media since 1869.[11] In fact, Anderson and Robertson assert in their introduction that, "with respect to Aboriginal peoples, the colonial imaginary has thrived, even dominated, and continues to do so in mainstream English-language newspapers."[12]

The imaginary to which they refer is the way in which Canada has created an image of itself, based not so much on historical fact as on ideological interpretation. In doing so, Canada has necessarily had to rely upon an image of Indigenous peoples, which, as expressed by Turcotte, Olsen, Klassen, et al., portrays us as pretty much useless. *Seeing Red* was published in 2005, and I would have no trouble at all finding you hundreds of examples since then of exactly the kind of racist, patronizing, anti-Indigenous propaganda Anderson and Robertson meticulously catalogued.

How is it that so little progress has been made to overcome this narrative in 147 years? Certainly, the colonial myths that continue to dominate media discourse have existed for much longer than this. Yet, one would hope that nearly a century and a half of technological and social development would see a corresponding shift in mainstream attitudes. Instead, we see the same arguments being made year after year after year.

Of course, the idea that Canadian society is evolving and progressing is an important part of the colonial imaginary. The myth is that progress is tied to the passage of time, thus, things are always inevitably getting better. When Canadians consider the injustices faced by Indigenous peoples, those injustices are nearly always located in the past. The irony is that every generation has located such injustice in the past, and only rarely in contemporary contexts. Were this actually true, no injustice could have possibly occurred ever, much less be understood to continue today!

Canadians who do recognize historical injustice seem to understand it in this way:

- Bad things happened.
- Bad things stopped happening and equality was achieved.
- The low social and political status held by Indigenous peoples is now wholly based on the *choice* to be corrupt, lazy, inefficient, and unsuited to the modern world. (More on this in the next chapter.)

In other words, there is no history of colonialism and systemic racism that informs the modern view of Indigenous peoples, because that problem was supposedly solved at some point in the past. The "real" racism is in conflating "legitimate" dislike for Indigenous peoples (based not on race or ethnicity, but rather on the "bad choices we make") with historic colonialism/racism "which is over." In continuing to discuss colonialism and racism as present-day concerns, Indigenous peoples are engaging in so-called "reverse-racism and oppressing blameless settlers."

Canada is hardly unique in this ahistorical approach. In the United States, slavery is also located in the distant past, and the belief that full equality was achieved, at some nebulous but definite point, is widely accepted (at least by settlers) as true. Thus, anti-Black sentiment is based not on race but on "true generalizations" of all the "bad choices Black people have made" since they became "equal." To even suggest this view as untrue raises hackles.

At least the United States admits slavery happened; in Canada, many still seem to think there was no enslavement here, believing only that Canada was a shining safe station on a glorious Underground Railroad.[13]

Flip the narrative.

The fact is that what we all learn about Canadian history is wrong. Every single one of us, Indigenous and non-Indigenous alike, has been fed a series of lies, half-truths, and fantasies intended to create a cohesive national identity. What is most startling about this is that a great many people are aware of the errors and omissions present in our system of education and in our public discourse, yet there has not been a national attempt to rectify this.

That is not to say no effort has been made. The inclusion of events into the mainstream consciousness – events I only heard rumours about when I was in school – has been incredibly important. Acknowledging Japanese internment, the Chinese Head Tax, residential schools, and a host of other less-than-inspiring events and policies has certainly taken us beyond the kind of starry-eyed propaganda served up for a long time in this country.

Nonetheless, integral to the colonial narrative is belief in the superiority of European contributions and the absence of any truly important contribution from non-European peoples to Canadian society – except when narrowly defined within examples of successful integration and "up by their bootstraps" stories. After all, if Black, non-Black POC, and Indigenous contributions were of any real value, wouldn't we see them everywhere? Instead, all that is good and modern originated in Europe!

Not everyone states this as baldly as Mr. Olsen, et al. but the sentiment is still widely shared. Which is incredibly sad, because Canada will not crumble and fall apart if we become more honest and aware of the history of these lands and the incredible diversity of contributions by peoples from all over the world.

The violence of national myths

A more accurate and less self-serving history, a more honest reality, is ours. It is our birthright, whether we have been in these lands for thousands of years or arrived yesterday. We are all being denied a real identity, one based on more than colonial myths intended to create a national identity out of thin air.

It is not only Indigenous peoples who want to reclaim that birthright. Millions of people living in this country are trying to come to grips with their own personal histories – histories that more often than not fail to accord with the official narrative. There are many such examples. Unwed mothers who were pressured into giving up their babies for adoption finding out that many of these babies were killed and buried instead.[14] Black orphans who were horrifically abused by those who were supposed to protect them.[15] Italians in Canada put into internment camps during WWII, and so very many more who have had to struggle to have their stories heard and believed.[16]

These are all horrific stories, and they are only the tip of the iceberg, because most of us have heard only a fraction of them. The violence that national myths commit is to delegitimize the very real pain that is the legacy of abuse and oppression. When these stories begin to surface, they are often treated as conspiracy theories. Even when incontrovertible proof is discovered and the information becomes freely available, the overarching Canadian narrative obscures and confuses, splitting these events up into disparate and unconnected "unfortunate incidents." Most Canadians will learn only a few of these stories and will be unable to connect them to a wider history of colonialism. This means that nothing can change, as is made so clear in the book *Seeing Red* and exemplified in articles like Klassen's. How can we possibly learn from the past when this country is so invested in whitewashing it?

We all need to work on reclaiming our histories, but this cannot be an individual exercise; it absolutely must be a national one. We must share our histories and learn the histories of others, and our curricula and media must reflect our evolving understandings.

Right now, Indigenous peoples are trying very hard to share our histories. For this to create a new chapter in Anderson and Robertson's research depends on whether or not Canadians are finally willing to listen.

NOTES

1. "Manitoba Newspaper Sparks Furor With Racist Editorial," *CBC News,* January 13, 2013, http://www.cbc.ca/news/canada/manitoba/manitoba-newspaper-sparks-furor-with-racist-editorial-1.1323976.

2. Travis Lupick, "Letter Titled 'Educate First Nations to Be Modern Citizens' Sparks Debate on Racism," *straight.com,* last modified March 28, 2013, http://www.straight.com/blogra/366901/letter-titled-educate-first-nations-be-modern-citizens-sparks-debate-racism.

3. Karin Klassen, "Klassen: Don't Blame 'Colonialism' for Aboriginal Tragedies," *Calgary Herald,* last modified July 29, 2013. To see this piece you have to use the Wayback Machine: https://web.archive.org/web/20130806093202/http://www.calgaryherald.com/life/story.html?id=8719563. Klassen specifically addressed herself to First Nations families.

4. Tamara Baluja, "Nanaimo Daily News Apologizes for Running 'Racist' Letter to the Editor," *j-source.ca,* last modified Marsh 29, 2013, http://j-source.ca/article/nanaimo-daily-news-apologizes-running-%E2%80%98racist%E2%80%99-letter-editor.

5. Danica Denommé, "Racist Nanaimo Newspaper Letter Rebuttal: Educate Canadians to Be Knowledgeable Citizens," *Huffington Post,* last modified May 28, 2013, http://www.huffingtonpost.ca/danica-denomma/nanaimo-daily-news-don-olsen-letter-racist-first-nations_b_2975065.html. This is a particularly good rebuttal that is well worth reading in classroom settings, as well as on your own. Denommé, a Black and Aboriginal activist, succinctly details some very important aspects of precontact life that Canadians should learn about and consider more often.

6. Obert Madondo, "BC NDP Candidate Resigns Over Racist Comments Against First Nations," *canadianprogressiveworld.com,* last modified April 16, 2013, http://www.canadianprogressiveworld.com/2013/04/16/bc-ndp-candidate-resigns-over-racist-comments-against-first-nations/.

7. Conrad Black, "Conrad Black: Canada's Treatment of Aboriginals Was Shameful, But It Was Not Genocide," *National Post,* last modified June 7, 2015, http://news.nationalpost.com/full-comment/conrad-black-canadas-treatment-of-aboriginals-was-shameful-but-it-was-not-genocide.

8. Réjean Morissette, "Dérives Autochtones," *ledevoir.com,* last modified June 11, 2015, http://www.ledevoir.com/politique/canada/442381/derives-autochtones. The most telling quote is this: "Au Québec, il n'y a jamais eu telle chose qu'un paradis terrestre autochtone détruit par l'arrivée de la civilisation européenne. Pas plus que n'ont existé ici des modes de vie traditionnels fondés sur une culture communautaire autochtone structurée. Ça, c'est l'histoire des Amérindiens américains et des grandes dynasties autochtones d'Amérique centrale et d'Amérique du Sud...Cessons de fabuler sur ce qui n'a jamais existé, à savoir l'occupation ancestrale du territoire." ("In Quebec, there was never such thing as an Indigenous earthly paradise destroyed by the arrival of European civilization. Nor did traditional lifestyles exist here, based on a structured, communal Indigenous culture. That is the history of the American Indians and of large Indigenous dynasties of Central and South America. Let's not fantasize about what never existed, namely the ancestral occupation of the territory.")

9. Jorge Barrera, "Conservative Director Booted From Riding Board Over Comments Describing 'Indians' as 'Self-Loathing,'" *APTN.ca,* last modified September 8, 2015, http://aptn.ca/news/2015/09/08/conservative-director-booted-from-riding-board-over-comments-describing-indians-as-self-loathing/.

10. This approach was taken by the son of a scientist behind nutritional experiments on First Nations children, who wrote to the media to justify the program. Andrew Livingstone, "Son Defends Scientist Behind Aboriginal Nutrition Experiments," *The Star,* last modified July 24, 2013, http://www.thestar.com/news/canada/2013/07/24/son_defends_scientist_behind_aboriginal_nutrition_experiments.html.

11. Mark Cronlund Anderson, and Carmen L. Robertson, *Seeing Red: A History of Natives in Canadian Newspapers* (Winnipeg: University of Manitoba Press, 2011).

12. Ibid., 3.

13. Marcel Trudel, *Canada's Forgotten Slaves: Two Hundred Years of Bondage* (Montreal: Vehicle Press, 2013). There were *at least* 4200 enslaved Africans in Canada. In addition, indentured servitude, as experienced by Black people in Canada, more closely resembled slavery than freedom in a way that was not equally experienced by settlers under the same system.

14. "Butterbox Babies," *Ideal Maternity Home Survivors,* last accessed October 26, 2015, http://www.idealmaternityhomesurvivors.com/the-story/.

15. Here is a link to a roundup of various articles about the Nova Scotia Home for Colored Children Restorative Inquiry and the history that led to an inquiry being called: http://thechronicleherald.ca/tags/nova-scotia-home-colored-children (accessed Oct. 26, 2015). The inquiry itself received its terms of reference and mandate in 2015. You can monitor its progress here: http://restorativeinquiry.ca/.

16. Marisha Lederman, "Shining Light on a Dark Secret: The Internment of Italian-Canadians," *The Globe and Mail,* last modified September 6, 2012, http://www.theglobeandmail.com/arts/shining-light-on-a-dark-secret-the-internment-of-italian-canadians/article551227/.

14

The Myth of the Level Playing Field

In 2014, the Supreme Court rendered its decision in *Tsilhqot'in*, after which a staggering amount of opinion pieces were spewed forth discussing this landmark case.[1] The interest was unsurprising given it had been 17 years since *Delgamuukw*, the case that first acknowledged the possibility of Canada recognizing Aboriginal title.[2] After all that time, we finally had the Court point to a specific tract of land and say, "and this is what Aboriginal title looks like."

Without going into exhaustive detail, here are some of the main points of the case:

- The decision removes the fear that Aboriginal title could only be found on postage stamp areas where people lived either permanently or semi-permanently, and instead extends the possibility of Aboriginal title to wider territories that were heavily used by a people.
- The Court reminds everyone that translating precontact Aboriginal practices into modern-day rights cannot be done by shoving everything into a common-law box. Aboriginal perspectives must inform the translation process.
- The Court admonishes everyone to remember that it is inappropriate to approach Aboriginal land/rights claims on an overly technical basis. The issue is *justice and reconciliation,* so don't try to undermine this with nitpicking over dotted *i*'s.
- *Terra nullius,* on which the Doctrine of Discovery heavily relies, was found to have never applied in Canada. So the Court has once again told us how Canada did *not* gain sovereignty over the lands, but remained consistently vague on how Canada *did* gain this sovereignty – other than saying, as always, that when sovereignty was asserted by the Crown, it crystallized. Colonial magic!

- The Court says the content of Aboriginal title is basically the right to "enjoy the economic fruits" of the land and resources. Aboriginal title is collective, not individual, and underneath it all still remains Crown title. Crown title consists of whatever is left over after Aboriginal title has been subtracted from the equation. Essentially remaining are: a fiduciary duty to deal fairly with Aboriginal peoples, and the right to infringe on Aboriginal title as long as the infringement meets section 35 test criteria (i.e., if it's important enough to Canada).

To keep this all in context, the *Tsilhqot'in* had Aboriginal title recognized in only 5 percent of their total claim area. Private properties within that area were left out of the claim and continue to exist as private properties. The territory in question did not overlap with other First Nations territory. And, Aboriginal title lands are still part of Canada and subject to justifiable infringement. Also important to remember is that this entire discussion is being framed within a context wherein we must accept that Canada has the right to recognize anything at all when it comes to Indigenous rights – a right hotly contested by Indigenous peoples themselves.

However, to hear some people talk, the *Tsilhqot'in* decision spells the end for modern democracy. It's really this fear-mongering and the Western liberal myth of a level playing field I want to address.

To give you a sense of the arguments I'm referring to, Gordon Clark wrote a perfect example in *The Province* after the ruling was released.[3] This quote sums up his argument well:

> They [Canadians] reject special arrangements for aboriginals, including court decisions like Tsilhqot'in, because they breach the fundamental tenets of modern liberal democracies – equal citizenship and equality before the law – and perpetuate the divisions between First Nations and other Canadians."[4]

Other pieces by other authors did a bang-up job of exposing a deeply racist reaction to the *Tsilhqot'in* decision and to Indigenous peoples in general, and are easily deconstructed for the distasteful, bigoted mess they are. Clark's piece, however, is arguably more insidious because it appeals to the progressive desire for equality within a liberal democracy, wherein all people are created equal and deviations from that philosophy constitute the real injustice.

However, the argument ends up betraying itself in the end, ignoring the way in which Canadian law has been (and continues to be) used to strip Indigenous peoples of their land and resources to the benefit of Canadians. It sidesteps the way Indigenous peoples were denied equal citizenship rights until very recently, and completely glosses over how deeply unequal the living conditions are for Indigenous peoples in this country. And, no, I do not mean unequal "in our favour." Decisions like *Tsilhqot'in* haven't created these divisions; hundreds of years of racist, colonial policies have.

For this reason, I would encourage progressive Canadians to critically reexamine this all too commonplace opinion and evaluate whether they truly wish to support such an approach.

Clark treads a well-worn path with his piece – and variations on this theme can fill volumes – so this is really not a response to the man himself. I want to challenge the ideas he expressed that are shared by so many well-meaning Canadians. Please permit me to break down for you what I find so problematic with the myth of the level playing field.

Acknowledging the past is good enough.

First, this argument invariably begins by acknowledging Europeans behaved very naughtily toward Indigenous peoples, and racism has certainly factored into that behaviour. Clark even mentions provincial and federal governments, so he does not contain these bad things in the distant past directly following contact. Starting with this position allows one to recognize the racism and abuse inherent in the residential-school system, for example, while ignoring how contemporary Aboriginal child-welfare policies are linked to that system.

However, in acknowledging the past but cutting it off from the present, there is a strong implication that, at some point, Canada got itself sorted out and began dealing fairly with Indigenous peoples. The exact date of this occurrence is never mentioned, so the driving events that led to "The Change" vary greatly in the opinions of those making this claim. The idea is that policies and actions taken in the past were driven by inexcusable racism, whereas policies of today, if they fail Indigenous peoples, fail because of incompetence rather than malice or structural design.

This is a central pillar of the Western liberal myth of a level playing field: recognizing Indigenous peoples have legitimate grievances stemming from awful things that were done in the past, but the advent of a modern democracy means we are now all equals and we have an obligation to behave as such.

What this part of the argument always relies upon is the implicit notion that any remaining problems faced by Indigenous peoples stem from an inability for people living in Canada to commit to a standard of "equal citizenship and equality before the law." This charge will be levied at First Nations leadership and Canadian politicians both. There is little need then to understand how historical injustice has moulded and shaped conditions today, and continues to find structural expression within the Canadian context. There is even less need to deconstruct how ongoing injustices are inextricably rooted in that history. Instead, a bright line is drawn between the past and the present we could all be living in if only everyone embraced liberal democracy wholeheartedly.

(Of course, all ideologies rely on the notion that if everyone wholeheartedly committed to living the ideology in question, there would be unity; a recursive notion that disregards the reality of differing perspectives.)

Ironically, this way of acknowledging the past is just as dismissive as pretending the actions of European governments after contact were justified. Both approaches refuse to acknowledge there is, in fact, no break between the past and the present, and current policies and structures differ only in appearance. Historical policies to assimilate Indigenous peoples and deny their rights were overt and irrefutably based on beliefs of Indigenous inferiority, while today's policies simply make assimilation into the Canadian body politic seem like an unintended consequence of ensuring everyone is equal under the law (regardless of social inequality).

Equal access to rights has been achieved.

The next step in this argument is everyone in a modern democracy has equal access to the same rights, and any policy or judicial decision that recognizes differences is, in fact, creating inequality. Thus, the progressive can criticize the deeply racist *Indian Act* while, at the same time, argue that recognizing Aboriginal title is equally as damaging to the notion of "equal citizenship and equality before the law." That is exactly what Jeffrey Simpson argued a year after the *Tsilhqot'in* decision:

> In this territory [of the Tsilhqot'in], with a few restrictions, the group now has de jure sovereignty, a precedent that, if extended over time, would leave B.C. pockmarked with little self-governing, largely sovereign aboriginal territories over which the Crown's writ would barely run.[5]

This position is only tenable if one believes equal access to the same rights has already been guaranteed. Again, this belief relies on an ahistorical view of the modern context. Not only does it dismiss outright the way in which Indigenous and colonial relations have shaped current political and legal structures in Canada, it also outright wholly rejects English common-law sociopolitical traditions.

Canadian law, be it English common law or French civil law, comes from a tradition that favours male landowners and is inherently set up so that the richer you are, the more rights you have. If we narrow the view of rights to include only the trappings of modern liberal democracies, such as the right to vote and the right to protections under the Charter, then one can claim with a straight face that we are all equal under the law. However, even liberal progressives are quick to acknowledge legal equality does not necessarily translate to social equality; so, why insist, in the context of Indigenous peoples, the one will naturally follow the other?

Equality before the law will solve any problem.

One way in which Western liberal thought attempts to address the reality of difference in modern democracies is through the notion of "equality before the law." Sometimes, you will see people arguing that it is imperative all people are treated exactly the same under the law; but, of course, modern democracies do not actually function that way, and this position crumbles easily.

Equality in this sense does not mean *sameness*. It does not insist all people are the same and are to be treated as such. In fact, accommodating differences is arguably a central tenet of modern liberal democracies.

For example, legal equality as sameness would require people in wheelchairs to use the stairs, a patently ridiculous and unjust notion. Instead, building codes throughout Canada require a certain number of wheelchair ramps and elevators to ensure equal access to all people regardless of their level of mobility. Less obvious accommodations are also normalized. For example, the Quebec building code requires women's bathrooms have more toilets installed to address issues with longer wait times experienced previous to these legislative changes. Neither wheelchair accessibility nor extra toilets in women's bathrooms are held out by liberal progressives to undermine modern liberal democracy, so why then is acknowledging Indigenous differences so threatening?

Many will argue there is no need for the category of Aboriginal, only Canadian, and equality before the law will address any accommodations needed via other individual categories (woman, wheelchair user, unemployed, single parent, and so on).

It is at this point that the argument requires Indigenous peoples to assimilate completely, voluntarily giving up the category of Indigenous (because it can be legislated away, but it must also be collectively rejected). Here is where the outcome (complete assimilation) mirrors the overtly racist historical approach, despite the philosophies (we are all equal versus you are inferior to us) differing considerably.

Canada has an official policy of multiculturalism, which would allow Indigenous peoples to exist as Canadians and celebrate surface culture (food/music/clothing) without existing as a separate legal category. Indigenous peoples would need to stop advancing their claims to Indigenous rights, and exist within a framework of Canadian rights. This can appear as completely nonproblematic to those who do not understand Indigenous sociopolitical orders continue to exist, and exist outside the context of any Canadian legislative or judicial sphere. Giving that up to *become Canadian* and to be folded into a Western liberal-rights framework is the definition of assimilation. No amount of frybread and community Cree classes can change that.

The other option, if Indigenous peoples refuse to voluntarily assimilate into the Canadian body politic, is for Canada to stop recognizing the category of Aboriginal. Abolish the *Indian Act,* abolish recognition of Aboriginal status, and simply stop discussing the notion of Aboriginal rights entirely.

Both of these options have been repeatedly called for since the beginning of Canadian politics. The rhetoric changes with the times, but the goal is still the same. Does it really matter if policies are outwardly racist or merely "progressive" if the outcome is the cultural destruction of Indigenous peoples?

Equal citizenship requires erasure of differences.

The underlying problem with this entire approach is that certain differences, or *acknowledging* certain differences, is seen as being inherently threatening to modern democracy. Further, the choice as to which differences threaten national cohesion is not value neutral, despite any possible claims to the contrary.

Divisions between us already exist in myriad unavoidable ways, and we do not attempt to erase those differences in the name of "equal citizenship and equality before the law." In fact, we constitutionalize many of those differences and legally require they be accommodated.[6] We attempt to get rid of ways in which those differences are penalized legally or socially, unless those differences are actively harmful (e.g., pedophiles).

For example, section 15 of the Charter of Rights and Freedoms acknowledges and protects differences based on the following enumerated grounds: race, nation or ethnic origin, colour, religion, sex, age, or mental or physical disability. Recognized analogous grounds have been found by the courts to include: pregnancy, sexual orientation, marital status, off-reserve Aboriginal status, and citizenship.

It is very unlikely the same people arguing that Indigenous differences threaten democracy would argue that differences between able-bodied and disabled people hold the same threat (though they will certainly differ on what level of accommodation is appropriate). Yet, Clark states, "As long as natives are treated differently, it will perpetuate divisions and even breed resentment, neither of which is good for Canada."[7]

Replace the word *natives* with any other descriptor of difference that exists in Canadian society and is legally accommodated, and try to argue that this category of difference should be erased for the sake of unity or to avoid resentment. This argument only works when discussing how that category of people should not be specifically discriminated against (such as within the *Indian Act*), but the argument quickly falls apart when arguing accommodations should no longer be made – unless the category is actively harmful. And here we arrive at the crux of the argument: indigeneity *is* seen as actively harmful.

The Indigenous danger is economic.

The harm of discriminating *against* Indigenous peoples is clearly recognized by liberal progressives, so we don't really differ on that account. The disagreement is rooted in the notion that *accommodating* Indigenous difference is actively harmful to a modern democracy.

Accommodating Indigenous differences is not seen as harmful *merely* because it creates resentment. No doubt people resent all manner of accommodations provided to various categories of differences within the Canadian liberal democracy. This resentment is not called upon as justification for abolishing those other categories altogether or for moving backwards on advances that have been made. Imagine, for example, resentment being used as an actual, legal reason to abolish gay marriage in Canada.

Rather, the danger lies in the fact that (1) of all groups in Canada, only Indigenous peoples (and possibly the Québécois, also mentioned by Clark) have prior legal claim to land and resources that are otherwise believed to belong to Canada, and (2) this prior legal claim is recognized by Indigenous law, and Canadian Aboriginal law is viewed as deeply problematic because it directly impacts Canada's economic power. There is great fear the *Tsilhqot'in* decision – and the entire body of Aboriginal law that recognizes Aboriginal rights as burdens, or limits on Crown title – will damage Canada economically.

That is *exactly* what Jeffrey Simpson argued a year after the *Tsilhqot'in* decision. To repeat:

> In this territory [of the Tsilhqot'in], with a few restrictions, the group [the Tsilhqot'in] now has de jure sovereignty, a precedent that, if extended over time,

would leave B.C. pockmarked with little self-governing, largely sovereign aboriginal territories over which the Crown's writ would barely run.[8]

This quote evokes an image of a disintegrating Canada, a modern democracy rent asunder and scattered to the winds by egregious and unjust accommodation of Aboriginal title.[9] Okay, but what is so terrifying about that exactly?

Simpson then quotes Professor Dwight Newman who laments that due to recent Aboriginal law decisions, "it has become extremely difficult to get major infrastructure projects done in Canada."[10] Ah. So, that's what this is *really* about.

The test: economy vs human rights

Notice that throughout, I have only been arguing within the Western liberal framework rather than from a position of Indigenous rights. I do this deliberately because I think the Western liberal approach needs to be self-critical, and these are the flaws I am seeing.

If a modern democracy wishes to ensure "equality of citizenship and equality before the law," then the law must become a tool to ensure equal access to rights and resources. That process is undermined when we ignore both a group that has been historically disadvantaged and how that history results in contemporary lack of access to rights and resources.

Engaging in this sort of blind-eye approach in the name of unity without admitting the real fear is economic is problematic enough, but the meat of the matter is people are suggesting a human-rights matter be overlooked for the sake of the Canadian economy.

Liberal democracies engage in this sort of balancing act all the time, so this concept of tempering human-rights concerns with economic concerns is hardly new or antithetical. However, much is assumed in taking the position that economic concerns must in this case trump the human-rights issue of Indigenous peoples in Canada.

It is assumed that abolishing the category of Aboriginal will be more cost-effective than acknowledging it. This is a major flaw in the argument that economic concerns should trump human rights. Billions of dollars are spent on providing Indigenous peoples with services such as health care, education, social services, infrastructure, and so on, not to mention the monies spent on court cases centred on Aboriginal rights.

However, the vast bulk of these monies (flowing constitutionally from the federal rather than provincial government) are already provided to Canadians.

Were we to abolish Aboriginal as a category, this cost would not disappear; it would simply shift onto the shoulders of the provincial governments. Making Indigenous peoples "Canadian" would not end their health care, education, social services, and infrastructure needs. In fact, given that Indigenous peoples are historically underfunded in all those areas, the cost would be higher once they were folded into the Canadian body politic, receiving funds equal to everyone else.

It is also assumed that abolishing judicially created obligations toward Indigenous peoples would be more cost-effective than continuing to engage in them. This includes obligations like the duty to consult, or the court costs involved in not wanting to acknowledge Aboriginal rights, as well as all the time and money put into negotiating outstanding land claims and comprehensive claims. Maybe just dropping all of this in the name of equality would save some big time sôniyaws?[11]

This ignores the well-studied economic and social impact that occurs when Indigenous peoples are denied Indigenous rights or not accommodated as a category of people. Whether the strategy is relocation from isolated communities to those with more accessible services, refusing to accommodate Indigenous peoples in the justice system, or ignoring how differences affect Indigenous children in the child-welfare system, it has been made very clear over the years that the social (and economic) cost of denial is shockingly high. In essence, abolishing Aboriginal as a category does not abolish the very real differences that exist, nor the social and economic costs associated with dealing with how those differences are manifested in Canadian society.

One would have to engage in a very thorough cost-benefit analysis to determine whether the supposed economic benefit of abolishing the category of Aboriginal would be worth it. In doing so, one would have to become much more familiar with the issues than most people making this argument are; so, in that sense, I recommend it. Just don't ignore data and skew your equation with preconceptions based on misunderstanding the situation.

More important, those advocating these kinds of arguments need to take a hard look at whether using an economic cost-benefit analysis to determine when to trump human rights is consistent with one's own beliefs. Is this really where people want "modern democracy," even within a capitalist economic system, to go?

Calling for a more honest discussion

For many, the answer to the question above might still be yes, but I would rather have them say it outright than pretend the call to abolish Aboriginal as a category is about fairness and equality rather than about the economy. Let's agree this conversation needs to become more honest.

There does not exist today a level playing field upon which Indigenous peoples can benefit equally. Historical injustice did not cease at some magical moment to be replaced by contemporary fairness.

There is no level playing field when it comes to the access of equal rights – not for Indigenous peoples, and not even within the wider Canadian public. A host of barriers exists preventing millions of Canadians from accessing the same rights and resources as other Canadians.

There is no level playing field when it comes to equality before the law, in the sense that due to the recognized lack of access to equal rights, accommodations are specifically written into Canadian law. There is an attempt to create a level playing field by recognizing, not ignoring, differences.

There is no level playing field when it comes to deciding which differences must be abolished for the sake of equal citizenship. Before gay marriage was legalized in Canada, did the exclusion of homosexual marriage threaten equal citizenship? Canada has now taken the position that, yes, it did, but, obviously, Canada did not take this position until very recently. Was it any less true when homosexual marriage was excluded? Recognition and accommodation are based on value judgments, and values shift over time. In an age where racism against Indigenous peoples is widespread and systemic, it is difficult to imagine someone arguing that weighing the decision to recognize or abolish the category of Aboriginal is a value-neutral, level-playing-field exercise.

There is no level playing field when the discussion becomes about how the colonization of land and resources, as the source of Canadian wealth, cannot be allowed to be threatened by the human-rights issue of Indigenous peoples within Canada. The ultimate irony of the progressive liberal fearing Indigenous peoples will take Canadian land cannot be lost on any of us when this discussion is engaged.

If you find yourself making these arguments, or you come across them, please do a little bit of digging to find the roots. I see too many surface arguments calling for unity without a shred of nuance to be found, and I think we ought to expect more from those who claim to be socially progressive.

NOTES

1. *Tsilhqot'in Nation v. British Columbia, 2014,* SCC 44.
2. *Delgamuukw v. British Columbia, 1997,* 3 SCR 1010.

3. Gordon Clark, "Gordzilla in the City: Native Court Rulings Perpetuate Unhealthy Divisions in Canada," *The Province* (blog), July 7, 2014, http://blogs.theprovince.com/2014/07/07/gordzilla-in-the-city-native-court-rulings-perpetuate-unhealthy-divisions-in-canada/.

4. Ibid.

5. Jeffrey Simpson, "Confusion Reigns on Aboriginal Rights When Court Rulings Meet Reality," *The Globe and Mail*, last modified July 11, 2015, http://www.theglobeandmail.com/globe-debate/confusion-reigns-on-aboriginal-rights-when-court-rulings-meet-reality/article25413801/.

6. *Canadian Charter of Rights and Freedoms*, Part I of the *Constitution Act, 1982*, Schedule B *Canada Act, 1982* (UK), 1982, c 11, s 15.

7. Clark, "Gordzilla in the City."

8. Simpson, "Confusion Reigns on Aboriginal Rights."

9. Apparently, 149 years of a sometimes-functioning "Confederation" (really a decentralized federal state, but never mind) is much more important than tens of thousands of years of prior occupancy and the sociopolitical systems that arose prior to contact.

10. Simpson, "Confusion Reigns on Aboriginal Rights."

11. A word for money in nêhiyawêwin, naturally.

15
The Myth of Taxation

Well, nitôtêmitik, now that we've addressed some structural issues, it's time to tackle some of the most widespread and pernicious myths out there – the kinds of myths that have become so rooted in the Canadian consciousness, they are taken as fact and rarely examined. Out of all the myths I have come across, the belief that Indigenous peoples do not pay taxes seems to be the most widespread. I'm here to tell you that you probably don't know what you think you know.

First off, let's acknowledge the obvious: no one really *likes* to pay taxes. In fact, many people are downright resentful about them. However, there is a grudging understanding that paying taxes allows there to be a pool of funds that make all manner of things available that would otherwise not be. The idea that any group of people can get away with not contributing, when everyone else is forced by law to do so, raises indignant ire unmatched by pretty much anything else.

So keenly is this injustice felt that identities are formed around whether one pays taxes or not. "As a taxpaying citizen" has been a standard starting point for all manner of arguments, apparently identifying the person who utters this formulaic phrase as hardworking, socially responsible, and worthy of being listened to. The corollary to this is the belief that people who do *not* pay taxes are lazy, socially parasitic, and unworthy of even the most basic human rights. If this feels like an exaggeration to you, stop by any comment section on an article about Indigenous peoples, and you'll soon see I tell no lies. This is really how some people think.

Tackling this myth is, therefore, fairly important. If some people out there justify their hatred of Indigenous peoples through the myth that we don't pay taxes, and therefore do not deserve basic human rights, then exposing this myth means yanking out a foundation stone. Yank enough of those stones, and the whole structure of justifications collapses. We are left with the fact that a lot of this is just "I don't like you" rather than "this is how you have failed to earn my respect."

So, let's get down to it. Do Indigenous people pay taxes?

The short answer first

- There is an *Indian Act* tax exemption for First Nations *only* that is very narrow and applies only to personal property and income located on a reserve.
- First Nations peoples pay all other taxes not covered by the narrow exemption.
- The tax exemption only involves about 192 005 First Nations peoples when you subtract the number of children aged 0–14 and people 65 and older from the potential tax-paying base.
- That number is actually *even lower* because a number of First Nations have exchanged tax exemptions for other benefits in self-governing Final Agreements, or have instituted their own taxation regimes.

Indians don't even pay taxes; why should they get my tax dollars?! *Blaaargh* (head explodes).

I'm sending you the dry-cleaning bill. Just saying.

This is one of the most common complaints that comes up in any discussion of any news story concerning First Nations. I am going to focus on the factual aspects of First Nations taxation more than on the philosophical discussions of "who should be taxed" and "where should my tax dollars go." Rather than being drawn off into a larger-issue discussion, I'm going to keep the focus narrow.

The first thing you need to know is that most Indigenous peoples *don't* get tax exemptions. The tax exemptions that do exist are linked completely to the reserves, so non-status Indians, Inuit, Métis, and most status Indians living off-reserve don't get any tax exemptions at all. That narrows down the people eligible for tax exemptions by a pretty huge margin.

In 2011, there were 1 400 685 First Nations, Métis, and Inuit.[1] Out of that, 637 660 were status Indians (also called "registered Indians," if you want to check these numbers yourself), 22 895 of whom, by the way, aren't Aboriginal at all.[2]

Regarding status Indians, only 314 370 were living on-reserve, give or take, based on incomplete census results.[3] It is this group that accounts for the majority of people who are eligible for the tax exemptions under discussion.

Yeah, about 300 000 Indians don't pay any taxes!

I hate to do this to you (no, I don't), but I can't start this discussion until I whittle the numbers down a little more for you. I think it's important we keep in mind the actual numbers at play here before we decide whether or not to get hysterical about money pouring out of our pockets like a river of multicoloured, polymer substrate bills.

In 2011, there were 105 230 status Indians between the ages of 0–14 living on-reserve.[4] The 0–14 population accounts for 30 percent of the total status-Indian population, representing a much higher birthrate than among the non-Aboriginal population; this significantly decreases the population of potential First Nations taxpayers.[5] There are also 17 135 status Indians who are 65 years and older living on-reserve.[6]

This means that of the total population, only 192 005, would actually be of an age to be eligible to pay taxes – unless you think kids aged 0–14 should be included in the labour force and pay income tax, and one should be forced to work essentially until one dies. Therefore, what we're actually talking about here is about 192 000, out of the almost 36 million people living in Canada, who have access to *Indian Act* tax exemptions. That is 0.5 percent of the total population in Canada.

Yet, I suspect the total numbers aren't the issue so much as the "principle" of the thing.

But wait, there's more, um, I mean less!

There are 139 First Nations communities – out of more than 600 across Canada – that have an on-reserve property tax regime, generating about $70 million in revenues annually.[7] The taxes are collected by the First Nation, and used for the First Nation.

In addition, there are communities that have negotiated self-governance and other alternate tax regimes with the federal government so that the band levies things like the First Nations Sales Tax, the First Nations Goods and Services Tax, and/or the First Nations Personal Income Tax.[8] In the Yukon, for example, 11 out of the 14 First Nations are no longer tax exempt under self-governing Final Agreements.[9]

All of this reduces the total number of people actually eligible for *Indian Act* tax exemptions even more. If we absolutely cared about the total numbers – as in, if folks who got upset about First Nations tax exemptions decided "under this number, it no longer matters" – then I would go through the process of figuring these numbers into the total. I strongly suspect, however, that *any* number of First Nations people accessing tax exemptions would still make some people very angry.

Whoop-de-doo, so a few of them pay property taxes (and a few other taxes) that don't benefit me at all; what's your point?

Well, the claim often made is that First Nations don't pay any taxes at all. That might not be the real issue, but it's certainly worth addressing so that more people understand the reality of the situation. I hope you don't mind if I continue, then.

I am going to quote Indian Affairs:

> In general, Aboriginal people in Canada are required to pay taxes on the same basis as other people in Canada, except where the limited exemption under Section 87 of the Indian Act applies. Section 87[10] says that the "personal property of an Indian or a band situated on a reserve" is tax exempt.[11]

All right. Do you have your Timmy's coffee ready? I feel like using a list format to break this down for you.

- Only status Indians are eligible for the *Indian Act* exemption. Non-status Indians, Métis, and Inuit are not covered.
- Status Indians who don't live on-reserve are generally not eligible for this tax exemption, unless they are purchasing goods and services on-reserve or are employed on-reserve.
- The *Indian Act* tax exemption applies to: federal and provincial taxes on property and income situated on-reserve, as well as federal and provincial sales taxes for goods/services purchased on a reserve.
- This exemption does not apply to provincial sales taxes on goods/services off-reserve. Unless there is an agreement with the province separate from the *Indian Act*, status Indians must pay provincial sales taxes even on goods being transported to the reserve.
- This exemption extends to federal sales taxes on goods purchased off-reserve if they are delivered to the reserve by the retailer's official agent. If a status Indian wants to transport goods back to the reserve, then under the *Indian Act* they are not exempt. Taxes on meals, movie tickets, and a host of other things that couldn't conceivably be brought back to the reserve are also not tax exempt.
- Services provided on-reserve are tax exempt. Services provided off-reserve are not tax exempt unless, under Section 90 of the *Indian Act,* the services were purchased with "Indian monies." That means official band monies used for things like off-reserve lawyer fees, accountant fees, and so on. Average band members aren't accessing those funds, so the services they purchase aren't tax exempt.
- Income is considered personal property if it's earned on-reserve. Once you work off-reserve, that exemption does not apply and you're paying income taxes even if your employer is situated on the reserve. If your duties are off-reserve in nature, it's off-reserve income and taxable. Are there some nitpicky exceptions? With taxation there always are, but this is the general rule.
- First Nations corporations and trusts don't qualify for the Section 87 tax exemption. Indigenous and Northern Affairs Canada (INAC) explains this

pretty well, pointing out that a corporation is a separate "legal person" and is not therefore an "Indian" legally.[12]

Hold on, I know for a fact that some people using their status cards for point-of-sale exemptions aren't living on-reserve or having goods delivered there. What gives?

There are a variety of provincial policies that attempt to make point-of-sales exemptions less painful for all involved. Some of these policies were created to deal with confusion surrounding the implementation of the Harmonized Sales Tax (HST), which blends provincial and federal sales taxes. These policies respect the specific exemption we've been discussing here, but may provide more relaxed enforcement policies for the provincial portion.[13]

For example, some provinces waive the enforcement of the delivery rule on the provincial portion of the sales tax, allowing a First Nations person to transport goods to the reserve himself or herself. Part of the reasoning here is that requiring delivery to be made by an agent of the vendor has the potential to negate the exemption, as any savings gained are eaten up by delivery fees. Other provinces have harmonized their provincial policies with federal policies.

To highlight just how confusing it can get, consider the situation in Quebec. Only the Mohawk Kahnawake have signed an agreement with the provincial government that includes a waiver of provincial sales tax. This is not an *Indian Act* exemption; it is a contract between the Mohawk Council of Kahnawake and the government of Quebec. Further, the contract only applies to retailers within a certain distance of Kahnawake, and does not apply to all off-reserve retailers in Quebec. To top this off, many retailers within the area to which this contract applies simply do not understand the exemption, or they refuse to honour it.[14]

I mention this because the issue is complex and poorly understood – like most anything related to taxes. Many salespeople do not really understand the exemption and the limitations on it, and some First Nations people aren't totally clear on it either. The implementation of this tax exemption can then run into practical problems when people either intentionally or unintentionally mess up how the exemption is applied.

However, the issue is: what the legal exemption actually *is* versus what many believe it to be. It is important to understand the actual legal exemption rather than characterize the issue by the instances of cheating.

Even if every single status Indian in this country (including infants at the breast) were to abuse point-of-sale rebates, we'd be talking about 600 000 people "cheating the system." How many non-Aboriginal people cheat the system beyond that – claiming fake work expenses, not declaring tips, not declaring other income, and so on?

Tax evasion is not unique to any group of people; it is a wider reality.

That still means a bunch of them aren't paying income taxes, which is big-time revenue!

I recognize personal income-tax revenue accounts for 48 percent of total revenue federally[15] and 15 percent on average provincially (with a range from 2.3 percent to 26.6 percent depending on the province or territory).

Sales taxes account for 11 percent of total revenue federally, and 8.4 percent on average provincially (with a range from zero percent to 16.2 percent depending on the province or territory).

This is what a lot of people think about: money that isn't there because of the tax exemption – potentially a lot of money not going into public coffers to help pay for social programs.

This argument dismisses the very small numbers of First Nations people who are eligible for a tax exemption. It also ignores other segments of the Canadian population that do not pay income taxes, either. I am not going to look up raw numbers on this because I think it is beside the point.

No way, sister! It *is* the point!

Here is why I disagree.

I think there are two possible arguments you are making here:

1. You think only people who do pay income taxes or sales taxes should be eligible for programs paid for from those tax revenues.
2. You want to have a say in where your tax dollars go.

If you are arguing point 1, then you aren't just talking about First Nations peoples – not if you want to approach the issue honestly. If you believe that only people contributing to these particular tax revenues should receive social programming, then you and I disagree on a fundamental philosophical level that is beyond the scope of First Nations taxation. I'd even suggest you disagree with a general Canadian belief that does not link individual taxation amounts to eligibility for social programming. That generalized discussion should be engaged in elsewhere, not merely trained on First Nations peoples.

If you are arguing point 2, then, again, you are engaging in a topic that is far beyond the scope of merely First Nations taxation. There are any number of arguments you could make about how you, the individual taxpayer, should be able to direct the spending of your tax dollars. "Why should I pay for programs I will never access?" is a common complaint. However, the fact is the Canadian government has set up a particular tax-spending regime you have minimal individual control over. Once more, this issue should not be narrowed to apply only to First Nations.

Okay, fine, even if I accept that, why do status Indians living on-reserve get this tax exemption in the first place?

Allow me to once again quote Indian Affairs on that:

- A tax exemption for Indian property situated on reserves has existed since before Confederation.
- The Supreme Court of Canada has stated this exemption is linked to the protection of reserve land and property.
- The Court has concluded the purpose of the exemption is to make sure tax does not erode the use of Indian property on reserves.
- The Court has indicated this tax exemption is not intended to remedy the economically disadvantaged position of Aboriginal peoples in Canada or bring economic benefits to them.[16]

This may not satisfy you. If that is the case, then you are going to have to delve deeper into the history of this country to understand why this tax exemption was set up.

What I have just said might also not satisfy you. Perhaps you came here figuring I would answer all your questions. So, can I ask you a question?

Why are churches tax exempt? Why are nonprofit corporations tax exempt? Can you provide me with a quick and satisfying answer *without* a historical and sociological explanation?

Fine, but I'm still not happy about this!

My main purpose here was to address the claim that "Indigenous peoples don't pay taxes." It isn't an accurate statement at all, and I hope you understand this better now. The various justifications for the narrow tax exemption that does exist are more of a historical and philosophical discussion that can be had elsewhere or at another time.

If you had anywhere near the amount of coffee I've ingested while writing this, you'll probably appreciate this being wrapped up now! May I suggest a break before the next chapter?

NOTES

1. Statistics Canada, "Aboriginal Peoples in Canada: First Nations, Métis and Inuit," last modified April 4, 2015, http://www12.statcan.gc.ca/nhs-enm/2011/as-sa/99-011-x/99-011-x2011001-eng.cfm. Keep in mind census numbers are not exact; incomplete enumeration of Aboriginal communities has always been a problem.

2. If you aren't sure how that is possible, it is explained in chapter 4.

3. See note 1.

4. You must filter area of residence to include only "on-reserve" populations to check these numbers.

5. Statistics Canada, "Aboriginal Peoples in Canada: First Nations, Métis and Inuit," last modified April 4, 2015, http://www12.statcan.gc.ca/nhs-enm/2011/as-sa/99-011-x/2011001/tbl/tbl04-eng.cfm.

6. First Nations (and Inuit) have the shortest life spans of any populations in Canada.

7. First Nations Tax Commission, "First Nations With Property Tax Jurisdiction," *fntc.ca,* last accessed November 1, 2015, http://fntc.ca/property-tax-fns/.

8. Indigenous and Northern Affairs Canada (INAC), "Fact-Sheet Taxation by Aboriginal Governments," last modified March 31, 2014, http://www.aadnc-aandc.gc.ca/eng/1100100016434/1100100016435.

9. Council of Yukon First Nations, "Agreements," *cyfn.ca,* last accessed November 1, 2015, http://cyfn.ca/agreements/.

10. *Indian Act,* RSC 1985, c I-5, s 87.

11. INAC, "Frequently Asked Questions About Aboriginal Peoples," last modified March 31, 2014, http://www.aadnc-aandc.gc.ca/eng/1100100013800/1100100013801.

12. Canada Revenue Agency, "Information for Indians," *cra-arc.gc.ca,* last modified January 30, 2015, http://www.cra-arc.gc.ca/brgnls/stts-eng.html#heading3.

13. Ontario Ministry of Finance, "Ontario First Nations Point-of-Sale Exemptions," *fin.gov.on.ca,* last modified October 2010, http://www.fin.gov.on.ca/en/guides/hst/80.html. This example illustrates the way Ontario deals with First Nations point-of-sale exemptions.

14. Christopher Curtis, "Mohawks Are Getting Tired of Explaining to Cashiers Why They Don't Have to Pay QST," *Montreal Gazette,* last modified September 11, 2015, http://montrealgazette.com/news/mohawks-are-getting-tired-of-explaining-to-cashiers-why-they-dont-have-to-pay-qst.

15. Department of Finance, "Annual Financial Report of the Government of Canada Fiscal Year, 2013–2014," *fin.gc.ca,* last modified October 6, 2015, http://www.fin.gc.ca/afr-rfa/2014/report-rapport-eng.asp.

16. See note 12.

16

The Myth of Free Housing

Another one of the most prevalent and enduring myths out there is that Indigenous peoples receive free housing. Many Canadians hold on to some very strong preconceived notions about Indigenous housing, all of which can be explored in some detail. However, for the purpose of this chapter, I'm going to focus specifically on the "free housing" aspect of the myth. This chapter then will not discuss housing *conditions* on-reserve; I'll save that topic for later.

So, I heard Natives get houses for free. How is that fair?

I know you want me to deal with the "how is that fair part" first, but really, I've got to remind you of some numbers before we can get there.

As of the 2011 census, there were 1 400 685 Aboriginal peoples in Canada. They included:[1]

- 59 445 Inuit
- 451 795 Métis
- 851 560 First Nations (637 600 status and 213 900 non-status)

Now, I'm hoping even the most rabid believer in the Free Housing for Natives Myth does not actually claim nearly a million and a half people are eligible for government-provided/paid-for housing. This myth really involves status Indians and on-reserve housing, though this distinction is not always clear when it's brought up.

Inuit and Métis do not have reserves and, as of 2011, 50 percent of status Indians were living off-reserve. We're talking 314 370 people actually living on-reserve.

Yeah, but that's still more than a quarter of a million people getting free houses when I have to work my ass off and –

Whoa, Nelly. Hold on! I was trying to tackle a gross generalization that gets thrown out there a lot, and clarify that being Indigenous does not mean "thanks for the free house!"

Yeah, but you think it should mean that, don't you?!

Okay, imaginary person, you seriously have to tone down the hostility (and I need to stop reading *Globe and Mail* comment sections before writing).

I think it's useful to acknowledge there are indeed different understandings of whether Indigenous housing is a right.

If you take a strictly legal, positivist approach, which assumes the only valid perspective is the one affirmed by current Canadian law, then that's fine. But I want you to recognize this is what you are doing, and legal positivism does not lead to objective truth outside of "this is what the law says right now."

I bring this up because part of learning about issues like housing, or education, or treaties, or what have you, is understanding Indigenous peoples do not necessarily agree with the Canadian state about how things were, are, or should be. This does not make us wrong, and it does not make the Canadian state right. I am not going to argue one way or the other in this chapter, because it would get very long. I am just going to summarize the positions.

Housing as an Aboriginal or treaty right

The Royal Commission on Aboriginal Peoples addressed the different perspectives on housing as a right in its final report:

> In a submission to the Standing Committee on Aboriginal Affairs in 1992, the Assembly of First Nations (AFN) asserted that "housing is a federal responsibility which flows from the special relationship with the federal Crown created by section 91(24) of the British North America Act of 1867 and treaty agreements themselves."
>
> The Federation of Saskatchewan Indian Nations stated that "[S]helter in the form of housing, renovations, and related infrastructure is a treaty right, and forms part of the federal trust and fiduciary responsibility. [This position derives] from the special Indian-Crown relationship dating back to the Royal Proclamation of 1763, enhanced by section 91(24) of the Constitution Act, 1867 and sections 25 and 35 of the Constitution Act, 1982."[2]

What "housing as an Aboriginal or Treaty right" means to different Indigenous peoples and organizations varies greatly. To some it means 100 percent paid-for, provided-at-no-cost funding. For others, it means guaranteed subsidies to help with construction and operation costs, with bands collecting rent or offering rent-to-own regimes as they wish.

Housing as social policy

The Royal Commission also states (italics mine):

> To date, the federal government has not recognized a universal entitlement to government-financed housing as either a treaty right or an Aboriginal right. *It has taken the position that assistance for housing is provided as a matter of social policy,* and its Aboriginal housing policy has been based on this premise. *Thus, assistance has been based on "need."*[3]

The Canadian government, then, argues that providing housing assistance to those in need (Indigenous or not) is a social policy objective for all Canadians. This is the current official approach to Indigenous housing in Canada.

Can you please get to the free housing issue now?

Yes, and thank you for being patient.

Contrary to popular belief, no one is handing out free houses on-reserve. When you hear about someone being on a housing list on the rez, you're not listening to people tell you they are waiting until someone hands them the keys to a brand-new home they now own, debt free.

There are two main categories of housing on-reserve:

1. market-based housing
2. nonprofit social housing

Market-based housing on-reserve

Market-based housing refers to households paying the full cost associated with purchasing or renting their housing. This is not free housing.

As of 2006, home-ownership rates on-reserve were at 31 percent, compared to 69 percent among off-reserve Canadians.[4] While the overall home-ownership rate is significantly lower on-reserve than off, many Canadians are not aware there is any home ownership on-reserve at all.

There are barriers to market-based housing on-reserve that you should understand. Land on-reserve is held in common; it is not split into individual properties owned by individual people. You can be given permission to possess a piece of land and use it, but this does not mean you own it.[5]

Most people require some sort of loan to purchase a home, and to secure that financing they must have collateral (something that can be seized and sold off in order to pay your debt). There are severe *Indian Act* limitations to seizing property on-reserve, making it extremely difficult to secure financing for anything, whether you intend to buy or build a house, start a business, do renovations, or what have you.[6] To be extremely clear, this is not an endorsement of attempts to unilaterally impose private-property regimes on reserve; I'm just explaining things.[7]

There are various programs in place, with new ones being developed on a community-by-community basis to address the issue of financing. Indian Affairs administers Ministerial Loan Guarantees, which are the most common and provide security for lenders.[8] However, the First Nation is ultimately on the hook if there is a default, and not all communities can cover that cost, so these loan guarantees are not always available.

In 2008, with great fanfare, the Harper government announced a program that was supposed to build 25 000 new homes on reserves across Canada by 2018. This First Nations Market Housing Fund had only managed to help build 99 houses by May of 2015.[9]

The First Nations Market Housing Fund:

> …will establish a Credit Enhancement Facility. This will help individuals on-reserve and on settlement lands where appropriate, to obtain loans, where their First Nation meets certain criteria, such as a demonstrated ability to manage their finances, loans and housing.[10]

The Fund adds another layer of protection to lenders compared to what is available through Ministerial Loan Guarantees. If the individual borrower defaults, then the band is on the hook with the Ministerial Loan Guarantees. If the band does not have the capital to guarantee the loan that way, it simply won't be issued. With the First Nations Market Housing Fund, if the band defaults, there is a 10 percent backstop that can come out of the fund, making it slightly more likely a lender will allow individual band members to borrow. However, the band has to be approved first, and as you can see from above, they have to be in good financial standing, which is not so easy when you are administering poverty.

In addition, there was a one-time only grant of $300 million into the fund in 2008, and administrative costs alone are $3.6 million a year, with $5.4 million being spent in 2014 alone on "capacity development."[11] Many people have pointed out that this is an inefficient and expensive way to encourage market housing on-reserve. Nonetheless, there are nearly 60 First Nations participating in the fund as of 2015, with many more in negotiations to join.[12]

So far, no one approach has been successful enough to work in every situation and home ownership on-reserve varies from "a lot" to "almost none" depending on the community.

Income is another obvious barrier to accessing market-based housing on-reserve, whether we're discussing building a new home, purchasing an existing home, or renting a home owned by the band. This brings us to the second category.

Nonprofit social housing

The Canadian Mortgage and Housing Agency (CMHC) delivers housing programs and services across the country, to all people living in Canada, under the National Housing Act.[13] It states:

> The purpose of this Act, in relation to financing for housing, is to promote housing affordability and choice, to facilitate access to, and competition and efficiency in the provision of, housing finance, to protect the availability of adequate funding for housing at low cost, and generally to contribute to the well-being of the housing sector in the national economy.[14]

Section 95 of this Act deals with social housing, and programs under this section include subsidies for nonprofit rental housing on-reserve (and elsewhere throughout Canada).[15] If I haven't pounded in this fact enough, let me do it once more: this is not a program only First Nations peoples benefit from. There are tens of thousands of Canadians living in co-op housing built with the help of subsidies under section 95.

The Co-Operative Housing Federation of Canada deals with social housing off-reserve, but these FAQ answers apply on-reserve, as well:

> The members do not own equity in their housing. If they move, their home is returned to the co-op [the band], to be offered to another individual or family who needs an affordable home.
>
> Some co-op households pay a reduced monthly rent (housing charge) geared to their income. Government funds cover the difference between this payment and the co-op's full charge. Other households pay the full monthly charge based on cost.
>
> Because co-ops charge their members only enough to cover costs, repairs, and reserves, they can offer housing that is much more affordable than average private sector rental costs.[16]

Nonprofit social housing is often called Band Housing on-reserve, and 57 percent of on-reserve people lived in these units as of 2006.[17]

Indian Affairs (alone or via the CMHC) does not cover the full cost of housing.[18] In addition to government funding, First Nations and their residents are expected to secure funding from other sources for their housing needs, including shelter charges and private-sector loans.

All people in Canada who are eligible for social assistance can be issued shelter allowances. This is meant to help low-income individuals meet their shelter expenses (rent, utilities), and amounts are based on provincial tables. Since 1996, shelter allowances for First Nations people living on-reserve tended to be calculated using provincial-rate tables, but, in 2010, there was a review of the shelter-allowance policy that exposed some problems.[19] Essentially, the issues identified were inconsistent application, lack of clarity, inadequate funding, and so on. So, in 2012, Indian Affairs issued a National Social Programs Manual that combined five social programs into one document and more clearly outlined eligibility requirements and rates available.[20]

All this really means is that for people living off-reserve, there are provincial-policy manuals explaining the labyrinthian process of getting a shelter allowance; for people living on-reserve, there is a federal-policy manual, which is equally as complicated. The reason for this division harks back to Constitutional division of powers wherein social programming like this is generally a provincial/territorial concern, but becomes a federal concern when it involves "Indians and lands reserved for Indians."

Before you go thinking everything is rosy, in 2012, the CMHC announced it was cutting funding for section 95 housing on-reserve in Saskatchewan by 30 percent.[21] These kinds of cuts have a huge impact on how many units can be built in First Nations communities, and greatly exacerbate the already unbelievably long waiting lists to access social housing on-reserve.

But I thought...

You thought wrong. While on-reserve home ownership lags behind off-reserve ownership, it does exist despite the considerable obstacles involved in securing financing. Band housing is built with the help of government subsidies available for similar projects all over Canada, and where low-income First Nations individuals need help to pay their rent in these social housing units, Indian Affairs provides social assistance similar to that available to all other Canadians.

We can and should delve into housing quality and conditions on- and off-reserve and understand the factors involved in overcrowding and inadequate shelter. But to have that discussion, I first needed us to get past the myth of free housing.

If you want to continue to call what I've described "free housing," then you need to recognize this situation is not unique to First Nations. If the only complaints on section 95 housing and/or shelter allowances you have are aimed at First Nations, then those arguments are inherently racist.

However, I think the real issue is that most people honestly don't understand housing on-reserve, and because the issue is complicated, people rely on word of mouth. I'm hopful this chapter helps clear up some of the confusion.

NOTES

1. Statistics Canada, "Table 3: Distribution of First Nations People, First Nations People With and Without Registered Indian Status, and First Nations People With Registered Indian Status Living On or Off Reserve, Canada, Provinces and Territories, 2011," last modified November 4, 2015, http://www12.statcan.gc.ca/nhs-enm/2011/as-sa/99-011-x/2011001/tbl/tbl03-eng.cfm.

2. Indian and Northern Affairs Canada, "Volume 3, Gathering Strength, Chapter 4- Housing," last modified February 8, 2006, http://www.collectionscanada.gc.ca/webarchives/20071211053819/http://www.ainc-inac.gc.ca/ch/rcap/sg/si37_e.html#2.2%20A%20Right%20to%20Housing.

3. Ibid. (my emphasis).

4. Canadian Mortgage and Housing Corporation, "Preconditions Leading to Market Housing on Reserve," last accessed November 2, 2015, https://www03.cmhc-schl.gc.ca/catalog/productDetail.cfm?cat=150&itm=18&lang=en&fr=1344275780406.

5. *Indian Act*, RSC, 1985, c I-5, s 20(1). "No Indian is lawfully in possession of land in a reserve unless, with the approval of the Minister, possession of the land has been allotted to him by the council of the band." The rest of s. 20 explains how one can acquire a Certificate of Occupation. None of this is the same as fee-simple land ownership. Fee-simple land ownership is the most common form of land ownership in common-law countries like Canada, and with fee simple you can rent your land, sell it, or pass it on to your heirs.

6. Ibid., s 89.

7. Thomas Flanagan, *First Nations: Second Thoughts* (Montreal: McGill-Queen's Press, 2008). This is one such regime promoted by former Kamloops Chief, Clarence T. (Manny) Jules, and then made into a proposed First Nations Property Ownership Act, which so far has only passed through one reading in Parliament.

8. INAC, "Ministerial Loan Guarantees," last modified July 4, 2012, http://www.aadnc-aandc.gc.ca/eng/1100100010759/1100100010763.

9. Dean Beeby, "First Nations $300M Federal Housing Fund Builds Just 99 Homes," *CBC News*, May 27, 2015, http://www.cbc.ca/news/politics/first-nations-300m-federal-housing-fund-builds-just-99-homes-1.3086954.

10. First Nations Market Housing Fund, "About the Fund," last accessed Nov. 2, 2015, http://www.fnmhf.ca/english/about/index.html.

11. Here, capacity development basically meant explaining to First Nations how the fund works. See note 8.

12. First Nations Market Housing Fund, "Participating First Nations," last accessed November 2, 2015, http://www.fnmhf.ca/english/participating_fn/index.html.

13. *National Housing Act,* RSC 1985, c N-11; Government of Canada, "National Housing Act," 1985, last modified November 5, 2015, http://laws-lois.justice.gc.ca/eng/acts/N-11/index.html.

14. Ibid., section 3.

15. Canada Mortgage and Housing Corporation, "On-Reserve Non-Profit Housing Program (Section 95)," last accessed November 2, 2015, http://www.cmhc-schl.gc.ca/en/ab/onre/onre_010.cfm.

16. The Co-operative Housing Federation of Canada, "What Is a Housing Co-op?," last accessed November 2, 2015, http://www.chfcanada.coop/eng/pages2007/about_1.asp.

17. See note 4.

18. INAC, "First Nation On-Reserve Housing Program," last modified September 15, 2010, http://www.aadnc-aandc.gc.ca/eng/1100100010752/1100100010753.

19. INAC, "Evaluation of Shelter Allowance as it Relates to On-Reserve Housing," last modified August 2011, https://www.aadnc-aandc.gc.ca/eng/1343849675000/1343849974382.

20. INAC, "National Social Programs Manual" January 31, 2012, https://www.aadnc-aandc.gc.ca/DAM/DAM-INTER-HQ-HB/STAGING/texte-text/hb_sp_npm_mnp_1335464147597_eng.pdf.

21. NationTalk, "Budget Cuts to On Reserve Social Housing Program," *nationtalk.ca,* August 7, 2012, http://nationtalk.ca/story/budget-cuts-to-on-reserve-social-housing-program.

17

The Myth of the Drunken Indian

Ah, yes. It's time to finally address the foundational stereotype of the drunken Indian, hopped up on the White Man's firewater. (Actually, in Cree it's called "iskotêwâpoy," which is more like "fiery liquid.")

This particular stereotype is *extremely* prevalent, and very ugly. It mashes together many important pieces that should be unpacked and examined. Whether trotted out as invective-laden generalizations or proffered as a supposedly kinder "it's not really your fault" genetic explanation, it has created some heavy baggage for Indigenous peoples. Many Indigenous people have internalized the stereotype, believing alcoholism is something genetically impossible to avoid. On top of this, Indigenous peoples often find themselves fearing becoming the face of the stereotype, feeling that drinking in public solidifies the stereotype in ways other populations simply do not have to worry about.

The stereotype itself is not as ubiquitous or damaging as it once was, due to many studies and publicly accessible articles that debunk commonly held misconceptions. In a 2008 CBC article, Katherine Walker discussed some of the ways the stereotype has lost its potency, at least in the sense that it is no longer as easy, or legal, to act on it by denying Indigenous peoples jobs, homes, or even entrance into certain establishments. In my opinion, she refocuses the issue best here:

> I do not want to deny the very real problems with addictions among aboriginal people. Far too many communities have high rates of alcohol and drug use and heartbreakingly high rates of Fetal Alcohol Spectrum Disorder among their children.
>
> The reasons why aboriginal people have struggled with addictions, individually and collectively, have been the focus of many a report or survey through the years. The root causes are pretty well documented at this point – residential schools,

the Indian Act, child welfare issues, Indian agents, geographic isolation, racism, intergenerational trauma – the list goes on.[1]

Nonetheless, it is clear the stereotype endures and continues to be passed down as truth often enough that it would be remiss of me not to address it. It isn't hard to find examples of the myth rearing its ugly head. In 2007, a teenage employee of Tim Hortons taped a sign to a drive-through window that stated, "No Drunken Indians Allowed."[2] In 2012, a Toronto restaurant faced serious backlash for its "Dirty Drunken Half-Breed" burger.[3] In 2014, Winnipeg mayoral hopeful Gord Steeves had to face some fallout when his wife's social-media comments invoked the drunken Indian stereotype.[4] That same year it was revealed a Manitoba fishing lodge had published a guide for its clientele, advising them not to offer alcohol to Cree guides because "like all Native Americans, they have a basic intolerance for alcohol."[5] These are just some of the incidents that gained media attention over the past few years.

The stereotype of the drunken Indian often confuses the *history* of alcohol in our communities with genetic theories. Separating these issues out from one another allows us to tackle the myth more effectively. It also gives us another piece of the picture that is colonialism, because alcohol has absolutely been weaponized against Indigenous peoples in Canada, and the history of this weaponization stretches back to contact.

I want to examine the stereotype and provide some of the research mentioned in Walker's article, quoted above. Maybe you'll learn some things about the issue that you never knew. More important, I'm hoping people will be more critical-minded when this stereotype is brought up.

Belief #1: Indigenous people cannot metabolize alcohol.

A very common belief is Indigenous people "can't handle their liquor" due to the lack of a specific gene that helps humans metabolize, or break down, alcohol. The basic idea is that because most Indigenous people living in Canada and the United States did not have a habit of drinking alcohol prior to contact, there was not enough time to develop a genetic resistance to it the way Europeans and other alcohol-drinking populations had. This idea *seems* to make sense, particularly if one compares lack of resistance to alcohol with lack of resistance to European diseases – *except the two situations aren't even remotely similar.* Alcohol is neither a virus nor a bacterium, and genes aren't antibodies, so step away from the pseudoscience, please.

First of all, the presence of fermented alcohol among various First Nations and Inuit is fairly well documented.[6] Some folks will concede this but then argue distilled liquors pack a heck of a lot more punch, so the absent-gene theory is still plausible.

Well, there are genes that have an impact on how a person metabolizes alcohol. Without getting into exhausting detail, there are actually a number of genes that influence the creation of two main enzymes responsible for breaking alcohol down. Those enzymes, alcohol dehydrogenase (ADH) and aldehyde dehydrogenase (ALDH), basically help your body turn alcohol into chemicals that are no longer as damaging to your vital organs. Humans have seven different genes (and many variations within them) that are responsible for ADH production, and two genes responsible for ALDH production. *All* human beings have some genes that allow these enzymes to be produced in the body.

You metabolize alcohol more quickly, or more slowly, depending on which gene(s) you have. The genes that are considered protective tend to produce enzymes that metabolize alcohol more slowly, meaning you cannot drink as much at a time because the effects last longer. So, you don't actually want the enzymes that clear the alcohol out of your system right away, as this tends to encourage heavier drinking, which can be a factor in developing an alcohol dependency.

Some of these genes are more common to specific ethnic groups. For example, the ADH1B*2 allele (gene variant) is found with high frequency in East Asians, but in low amounts among many First Nations people *and* among Europeans. It has some of the best protective effects against developing alcoholism.[7] However, "high frequency" is no guarantee. Other populations will also have this gene, and specific East Asians may not carry it. We're talking about probabilities here, not certainties. Add to this the fact that genetic differences within specific ethnic populations (e.g., between two East Asians) can be as high as variations *between* ethnic populations (e.g., between East Asians and Europeans), and the "they just lack the gene" theory starts crumbling to itty-bitty bits.[8]

To sum up, Indigenous people *have* genes that help them metabolize alcohol, just like all human beings do. Some of these genes work better than others and can *help* protect against alcoholism, but none of these genes can *prevent* alcohol dependency. Specific ethnic groups tend to have certain genes in higher frequencies, but genetic diversity within ethnic groups is also very high, thus generalizations about alcohol dependency cannot accurately be made based on genetics.

Overall, the research shows First Nations people react to alcohol much like any other peoples. As the Wisconsin Department of Health Services puts it:

> Metabolism of alcohol among all people groups is related to prior drinking history and body weight, not race or ethnicity.

Drinking patterns and problems among American Indians are influenced by the same factors as other people groups. These factors include genetics, age, social norms and laws, social involvement, economics, mental health, emotional pain or trauma, self-esteem, and environment. Substance abuse is not caused by race.[9]

For Indigenous peoples, it is important not to internalize the idea there is a genetic predisposition to alcoholism based on an inability to metabolize alcohol as efficiently as other populations. Simply accepting this can lead to a sort of fatalism – after all, if it's in your genes, how can you fight it? For Canadians, it is important to avoid perpetuating junk science, regardless of whether the intention is malicious or benign. Why? Well, "junk science" sort of says it all, doesn't it?

Belief #2: All Natives are drunks.

The cause of death due to alcohol use is 43.7 per 100 000 among Indigenous peoples in Canada, which is twice the rate of the general population.[10] There is no doubt alcohol abuse in our communities is a huge problem. However, there is a fairly common belief that *all* Indigenous people drink.

Although getting updated statistics is difficult, the 2002–2003 and 2008–2010 First Nations Regional Longitudinal studies give us the following information:

- More First Nations adults abstain from drinking than the general population (34.3 percent versus 23 percent among non-Natives).[11]
- Most First Nations adults who do drink do so less frequently than the general population (17.8 percent using alcohol on a daily/weekly basis compared to 44 percent in the general population; males twice as likely as females to be weekly drinkers.)[12]
- The proportion of heavy drinkers in First Nations adults is higher than the general Canadian population (16 percent versus 6.2 percent).[13]

To sum this up, more Indigenous people abstain from alcohol than the general Canadian population. Some studies suggest Indigenous people are twice as likely to abstain as their non-Indigenous counterparts. Indigenous people who do drink alcohol tend to do so less frequently than their non-Indigenous counterparts, but they also tend to drink more extremely when they *are* consuming alcohol.

There are two extremes represented here that are important to understand. Many Indigenous people do not drink at all, and consider alcohol to be a very serious problem in our communities. Heavy drinking is more common among Indigenous drinkers than among non-Indigenous people, however.

As expressed in all of the studies cited in this section, Indigenous people tend to have a more negative view of the use of alcohol compared to non-Indigenous people, which is no doubt linked to the damage that alcohol abuse continues to wreak on our communities.

Belief #3: Alcohol abuse is an Indigenous cultural trait.

Most people won't say this openly anymore, but this belief has hardly gone the way of the dodo. As with any population, substance abuse is a complex issue. Some people do not want to accept those complexities, however, and wish to merely attribute it to some sort of inherent weakness on the part of a specific population. This particular belief has existed since contact, and continues to inform public opinion today.

Earlier on, I mentioned the way alcohol has been weaponized against our communities. Well, I'm not just going to keep you hanging; this is something we need to discuss. Early European colonists demonstrated excessive drinking and violence, so much so that alcohol consumption among early settlers was considered a serious problem by colonial authorities.[14] Settler voyageurs, in particular, were notorious for excessive drinking, and these men were the first to contact many Indigenous peoples. Sexual violence against Indigenous women by European colonists and soldiers, a horrifically common part of colonial expansion, was very much linked to alcohol abuse.[15] From the early days of contact, right up until the end of the 19th century, Indigenous peoples were consistently exposed to models of violence associated with binge-drinking by fur traders, soldiers, and, later on, miners.[16]

It is important to note that temporary groupings of single, settler men – unattached to the communities they are interacting with, living without families or kinship obligations – have consistently enacted violence against Indigenous peoples (particularly against Indigenous women and girls) since contact. Alcohol and, later, drugs have almost always been part of the way in which this violence is enacted and continues to be experienced. The boomtowns of the gold rush have become the man camps of oil and shale-gas extraction.[17]

Colonial authorities were not successful in restricting alcohol consumption among their colonists, traders, and soldiers.[18] Attention then became focused on controlling or banning the provision of alcohol to Indigenous peoples (a population that was much more vulnerable to colonial domination), as well as legislating the consumption of alcohol by Indigenous peoples for their "protection." In 1874, for example, legislation was passed making it an offence for an Indian to be intoxicated.

The punishment was one month in jail![19] This led to a number of outcomes, including a booming and unhealthy underground trade.

As the historian Brian Maracle writes:

> The law didn't stop or prevent Indians from drinking, but it did change the way they drank – for the worse. Since Indians were forbidden to buy liquor, they frequently resorted to drinking other far more dangerous intoxicants. More ominously, Indians also had to guzzle their beer, wine or liquor as quickly as possible to keep from being arrested.[20]

In Canada, the *Gradual Civilization Act of 1857* and the *Gradual Enfranchisement Act of 1869* (which later became consolidated into the *Indian Act*) gave the Superintendent General of Indian Affairs the power to determine who was of "good moral character," and the consumption of alcohol figured greatly into this determination.[21] This had immediate impact on Indigenous peoples, as this determination was directly linked to certain benefits. Widowed Indian women could even have their children taken away if they were found lacking "good moral character."

This is what I mean when I say that alcohol has been weaponized against Indigenous peoples. First, it was deliberately introduced into our communities in highly destructive and violent ways by settlers. After that, it was banned on the pretext that Indigenous peoples were too racially weak to have a healthy relationship with alcohol. This bloomed into a widespread belief that alcohol abuse is an inherent trait of Indigenous peoples (whether cultural or genetic, it doesn't seem to matter), despite the fact that alcohol abuse is just as (if not more) widespread in settler populations. The use of alcohol among Indigenous peoples led to children being removed from the home, rations and annuities being withheld, and even imprisonment. These kinds of consequences remained in place in *Indian Act* legislation up until the 1980s and, it can be argued, are still in play, particularly when it comes to the removal of children from the home.[22]

Some closing thoughts

The Aboriginal Healing Foundation (AHF) has an excellent publication called *Addictive Behaviours Among Aboriginal People in Canada,* which I highly recommend.[23] To get a real sense of the problem, you have to understand the history of colonization in this country. While embarking on that exploration can take years, AHF does a good job of distilling some main points, as well as explaining why that history really does matter:

No other population group in Canada's history has endured such a deliberate, comprehensive, and prolonged assault on their human rights as that of Aboriginal people. Yet, despite growing recognition of past wrongs, many Canadians remain unaware of the full scope of these injustices or their impacts.

To understand how Indigenous cultures that had flourished for thousands of years began breaking down, giving rise to epidemic levels of addictive behaviours, it helps to look back at history through an Aboriginal lens.[24]

There is nothing inherent in our cultures (or our genes) that makes us more likely to become alcoholics than non-Indigenous people. In fact, the most successful substance abuse prevention and treatment strategies have been those that integrate Indigenous traditions, rather than external programs that pay no mind to our cultural context.

Alcohol abuse among Indigenous peoples is not a myth. But, there are some pernicious stereotypes out there that have a very real impact on the way people regard alcohol use by Indigenous peoples, and also on the way we ourselves view our relationship with alcohol. Obviously, these views need to be dealt with and examined, particularly among those who work with Indigenous populations.

It is not helpful to claim we are genetically weak and unable to avoid becoming dependent on alcohol. Nor is it helpful to imagine all of us have an alcohol problem, or will eventually develop one. More important, it is unhelpful to ignore our cultural and historical context in the belief this context is unrelated.

I grew up believing many of these myths, and it's taken many years to see alcoholism is not a foregone conclusion among our people. We can take steps to prevent it and treat it. I'm hopeful that dispelling some of these stereotypes will help to keep the focus on what we can do, rather than on what is supposedly out of our hands completely.

NOTES

1. Katherine Walker, "The Drunken Indian Stereotype and Social Healing," *CBC News,* last modified October 22, 2008, http://www.cbc.ca/news/canada/the-drunken-indian-stereotype-and-social-healing-1.729514.

2. Dawn Walton, "Tim Hortons Serves Up Some Controversy," *The Globe and Mail,* last modified March 13, 2009, http://www.theglobeandmail.com/news/national/tim-hortons-serves-up-some-controversy/article17996444/.

3. Jayme Poisson, "'Half-Breed' and 'Dirty Drunken Half-Breed' Chucked from Burger Menu," *The Star,* last modified August 29, 2012, http://www.thestar.com/news/gta/2012/08/29/halfbreed_and_dirty_drunken_halfbreed_chucked_from_burger_menu.html.

4. "Political Expert Says It's Too Soon To Know Impact of 'Drunken Natives' Comments," *Global News,* last modified August 9, 2014, http://globalnews.ca/news/1500278/wife-of-mayoral-candidate-under-fire-for-drunken-natives-comments/.

5. Mary Agnes Welch, "Drunk Indian Myth Surfaces," *Winnipeg Free Press,* last modified May 29, 2014, http://www.winnipegfreepress.com/local/drunk-indian-myth-surfaces-261044871.html.

6. Patrick J. Abbott, "American Indian and Alaska Native Aboriginal Use of Alcohol in the United States," *American Indian and Alaska Native Mental Health Research* 7, no. 2 (1996): 1–13, http://www.ucdenver.edu/academics/colleges/PublicHealth/research/centers/CAIANH/journal/Documents/Volume%207/7%282%29_Abbott_Use_of_Alcohol_1-13.pdf.

7. Howard J. Edenberg, "The Genetics of Alcohol Metabolism: Role of Alcohol Dehydrogenase and Aldehyde Dehydrogenase Variants," *Alcohol Research & Health* 30, no. 1 (2007): 5–13, http://pubs.niaaa.nih.gov/publications/arh301/5-13.pdf.

8. Ian R. Gizer, Howard J. Edenberg, David A. Gilder, Kirk C. Wilhelmsen, and Cindy L. Ehlers, "Association of Alcohol Dehydrogenase Genes with Alcohol-Related Phenotypes in a Native American Community Sample," *Alcoholism, Clinical and Experimental Research* 35, no. 11 (2011), http://www.ncbi.nlm.nih.gov/pmc/articles/PMC3197765/; Tamara L. Wall, Lucinda G. Carr, and Cindy L. Ehlers, "Protective Association of Genetic Variation in Alcohol Dehydrogenase With Alcohol Dependence in Native American Mission Indians," *American Journal of Psychiatry* 160, no. 1 (2003): 41–46, http://ajp.psychiatryonline.org/doi/full/10.1176/appi.ajp.160.1.41. If you are interested in these gene variations and their prevalence in Native Americans, check out these sources.

9. Rosalie A. Torres Stone, Les B. Whitbeck, Xiaojin Chen, Kurt Johnson, and Debbie M. Olson, "Traditional Practices, Traditional Spirituality, and Alcohol Cessation Among American Indians," *Journal of Studies on Alcohol* 67, no. 2 (2006): 236–244, https://www.dhs.wisconsin.gov/publications/p0/p00806.pdf.

10. Deborah Chansonneuve, "Addictive Behaviours Among Aboriginal People in Canada" (Aboriginal Healing Foundation, 2007), 25, http://www.ahf.ca/downloads/addictive-behaviours.pdf.

11. First Nations Information Governance Centre (FNIGC), "National Report on Adults, Youth and Children Living in First Nations Communities," *First Nations Regional Health Survey (RHS) 2008/10* (Ottawa: FNIGC, 2012), 97, http://fnigc.ca/sites/default/files/docs/first_nations_regional_health_survey_rhs_2008-10_-_national_report.pdf.

12. First Nations Regional Longitudinal Health Survey (RHS) 2002/03, "Results for Adults, Youth and Children Living in First Nations Communities," (First Nations Centre, 2005), 115, http://fnigc.ca/sites/default/files/ENpdf/RHS_2002/rhs2002-03-technical_report.pdf.

13. Ibid., 116. Heavy drinking is defined as binge drinking (five or more drinks per sitting) at least once a month for the last year.

14. Paul Aaron, and David Musto, "Temperance and Prohibition in America: A Historical Overview," in *Alcohol and Public Policy: Beyond the Shadow of Prohibition,* eds. M. H. Moore and D. R. Gerstein (Washington, DC: National Academy Press; 1981), 127–181.

15. Andrea Smith, *Conquest: Sexual Violence and American Indian Genocide* (South End Press, 2005). This offers a more thorough account of how colonialism has relied on sexual violence against Indigenous women.

16. A. M. Winkler. "Drinking on the American Frontier," *Quarterly Journal of Studies on Alcohol* 29, no. 2 (1968): 413–445.

17. A. C. Shilton, "The Human Cost of Keystone XL," *psmag.com*, last modified May 14, 2015, http://www.psmag.com/nature-and-technology/the-human-cost-of-keystone-xl.

18. W. E. Unrau, *White Man's Wicked Water: The Alcohol Trade and Prohibition in Indian Country, 1802–1892* (Lawrence: University Press of Kansas, 1996).

19. Royal Commission on Aboriginal Peoples, "Volume 1: Looking Forward, Looking Back," *Report of the Royal Commission on Aboriginal Peoples* (Ottawa: Queen's Printer, 1997), 293–294.

20. Brian Maracle, *Crazy Water: Native Voices on Addiction and Recovery* (Toronto: Viking, 1993), 44–45.

21. *An Act to Encourage the Gradual Civilization of Indian Tribes in this Province, and to Amend the Laws Relating to Indians*, 3rd Session, 5th Parliament, 1857; *An Act for the gradual enfranchisement of Indians, the better management of Indian affairs, and to extend the provisions of the Act 31st Victoria*, chapter 42.

22. This is discussed in further detail in chapter 21.

23. Deborah Chansonneuve, *Addictive Behaviours Among Aboriginal People in Canada* (Aboriginal Healing Foundation, 2007), http://www.ahf.ca/downloads/addictive-behaviours.pdf.

24. Ibid., 5–6.

18

The Myth of the Wandering Nomad

I've read pretty much every book written by Robert J. Sawyer over the past few years, because, as pointed out in an editorial by Adam Shaftoe and Matt Moore in the fall 2011 edition of *On Spec,* he's a Canadian sci-fi author who is surprisingly optimistic in his writing, in an age where so much science fiction is dystopian and disaster-themed.[1] Also, I really get a kick out of his Canadian references, despite the fact that they are mostly related to Ontario.[2] I'd love some more Prairie references, but you've got to write what you know, n'est ce pas? Sawyer lives in Mississauga, after all.

As a related aside, my husband was reading the final book in the Sawyer trilogy I'm about to discuss, at the same time as he was reading the final instalment of the *Hyperion Cantos* by United States sci-fi author Dan Simmons.[3] He noted that within the first few chapters of the Simmons book, there had already been a number of fights and all sorts of adrenaline-pumping action, while he was nearly through the Sawyer book and the most shocking thing that had happened so far were some really great intellectual conversations about the nature of what it means to be human. I want to stress that this does not make Sawyer's book any less interesting, but it is certainly more *Canadian* somehow.

My ears always perk up (figuratively, obviously, since I'm reading, not listening) when Sawyer mentions "Native Canadians." It's a term I think he chose over First Nations because it would be more familiar to readers in the United States, which is, let's be honest, a *way* bigger market than Canada. I'm interested in how writers portray Indigenous peoples, and what attitudes are expressed in these portrayals – something you've already seen me deal with in chapter 8. Sawyer introduces Indigenous characters fairly often, but never in stereotypically negative ways – nor, to his credit, in stereotypically positive, "noble savage" ways. Since he's writing sci-fi, many of the Indigenous characters end up being scientists, or other professionals interacting with the scientist protagonists.

The trilogy in question is The Neanderthal Parallax, where contact is made with an alternate earth in which Homo sapiens did not become the dominant humans, but rather Neanderthals did.[4] Sawyer explores all sorts of interesting cultural dissimilarities, related to differences in physiology, historical development, and even the ability to believe in a God. It's a good read; I recommend it.

Two passages in this trilogy really caught my eye, and I wanted to share them with you.

In the second book, *Humans*, on page 35, one of the protagonists (geneticist Mary Vaughan) is being asked to develop some sort of test to determine who is Neanderthal and who is Homo sapiens (you know, for possible immigration purposes). She has her reservations, but Sawyer has her thinking this:

> Mary nodded slowly. It did, sort of, make sense. And, after all, there was a benign precedent: the Canadian government already put a lot of work into defining who is and who isn't a Status Indian, so that social programs and entitlements could properly be administered.[5]

I'll admit I bristled at the characterization of this being benign. Nor, upon further reflection, has my reaction changed. To me, benign is something that is both well-meaning and does not cause harm. I don't think either of these criterion is met by the current government policies that define who is, and who is not, a status Indian – unless he meant benign like a tumour.

This struck me as one instance where Sawyer is perhaps too optimistic and forgiving, but it's also entirely possible he had Mary Vaughan thinking this to highlight her naïvety. I think this would require a wide understanding among his readership since the example given is not actually all that benign, but I doubt most Canadians (or United States citizens) give it any thought at all. Anyway, I don't want to get into that trap of double or triple guessing what the author was trying to convey with what was a very small bit of Canadian context.

I do want to point out the fact that being mentioned at all in a mainstream work of fiction is rare enough, and here I am, talking about it like it's a big deal!

That wasn't actually the passage that got most of my attention, though. Later on in the book, there is a conversation about a statement made that agriculture is a prerequisite to civilization. You see, the Neanderthals in this trilogy do not practise agriculture, yet had clearly developed a civilization including the development of technologies that impressed their Homo sapiens counterparts. (Failure to develop impressive technologies may cause people to dismiss you as primitive, even if you have civilization, so be warned!)

In this conversation, the Neanderthal protagonist, Ponter Boddit, notes hunting and gathering requires only about 9 percent of one's time (15–20 hours a week), a claim that astonishes the assorted professionals present.[6]

At this point, a Native American named Henry Running Deer (apparently a professor at the University of Chicago) confirms this and goes on to say some interesting things I want to share. This might be a longish quote, but it bears reading:

> "But how do you get permanent settlement without agriculture?" asked Angela.
>
> Henry frowned. "You've got it wrong. It's not agriculture that gives rise to permanent habitation. It's hunting and gathering."
>
> "But – no, no. I remember from school–"
>
> "And how many Native Americans taught at your school?" asked Henry Running Deer in an icy tone.
>
> "None, but –"
>
> Henry looked at Ponter, then back at Mary. "Whites rarely understand this point, but it's absolutely true. Hunter gatherers stay put. To live off the land requires knowing it intimately: which plants grow where, where the big animals come to drink, where the birds lay their eggs. It takes a lifetime to really know a territory. To move somewhere else is to throw out all that hard-won knowledge."
>
> Mary lifted her eyebrows. "But farmers need to put down roots – umm, so to speak."
>
> Henry didn't acknowledge the pun. "Actually, farmers are itinerant over a period of generations. Hunter-gatherers keep their family sizes small; after all, extra mouths to feed increase the work that an adult has to do. But farmers want big families: each child is another laborer to send out into the fields, and the more kids you have, the less work you have to do yourself… But as the farmers' offspring grow up, they have to move on and start their own farms. Ask a farmer where his great-great-grandfather lived and he'll name some place far away; ask a hunter-gatherer, and he'll say, 'right here.'"[7]

How many of you were taught that all Indigenous peoples were nomadic – of no fixed address? Perhaps you may have learned that some, like the Haudenosaunee, farmed and stayed put, but, in general, the perception is that we all just roamed the lands aimlessly, never really settling down permanently.

You've probably heard of our territories, which, perhaps in your mind, mark some sort of hazy boundary within which we did all this roaming. You've no doubt also heard about our ties to the land, blah, blah, blah, but perhaps you never really considered what that actually means, and what knowledge (and stability) it requires us to have.

As the fictional Henry Running Deer points out, being a successful hunter-gatherer requires an intimate knowledge of a specific territory, a knowledge that does not come quickly and is very vulnerable to relocation. When hunters from the United States come up to Canada, what do they do? They hire someone who knows the land. If they don't, they don't get their precious trophies. (Down with trophy hunting, arrrrrgh!)

Now, nothing Sawyer's character said came as a surprise to me, except for the fact that he had a character discuss this at all. To me, and probably most Indigenous people, this is common-sense knowledge. Yet, it means Sawyer has pondered this issue in a way few Canadians ever do, because this approach flies directly in the face of what the Canadian system of education has taught students since that system was created. Sawyer suggests being nomadic doesn't mean what you probably think it means; in fact, he goes on to propose permanent settlement might not mean what you think it means, either.

If permanent settlement is building-specific, then simply constructing a structure that will last a decade or longer may fulfill the criterion, but this is a fairly feeble definition. If, instead, it refers to successive generations inhabiting the same area over a significant period of time (like thousands of years), then folks, few people do permanent settlement like Indigenous peoples!

Basically, Sawyer is challenging the ladder theory, or unilineal theory, of civilization and development.[8] I'm talking about the Sid Meiers' *Civilization* game-type theory that has all people progressing through certain stages until they basically become like Europeans.[9] It goes something like this: first, you're an animist, then you're into polytheism, then you get with the program and believe in only one god. All the while, you're developing agriculture, metallurgy, building cities – becoming civilized! (It's okay if you like the *Civilization* computer games; I do, too! I even bought the expansion pack so I could play various Indigenous peoples – even though my game play relies heavily on armed expansion and colonization – to the dismay of all my ancestors, no doubt.)

Sawyer questions what most of us were taught in school (something we should all do more of). The ladder, or unilineal, theory has been pretty soundly discredited, but like so many things we were taught (but never confirmed were actually true),[10] it's had immense staying power in the minds of most Canadians, and it has certainly continued to influence opinions and policy.

Sawyer's characters are surprised by this different way of looking at the issue, and I imagine many people who have read this book were surprised, as well. That surprise comes from the fact that we have all been so "well educated" on the matter, we don't tend to question these outmoded assumptions. I'm grateful Sawyer did. I find it slightly ironic that more people are likely to have these beliefs questioned in the context of science fiction than in so-called real life, but then again, sci-fi is great for that sort of thing.

Now, if I could chat with him on the pesky matter of what constitutes benign in the context of the *Indian Act*....

NOTES

1. Brent, "2015 Alberta Book Awards," *On Spec* (blog), September 11, 2015, https://onspecmag. wordpress.com/.

2. As a geeky aside, in 2015, I had the opportunity to attend ceremony in Serpent River First Nation, and we drove by Sudbury, which is close to the neutrino observatory that was housed in INCO's Creighton Mine (in operation between 1999–2006). This is the crucible of Sawyer's Neanderthal Parallax, and well... It was really cool. Hush.

3. Dan Simmons, *The Rise of Endymion* (New York: Bantam Books, 1998).

4. Robert J. Sawyer, *Hominids* (New York: Tor, 2002); Robert J. Sawyer, *Humans* (New York: Tor, 2003); Robert J. Sawyer, *Hybrids* (New York: Tor, 2003).

5. Sawyer, *Humans*, 35.

6. The "original affluent society" theory was first put forth by Marshall Sahlins in 1972, suggesting early hunter-gatherers only worked between three to five hours a day in food production, and the remaining time was possible to spend in leisure. As you can imagine, some people dispute this theory.

7. Sawyer, *Humans*, 173–174.

8. A 19th-century social theory about the evolution of cultures and societies wherein Western civilization is the pinnacle of evolutionary achievement and one can get there by following a single line moving from most primitive to most civilized.

9. Sid Meier, *Civilization*, video game, 1995, http://www.civilization.com/en/home/. If you'd like a video game with a more Indigenous point of view, try my game, *Idle No More: Blockade*. It's free! Sorry, it only works on PCs. When you click the download link, you'll be sent to a dropbox link and asked to download an exe. file. I promise it isn't a virus! Download it here: https://www.dropbox.com/s/kogvjst7inm54j6/Idle%20No%20More.exe?dl=0. As Hugh Goldring of Ad Astra Comix points out, it's "not much of a video game, but it's a hell of a story!" Heh.

10. Christopher Wanjek, "The Tongue Map: Tasteless Myth Debunked," *livescience.com* (blog), August 29, 2006 (04:19am), http://www.livescience.com/7113-tongue-map-tasteless-myth-debunked.html. The same goes for the tongue map! The idea that your tongue has four areas to taste – sweet, sour, salty, and bitter – is all wrong!

19
The Myth of Authenticity

Okay, folks, it's time. Say it with me: traditions aren't technology-dependent.

I feel like I've said this so often, it should be indelibly emblazoned on the mind of every person who has ever lived, but the sad fact of my limited vocal reach requires me to repeat myself – and really, it's okay. I like exploring this concept.

What the heck am I talking about, you ask? As always, I'm talking about misconceptions. Some of them are even funny!

Often they're hunting-related:

A: That wasn't a *traditional* hunt; they used high-powered rifles, not bows and arrows!

B: And they should have dragged the deer home with their teeth, too, right?

A: Well, I guess if that's the tradition....

Sometimes they're communication-related:

A: Some *traditional* Indian she is, with her Facebook and iPhone.

B: You're going to say something about smoke signals, right?

A: Well, you know, however you guys traditionally used to talk to each other, sure....

Often they are related to living conditions:

A: Oh, a house, hey, real *traditional* that! How do you like all that nontraditional running water, anyway?

B: You mean the nonpotable water that isn't safe to drink? Oh, man, I hate that stuff.

A: You know what I meant....

Aaaaaand there are plenty of other examples. I am always amazed how much people seem to know about our traditions. You know, the next time you're not sure about a traditional practice, I suggest skipping the whole thing with the Elders. I bet you could zip on over to the Internet and get the real scoop in nanoseconds! Try the *National Post* comments section – it's full of ancient wisdom!

Okay, but for serious.

The idea that Indigenous traditions require us to use technologies that were only available to us precontact, or more generously, slightly post-contact, is silly. If silly was all we were dealing with, then I'd let it be. But silly ends up translating into policy, and I have to take that seriously. I'll give you an example.

Back in 2004, King Ralph[1] signed an Interim Métis Harvesting Agreement (IMHA) with the Métis Nation of Alberta.[2] Now, this former Premier of Alberta didn't always act with class,[3] but this was a pretty groundbreaking agreement. If you are unaware of this, until the Powley decision in 2003, neither the federal nor provincial governments really recognized a Métis right to hunt.[4] Powley was applied pretty narrowly, so it still did not grant province-wide hunting rights, but the IMHA was the first step toward doing exactly that. Sort of. (Oh, please, don't make me go into the many problems with having a provincially legislated framework for the exercise of inherent Aboriginal rights. It's late and I just want to pretend it's simple, okay?)

Before you anticipate the swelling music of victory, you should know the IMHA was scrapped once Steady Eddy[5] took over, and things have gone back to the traditional tale of Métis hunters having to fight their cases out individually (and at much greater expense to the taxpayer than a negotiated agreement) in the courts.

Back to the point. Although the IMHA seemed like a better way to approach the issue than forcing us into the courts every time we wanted to assert our right to hunt, there were some silly interpretations being applied, based on notions of what is "traditional."

The IMHA mentioned fishing with nets, specifically. Some Métis were being ticketed for fishing with a rod and reel instead of the more "traditional" gill nets.

That sound you're probably not hearing is me rolling my eyes.

Many of the men from my community were traditional fishers. They fished back when you could actually eat what you caught from Lac Ste. Anne. You can bet that as the technology improved, they were right there using it. I'm not talking about camping out for a week to get the new iRod, and they kept the know-how so that when all they had were the materials at hand, they weren't left without a way to fish. The point wasn't *what* they were fishing with; it was that they were catching fish.

The arbitrary decision to say, "That isn't a traditional practice if you're using 'new' technology," freezes us in time, and for no good purpose. It would be like me telling you that you don't get to travel anywhere if you're not doing it in a horse and buggy. Or, that unless you wear your powdered wig, you don't get to dance if you wanna, so just leave your friends behind.

It would be like me saying your legal system is invalid because you no longer have the Courts of Chancery, and I have decided only your pre-1740 way of life is "traditional."

Just look at Canadian property law if you'd like a sense of how you can be both traditional *and* modern. The rules governing what you can do with your land, what rights you have in your land, and who you can pass it along to are all based in feudal notions of ownership. I'm a geek, so I think this history is actually pretty fascinating, but I'm not going to insist you ditch computers and start administering the Torrens system via clerks with quills and ink bottles, and reinstate the feudal system in the meantime. That would be pointless.

I'm not going to belabour the frozen-in-time approach and how flipping bizarre it is to read about people telling us not to haul game home in pick-up trucks, or use kitchen appliances to make frybread, or use gasoline in our motorboats, because once you think about it, the weirdness should be self-evident. I do want you to think about this conversation the next time you think to yourself, "Oh, hey, that can't be traditional because they used [*insert some new technology*]."

We are just as capable of adapting to new technology and using it according to traditional beliefs and philosophies as you are. It'd be cool if you thought of a few ways in which your culture has used new technologies in a traditional way so you really get what I'm saying here.

And if you're still sticking to the whole, "Nope, you've got to do it the way your ancestors did way back when," then I'd like you to name a specific date after which any technological innovation renders our traditions invalid. Then we can *both* agree that from now on, all peoples living in Canada will only be allowed to do things the way they did it before that date, and we'll see how that works, okay?

NOTES

1. Ralph Klein, Progressive Conservative Premier of Alberta from 1992–2006. The nickname is a reference to his style of governing, and how long he stayed in office. He passed in 2013.

2. "Interim Métis Harvesting Agreement," University of Alberta (PDF), September 31, 2004, http://www.ualberta.ca/~walld/gciha.pdf.

3. Lee Parsons, "Canada: Alberta Premier Berates Homeless in Visit to Shelter," *wows.org*, last modified December 22, 2001, http://www.wsws.org/en/articles/2001/12/can-d22.html.

4. *R. v. Powley, 2003*, SCC 43, [2003] 2 SCR 207.

5. Ed Stelmach took over as Premier of Alberta in 2006 when Ralph Klein resigned. He got his nickname from his low-key style.

PART 4
State Violence

20

Monster

The Residential-School Legacy

> I hate you residential school, I hate you.
> You're a monster.
> A huge hungry monster.
> Built with steel bones. Built with cement flesh.
> You're a monster.
> Built to devour innocent Native children.
>
> —*Dennis Saddleman*[1]

Numbers; I deal best with numbers:

- 150 years of operation
- 150 000 children who attended
- 6000 children (at least) who died while in the system
- 67 percent of schools run by the Roman Catholic Church, 20 percent by the Anglicans, 10 percent by the United Church, 3 percent by the Presbyterian Church[2]
- 1996 – the year the last school closed
- 7000 interviews with survivors
- 6 volumes in the final Truth and Reconciliation report[3]

This is as dispassionate as I can get, but even broken down into numbers, this hurts.

Of all the topics I have covered in this book, none is more difficult for me to give voice to than this one. In fact, although I have tried to write about the residential-school system, I have never been able to bring myself to do more than skirt around the topic; I need to focus on what we can do to change things. I feel like someone who, after long exposure, has become so raw that the barest whisper feels like acid on my spirit. Rather than developing calluses, I am a flayed nerve.

I never attended residential school. My experiences are all secondhand. Mine is the first generation to be schooled entirely outside of that system, and yet I cannot think of any Indigenous people of my generation who have not been touched by it, one way or another.

A term was coined in the 1980s for this impact: *historic trauma transmission.* It refers to the "cumulative emotional and psychological wounding across generations."[4] There is no one response to this, no one way of feeling or expressing it. For me, it has meant being utterly incapable of thinking about residential schools without imagining my own children being forcibly removed from me and put into such situations. The residential-school system is gone, but my fear never leaves me. This was *legal.* This was *acceptable.* This *happened.*

And so I apologize if this chapter ends up being unsatisfying. I will do my best, but if you want details of what children endured in those schools, you should hear it from survivors, not from me. There is now a large, publicly accessible record that exists that can fill in any gaps you are left with after I am drained of my words here.

The Truth and Reconciliation Commission of Canada (TRC) was established in 2008 to look into the legacy of the residential-school system. It issued an executive summary in the summer of 2015, and released all six volumes of its final report on December 15th of the same year.[5] Its work has now been transferred to the National Centre for Truth and Reconciliation housed at the University of Manitoba, which will be a permanent home for all statements, documents, and materials gathered by the TRC.

Over the last few years, it has become common to hear former students of residential schools telling their stories. These former students are called "survivors," and this is not just some trite label. Many did not survive, either because they died in the system or the trauma they experienced eventually ended in their deaths years later. Those who remain *survived.*

It is important to understand that the outpouring of survivor testimonies is a very recent phenomenon. For so long, survivors often did not discuss their experiences. In the 1980s, there was some limited recognition of how deeply these experiences had impacted both survivors and their families, and slowly people started talking about it.

Between 1986 and 1994, various churches issued apologies for their role in residential schools. In 1996, the Royal Commission on Aboriginal Peoples (RCAP) released its final report, addressing residential schools in volume one, chapter 10. In 1998, the Canadian government made a Statement of Reconciliation and established the Aboriginal Healing Foundation (AHF) to manage a healing fund of $350 million.[6]

Throughout this time, survivor stories began to trickle in, at first during AHF-funded healing circles. After a while, it became common for survivors to publicly relate some of their experiences at almost any Indigenous conference or gathering. These testimonials were often spontaneous, provided not by panelists, but, more often, by people in the audience. You never really knew when it was going to come up, but as I got older, it came up more and more. Survivors were breaking their silence, many of them for the first time. There was no dedicated forum to tell these stories, so they could spill out anywhere. A trickle became a steady flow.

Because I have heard so many accounts over the years, I often forget that, up until recently, most Canadians knew next to nothing about residential schools. In 2005, a miniseries called *Into the West* was produced in the United States, and was fairly popular in Canada.[7] Episode 5 introduced viewers to the infamous Carlisle Indian Industrial School in the United States.

All of a sudden, through television, residential schools entered the public consciousness in a way that official reports and statements hadn't been able to accomplish. The experiences portrayed in that episode were being discussed in cafes, online in debate forums – everywhere. It was in 2005 that I realized just how hidden these experiences had remained, despite the fact Indigenous people had been telling their painful stories for decades by that point.

I certainly wasn't the only one who entered these discussions and pointed out the same had been done in Canada. I must have given an overview of residential-school history hundreds of times in the next few months. It still boggles my mind to remember the shock on people's faces. Non-Indigenous faces, mind you. I silently asked so many times, "How did you not know this?!" But, of course, they didn't. This was still three years before Canada's official apology.[8]

Maybe I'm wrong. Maybe I'm overstating the impact of a television series. But for me, it marked the beginning of a wider awareness that has only continued to gain momentum with the 2008 apology, the Indian Residential Schools Settlement, and the Truth and Reconciliation Commission of Canada's work.[9]

The TRC Report

For over a century, the central goals of Canada's Aboriginal policy were to eliminate Aboriginal governments; ignore Aboriginal rights; terminate the Treaties; and, through a process of assimilation, cause Aboriginal peoples to cease to exist as distinct legal, social, cultural, religious, and racial entities in Canada. The establishment and operation of residential schools were a central element of this policy, which can best be described as "cultural genocide."[10]

The above quote is the first paragraph of the TRC's executive summary. Many people have found the inclusion of the term *cultural genocide* to be off-putting; some object to it because they feel it unnecessarily modifies the word *genocide*, while others insist genocide must only be used to refer to the mass killing of a specific group. The TRC certainly makes a thorough case for its inclusion of this term, and I do not feel the intent is to either inflate the circumstances or downplay them.

After the release of the TRC executive report, Zoe Todd (Métis), Erica Violet Lee (First Nations, nêhiyaw), and Joseph Murdoch-Flowers (Inuk) created the "Read the TRC Report" project, organizing volunteers to read excerpts from the summary report in a series of videos available online.[11] All across Canada, there has been an incredible surge of interaction with the final report, both on social media and in communities, as Indigenous and non-Indigenous peoples commit to reading the report and, more important, try to find ways to further the TRC's 94 Calls to Action.

If you commit to anything, please commit to reading at least the summary. There are five sections, all well worth reading. The Introduction explains why the TRC was necessary and, more important, it defines how it is using the controversial term *reconciliation*. The Commission Activities section lays out exactly what lengths the TRC went to in order to gather survivors' stories, and how it began laying the groundwork for wider education on the topic. I personally had no idea so many events were held across the country! This section also discusses how the Canadian government had to be taken to court repeatedly in order to force the disclosure of documents essential to the TRC's mandate.

The History section does an amazing job of laying out global colonial history as a backdrop to the development of the residential-school system, as well as providing concrete details about the way these schools were designed and operated. In particular, the Imperial Context subsection (which begins on page 47) should be essential reading for everyone. While many of us have learned this history in fits and starts, this section brings together the history of global colonialism in a way I've never quite seen before: clearly, succinctly, and briefly. It provides an excellent counter narrative to the one of colonial superiority, which so many of us have been inculcated with over our many years of schooling in the Canadian system. The utility of this section goes far beyond the issue of residential schools, and should be used in all educational settings. It is followed by the Assimilation Policy subsection, about which all Canadians should no longer remain ignorant.

When I began reading the History section, I was worried I would not be able to handle the excerpts from survivor testimonies that are included. To be honest, sometimes I couldn't. I needed to take many breaks to go hug my kids and just think of less awful things. If you undertake to read this summary, treat yourself kindly. Take the breaks you need; take the time you need.

If you have ever asked, "What does all this have to do with the present?" then the Legacy section will provide you with clarity. The impact of residential schools on those of us living right now is fleshed out and clarified for all who have been confused by this. The TRC also begins its recommendations in this section, nesting those recommendations in the exploration of the issues. You will find the first five recommendations deal with the child-welfare system as it exists *today*. Huh? Why? Well, you'll have to read to understand; and, please do.

The final section is The Challenge of Reconciliation. This section further lays out a path to follow, with more concrete recommendations and reasons for those recommendations being given.

So often we, as Indigenous people, are asked, "What is it you people *want*?" Well, this summary gives concrete answers to that question. We are not asking that money simply be thrown at us, as is frequently claimed. We are explaining what is wrong, why it happened/happens, and what has to be done in order to create real change. There is no need for further confusion, no need to keep asking what we want. Many of the recommendations echo what Indigenous peoples have been asking for on many levels, for decades and, in some cases, centuries.

Justin Trudeau has committed his government to full federal action on the TRC final report.[12] Whether this promise is ever fully realized or not, it is a fact that the TRC's 94 Calls to Action are something all Canadians need to become more familiar with. Already, these Calls to Action are having a profound impact on Canada, particularly in terms of the TRC's call for systemic educational inclusion of Indigenous topics in K–12 and post-secondary curricula. Predictably, there has been some backlash against making any of these changes mandatory.

Education for reconciliation

Much of the current state of troubled relations between Aboriginal and non-Aboriginal Canadians is attributable to education institutions and what they have taught, or failed to teach, over many generations. Despite that history, or, perhaps more correctly, because of its potential, the Commission believes education is also the key to reconciliation.[13]

The Commission does an excellent job of reviewing the ways in which Indigenous peoples have been taught about (or excluded) in Canadian schools over the last few decades. A number of Calls to Action address the need to ensure all people living in Canada learn substantially more about Indigenous peoples, with the goal of creating a population educated enough on the issues that a respectful relationship can be formed between Indigenous and non-Indigenous peoples.

Not long after the executive summary was released, Lakehead University and the University of Winnipeg announced they would be creating a requirement, as of the 2016–2017 year, that all students, regardless of their program of study, must take one Indigenous studies course in order to graduate.[14] A number of other postsecondary institutions have openly discussed doing the same. As you can imagine, not everyone is thrilled with the idea of having to learn Indigenous topics.

Don't we learn enough about Indigenous peoples in elementary and secondary school?

Whenever there is talk about the need for systemic changes to ensure Canadians learn about Indigenous peoples, a veritable tsunami of anecdotes pour in. To hear some tell it, Canadians are already experts on Indigenous cultures, history, and contemporary realities.[15]

One person, for example, insists, "Indigenous issues were the primary focus of [his] social science and history classes from kindergarten to graduate school at UBC."[16] Wow! The primary focus! Sounds amazing! So, what did this person learn? In fourth grade he filled out a linguistic map, the next year he made bannock, and the year after that a residential-school survivor spoke to his class. He even learned about Louis Riel in high school! Poor guy wasn't "allowed to even consider anyone else's history until his second year of University." Someone, please give this guy the degree in Indigenous Studies he has so clearly earned!

On my Twitter feed, another person claims she didn't learn European history in high school because "Indigenous studies [were] mandatory and WW2 was not."[17] That this is provably untrue doesn't really matter if the purpose of such claims is merely to bolster a rhetorical point: forcing people to learn more than they already apparently know about Indigenous peoples is akin to "brainwashing," "fascism," and any number of other less repeatable terms.[18]

There is much to unpack here, but I want to focus specifically on what Canadians are actually learning about Indigenous peoples. Is it enough? Are the Truth and Reconciliation Commission's educational Calls to Action unnecessary?

Well, the TRC's Call to Action 62.1 exhorts governments in Canada:

> …in consultation and collaboration with Survivors, Aboriginal peoples, and educators, to make age-appropriate curriculum on residential schools, Treaties,

and Aboriginal peoples' historical and contemporary contributions to Canada a mandatory education requirement for Kindergarten to Grade Twelve students.[19]

According to claims like those above, this happened years ago; job done!

Since the current debate centres around mandatory courses at the postsecondary level, such as those recently announced at the University of Winnipeg, I thought it made sense to look at what Canadians are learning before they get to that point.[20] Perhaps we will discover, after all, that these kinds of courses are not needed!

Educational curricula are provincial concerns, so what is taught in Canada varies greatly. To know what elementary- and secondary-level students in any given province or territory are learning about Indigenous peoples, you need to access Ministry of Education sites and look through the curricula. When it comes to elective courses, you also have to look at each school board to see which schools actually offer those courses.

In most of Canada, there are no mandatory Indigenous Studies courses, meaning one can graduate from high school without ever having to take such a class. Only six provinces even offer *elective* Indigenous Studies courses, and there is no guarantee these elective courses will be available in any given school. Interested students in Manitoba, Quebec, Newfoundland, and Prince Edward Island cannot even choose to take an Indigenous Studies course. Seven provinces have developed curricula to teach an Indigenous language, but these courses tend to be even less available due to lack of qualified language teachers.[21]

What about inclusion of Indigenous topics in K–12?

Surely, there are no mandatory Indigenous Studies courses because these topics are already a "primary focus of social science and history classes from kindergarten on"?

In October 2015, KAIROS (Canadian churches working together for justice and peace) took a look at how much Canadian students are actually learning about Indigenous peoples in elementary and secondary school. They issued a report card on provincial and territorial curriculum using the TRC's Call to Action 62.1.[22] They examined whether or not curricula include the four elements identified: residential-school legacy, treaties, historical contributions, and contemporary contributions.

KAIROS also looked at whether these elements are mandatory, and at what grade levels they are offered. Further, public commitment by provinces and territories was measured against actual implementation.

It turns out that *no* provinces or territories received top marks for their public commitment to Call to Action 62.1. Only the Prairie provinces received a passing grade; all other jurisdictions have so far failed to make significant public commitment to integrating these topics into the general-learning outcomes. That means most places in Canada aren't even issuing empty promises to follow the TRC's recommendation!

In terms of actual implementation, seven of the provinces and territories have one of the four elements included in their learning outcomes, and only Saskatchewan can boast teaching more than one of the four elements (though not all). In our most populous provinces, Ontario and Quebec, none of the four elements is adequately covered in the curricula.

In seven of the eight provinces that cover at least one of the recommended topics, this learning is mandatory in only a few grades. Saskatchewan outperforms all other provinces and territories in Canada and still does not even come close to K–12 integration of mandatory coverage of the four elements recommended by the TRC.

It seems that anecdotes do not translate into actual Canada-wide learning outcomes. Maybe those mandatory Indigenous Studies courses at the postsecondary level are necessary after all, at least until K–12 curricula are revamped.

Remember, the TRC did not call for only the residential-school legacy to be taught to all people in Canada. Learning about the treaties and the historic and contemporary contributions of Indigenous peoples is also vital if Canadians are ever going to achieve a base level of knowledge necessary to enter into any form of "new relationship" with us. Education like that envisioned by the TRC would make books like this obsolete – something that would bring me endless joy.

You can start this process now.

I've provided a number of resources to get you started. You have complete access to the entire TRC report, and if going through all six volumes is too daunting, please at least make it a priority to read the executive summary. If you'd rather listen to it, check out the "Read the TRC Report" videos. Canadians have been coming together in their respective communities to help one another through this difficult material, so see if such a group exists where you live. If you have children, or work with children, educators have identified a number of books that are appropriate for kids under 12.[23] Most of all, please do not push this learning aside as unimportant. If there is ever going to be change in this country, it will come because individuals made it happen.

NOTES

1. Dennis Saddleman, "Monster," *CBC Radio,* accessed December 26, 2015, http://www.cbc.ca/radio/thecurrent/apr-3-2014-1.2908353/monster-by-poet-dennis-saddleman-i-hate-you-residential-school-i-hate-you-1.2908356.

2. Marie Wilson, Commissioner, TRC of Canada.

3. With the additions of a summary and many documents, the *TRC Report* now actually exceeds six volumes.

4. Eyaa-Keen Healing Centre, "Historic Trauma Transmission," accessed December 26, 2015, http://eyaa-keen.org/resources/historic-trauma-transmission/.

5. Truth and Reconciliation Commission of Canada, "Honouring the Truth, Reconciling for the Future: Summary of the Final Report of the Truth and Reconciliation Commission of Canada," 2015, http://www.trc.ca/websites/trcinstitution/File/2015/Findings/Exec_Summary_2015_05_31_web_0.pdf. Truth and Reconciliation Commission of Canada, Final Report of the Truth and Reconciliation Commission of Canada, 2016, http://www.trc.ca/websites/trcinstitution/index.php?p=890. All reports are available in complete form, for free, online: http://nctr.ca/reports.php.

6. Indian Affairs and Northern Development, "Gathering Strength: Canada's Aboriginal Action Plan," 1997, accessed December 26, 2015, http://www.ahf.ca/downloads/gathering-strength.pdf.

7. "Into the West," TV mini-series, http://www.imdb.com/title/tt0409572/.

8. Government of Canada, "Statement of Apology to Former Students of Indian Residential Schools," June 11, 2008, accessed December 26, 2015, https://www.aadnc-aandc.gc.ca/eng/1100100015644/1100100015649.

9. Indian Residential School Settlement, official court website, accessed December 26, 2015, http://www.residentialschoolsettlement.ca/english_index.html.

10. Truth and Reconciliation Commission of Canada, "Honouring the Truth, Reconciling for the Future: Summary of the Final Report of the Truth and Reconciliation Commission of Canada," 2015, http://www.trc.ca/websites/trcinstitution/File/2015/Findings/Exec_Summary_2015_05_31_web_0.pdf.

11. Zoe Todd, "Read the TRC Report," YouTube video, June 7, 2015, accessed December 26, 2015, https://www.youtube.com/watch?v=vW4lQfOfl3I&list=PLxPr_RIsvg9JJWoiRx2kl2v24r_pu7JbR.

12. Elizabeth McSheffrey, "Trudeau Promises Full Federal Action on Final TRC Report," *National Observer,* December 15, 2015, accessed December 26, 2015, http://www.nationalobserver.com/2015/12/15/news/trudeau-promises-immediate-action-final-trc-report.

13. TRC, "Summary of the Final Report," 234.

14. Nancy Macdonald, "Required Reading: Making Indigenous Classes Mandatory," *Maclean's,* November 19, 2015, accessed December 26, 2016, http://www.macleans.ca/education/making-history-2/.

15. This section of the chapter was first published in a modified form by *CBC Aboriginal,* accessed December 26, 2015, http://www.cbc.ca/news/aboriginal/debunking-myth-canadian-schools-teach-indigenous-peoples-1.3376800.

16. Josh Dehaas, "Why Indigenous Studies Shouldn't Be Mandatory," *Maclean's*, February 23, 2012, accessed December 26, 2015, http://www.macleans.ca/education/uniandcollege/why-indigenous-studies-shouldnt-be-mandatory/.

17. Lauren Southern, Twitter post to âpihtawikosisân (Twitter account), December 10, 2015, accessed December 26, 2015, https://twitter.com/apihtawikosisan/status/675143351042228225.

18. Here is the social studies curriculum for grade 11 in British Columbia: https://www.bced.gov.bc.ca/irp/pdfs/social_studies/2005ss_11.pdf. World War II figures prominently; and it does again in grade 12.

19. See note 10.

20. Heather Steele, "University of Winnipeg Approves Mandatory Indigenous Course for All," *Global News,* November 20, 2015, accessed December 17, 2015, http://globalnews.ca/news/2352776/university-of-winnipeg-approves-mandatory-indigenous-course-for-all-students/.

21. In the northern Territories, with the highest per capita residential-school participation in the country, a mandatory new course for all high-school students has been developed. Co-created with residential-school survivors, the course covers the northern residential-school story, as well as the history of northern colonization, treaties, and modern-day Indigenous-led governance.

22. "Report Card: Provincial and Territorial Curriculum on Indigenous Peoples," KAIROS Canada, October 2015, http://www.kairoscanada.org/what-we-do/indigenous-rights/windsofchange-report-cards.

23. Chantelle Bellrichard, "10 Books About Residential Schools to Read With Your Kids," CBC *News,* September 26, 2015, http://www.cbc.ca/news/aboriginal/10-books-about-residential-schools-to-read-with-your-kids-1.3208021. Those books are: Nicola Campbell, *Shi-shi-etko* (Toronto: Groundwood Books, 2005); Nicola Campbell, *Shin-chi's Canoe* (Toronto: Groundwood Books, 2008); Michael Kusugak, *Arctic Stories* (Winnipeg: Pemmican Publications, 2015); Peter Eyvindson, and Sheldon Dawson, *Kookum's Red Shoes* (Winnipeg: Pemmican Publications, 2011); Christy Jordan-Fenton, and Margaret Pokiak-Fenton, *Fatty Legs: A True Story* (Buffalo: Annick Press, 2010); Christy Jordan-Fenton, and Margaret Pokiak-Fenton, *A Stranger at Home: A True Story* (Buffalo: Annick Press, 2011); Sylvia Olsen, *No Time to Say Goodbye: Children's Stories of Kuper Island Residential School* (Winlaw: Sono Nis Press, 2002); Larry Loyie, *As Long as the Rivers Flow* (Toronto: Groundwood Books, 2005); Shirley Sterling, *My Name Is Seepeetza* (Toronto: Groundwood Books, 1992); Julie-Ann André, and Mindy Willett, *We Feel Good Out Here = Zhik gwaa'an nakhwatthaiitat qwiinzii (The Land Is Our Storybook)* (Markha: Fifth House Publishers, 2008). A longer reading list for all ages can be found at Where Are the Children, http://wherearethechildren.ca/en/resources/.

21

Our Stolen Generations
The Sixties and Millennial Scoops

If you've ever heard the term *Sixties Scoop* and thought it had something to do with ice cream in the old days, I'm here to enlighten you.

I prefer the term *Stolen* or *Lost Generations* because the scooping I'm about to discuss did not end in the 1960s. In fact, many argue that it didn't end with a single generation, either, and perhaps hasn't actually ended at all – hence, the title. Similar policies were put into place in Australia with equally unhappy results.[1]

You could delve into this sordid history and lose many hours uncovering details, but I'll provide you with a brief outline and enough resources in the endnotes to allow you to do that digging if you wish. This is an ongoing chapter of Canadian history that has yet to receive attention comparable to that finally given to the residential schools, but it is slowly leaking into the public consciousness due to the efforts of advocates and adoptees.

In short, *Sixties Scoop* is the term used to refer to the adoption of First Nations and Métis children here in Canada, beginning in the 1960s and continuing up until the mid-1980s. It is not a specific policy, but rather a series of outcomes of various child-welfare practices. The 1960s saw the largest number of Indigenous children being adopted out in this way, in too many cases without the consent or even knowledge of their families or communities. Some of these children were adopted out internationally.

Adoption as cultural annihilation

It is important to remember many of the services Canadians take for granted – such as education, health care, and social-welfare programs – are mainly designed and administered by the provinces and territories.

However, the federal government has been asserting its authority over "Indians, and Lands of the Indians" since 1763.[2] While it still remains unclear whether this includes all Inuit, Métis, and non-status Indians, it is true that status Indians must turn to the federal government – not the provinces – for many services.

Canada did not spring from the skull of Zeus fully formed. The development of social programs and services has been incremental. Before the mid-1960s, there was no organized federal child-welfare system.[3] The provinces each had their own system, but nothing was in place for First Nations people.

In the mid-1960s, agreements started to be formed between the federal and provincial governments to provide some child-welfare coverage in First Nations communities. To be brief, the approach was "take first, ask questions later (if ever)."

The similarity to tactics used during the height of the residential-school system is eerie. Aboriginal children were taken en masse from their families and adopted out into non-Indigenous families:

> Child welfare workers removed Aboriginal children from their families and communities because they felt the best homes for the children were not Aboriginal homes. The ideal home would instill the values and lifestyles with which the child welfare workers themselves were familiar: white, middle-class homes in white, middle-class neighbourhoods. Aboriginal communities and Aboriginal parents and families were deemed to be "unfit."[4]

Research has shown that in British Columbia alone, the number of Indigenous children in the care of the child-welfare system went from almost none to *one third* in only 10 years as a result of this expansion.[5] This was a pattern that repeated itself all across Canada.

There is evidence that at least 11 132 status-Indian children were removed from their homes between 1960 and 1990. However, it is clear the numbers are, in fact, much higher than this, as birth records were often closed and status not marked down on foster records. Some estimate the number, which included non-status and Métis children, was close to 20 000.[6] Across the country, 70 to 90 percent of Indigenous children were placed in non-Indigenous homes.[7]

Being from an Indigenous family was often enough to have a child declared in need of intervention. This process resulted in thousands of Indigenous peoples being raised without their culture, their language, and without learning anything about their communities. Reclaiming that heritage has been a painful and difficult journey not only for the adoptees, but often also for their families.[8]

The Sixties Scoop picked up where residential schools left off, removing children from their homes, and producing cultural amputees.

Child-welfare reforms not working

In the late 1970s, it was recognized that the approach up to that point was inadequate, and an Indian Child Welfare Sub-Committee was struck to address the problems and provide recommendations. The working committee was a joint effort by federal and provincial governments, as well as the Manitoba Indian Brotherhood.[9] There were efforts made to turn more power over to First Nations themselves and to keep children in their communities rather than being adopted out across Canada, into the United States, and even overseas.[10]

In 1982, Manitoba Judge Edwin C. Kimelman was appointed to head an inquiry into the child-welfare system and how it was impacting Indigenous peoples.[11] He had this to say:

> It would be reassuring if blame could be laid to any single part of the system. The appalling reality is that everyone involved believed they were doing their best and stood firm in their belief that the system was working well. Some administrators took the ostrich approach to child welfare problems – they just did not exist. The miracle is that there were not more children lost in this system run by so many well-intentioned people. The road to hell was paved with good intentions, and the child welfare system was the paving contractor.[12]

Nor was this his strongest condemnation of the process, and he made it clear in his report that the system was a form of cultural genocide.

Unfortunately, by 2002, over 22 500 Indigenous children were in foster care across Canada – more than the total taken during the Sixties Scoop and certainly more than had been taken to residential schools.[13] Indigenous children are six to eight times more likely to be placed in foster care than non-Indigenous children.[14] To ignore the repeated attempts to annihilate Aboriginal cultures and instead place the blame solely on "dysfunctional Native families" is to take an utterly ahistorical and abusive view. As Valerie Galley wrote in a 2010 paper prepared for the Saskatchewan Child Welfare Review panel:

> [This] over representation…is not rooted in their indigenous race, culture and ethnicity. Rather, any family with children who has experienced the same colonial history and the resultant poverty, social and community disorganization…may find themselves in a similar situation.[15]

Systemic discrimination and underfunding

On April 18, 2012, an important ruling came down from the Federal Court.[16] This case was a judicial review of a decision made by the Canadian Human Rights Tribunal (CHRT), which had used a technicality to dismiss allegations that the federal government racially discriminates against First Nations children by chronically underfunding child welfare on-reserve.[17] The Federal Court sent the human rights case *back* to the CHRT with the instructions to give it a full hearing. The original case, launched in 2007 by the First Nations Child and Family Caring Society and the Assembly of First Nations, is still ongoing.

Study after study has shown that child-welfare systems on-reserve are funded at levels far below those available to off-reserve populations, which inevitably leads to lower levels of service. As a result, less focus is put on helping families *before* children are removed, or on reuniting families once removal has taken place. In 2008, then Auditor General, Sheila Fraser, noted the rate of foster care for children on-reserve is eight times that of non-Indigenous children.[18] When the original CHRT complaint was filed, the federal government was spending about 78 cents for child welfare on-reserve for every dollar spent by provinces for children off-reserve.

Also troubling was the way in which Cindy Blackstock, president of the First Nations Child and Family Caring Society, faced retaliation and intense monitoring by the federal government after the human-rights complaint was filed. Her personal social media was spied on by federal officials and she was surveilled during public appearances.[19] In June 2015, the CHRT ruled in favour of Blackstock on the issue of retaliation and awarded her $20,000.[20]

The millennial scoop

No situation involving children in need of protective services is a happy one. Many of the stories, regardless of the background of the child, will chill your blood, and rightfully so. However, when only 21 percent of children in a province like Manitoba are Indigenous, yet account for 84 percent of children in permanent care, something is deeply, and terribly, wrong[21] – something that cannot be chalked up to just bad parenting.

Despite the fact that changes to the child-welfare system have been made, and Indigenous communities and families certainly have more control and input than was the case during the height of the Sixties Scoop, the number of Indigenous children being placed out-of-home does not seem to be decreasing. The trend is to place Indigenous children in group or institutional care – some at shockingly young ages.

Recently, Cora Morgan, Manitoba's First Nations family advocate, raised the alarm on the seizure of Indigenous infants, stating social workers are removing an average of one newborn a day in that province, despite not having adequate facilities or caretakers to deal with the influx of infants. Morgan pointed to one case where a three-day-old boy was taken from his mother simply because the mother had been a ward of Family Services until she was 18.[22] If anything, this seems like a stunning indictment by child-welfare workers of the child-welfare system itself; if it is assumed children passing through the system are incapable of becoming adequate parents, then that system is failing them utterly.

For years, a number of provinces have been housing foster children (a disproportionate number of which in *all* provinces are Indigenous children) in motels and hotels when no other accommodations are available.[23] These placements, which are meant to be temporary, have come under scrutiny after the murder of 15-year-old Tina Fontaine. She ran away from one such placement after a vicious sexual assault of another 15-year-old Indigenous girl outside the hotel where both target and attacker were housed.[24]

So, what is happening? Why are so many Indigenous children being removed from their homes?

I am going to focus for a moment on First Nations statistics both on- and off-reserve because I am pulling numbers from the incredible *Kiskisik Awasisak* report, which looks specifically at overrepresentation of First Nations children in the child-welfare system. If you want information specific to Métis and Inuit children, I've listed a good resource in the endnotes.[25] The numbers I'm going to discuss cannot be generalized across the board for all Indigenous children, but they at least gives us some idea as to what is going on in this country.

The main reason First Nations children enter the child-protection system is due to "neglect," representing 46 percent of substantiated investigations compared to 29 percent among non-Indigenous households. There are significantly lower rates of physical abuse among First Nations: 9 percent compared to 23 percent in the non-Indigenous population. Exposure to intimate partner violence is roughly equal: 33 percent among First Nations homes investigated versus 36 percent in the general population.[26]

Since the category of neglect is overwhelmingly the cause of removal of First Nations children from their homes, it is vital to understand what this entails. Neglect in cases involving First Nations children is "driven primarily by 3 structural risk factors: poverty, inadequate housing and substance misuse."[27]

PRIMARY CATEGORIES OF MALTREATMENT IN SUBSTANTIATED MALTREATMENT INVESTIGATIONS, INVOLVING FIRST NATIONS AND NON-ABORIGINAL CHILDREN, CONDUCTED IN SAMPLED AGENCIES IN 2008

(rate per 1000 First Nations or non-Aboriginal children in areas served by sampled agencies and percent)

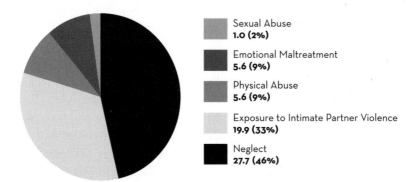

Sexual Abuse
1.0 (2%)

Emotional Maltreatment
5.6 (9%)

Physical Abuse
5.6 (9%)

Exposure to Intimate Partner Violence
19.9 (33%)

Neglect
27.7 (46%)

FIGURE 21.1A. FIRST NATIONS

59.8 substantiated maltreatment investigations per 1000 children in areas served by sampled agencies

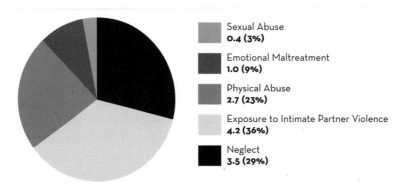

Sexual Abuse
0.4 (3%)

Emotional Maltreatment
1.0 (9%)

Physical Abuse
2.7 (23%)

Exposure to Intimate Partner Violence
4.2 (36%)

Neglect
3.5 (29%)

FIGURE 21.1B. NON-ABORIGINAL

11.8 substantiated maltreatment investigations per 1000 children in areas served by sampled agencies

Source: Vandna Sinha, Nico Trocmé, Barbara Fallon, Bruce MacLaurin, Elizabeth Fast, Shelley Thomas Prokop, et al. (2011). *Kiskisik Awasisak: Remember the Children. Understanding the Overrepresentation of First Nations Children in the Child Welfare System.* Ontario: Assembly of First Nations.

Poverty affects First Nations children removal because:

Parents with fewer financial resources face greater difficulties in providing the safe environments, adequate clothing and nutrition, appropriate child care and other assets which foster healthy child development.[28]

Poverty is compounded by intergenerational trauma and poor structural conditions. As the *Kiskisik Awasisak* report notes, First Nations children and families have complex needs, which are very expensive to provide for, particularly in the more remote communities.

Inadequate housing is a serious, systemic problem in many First Nations communities.[29] Overcrowding, lack of indoor plumbing or potable water, mould-infested homes, and crumbling infrastructure all play a part in what constitutes "inadequate housing." The fact that deplorably common conditions found on-reserve work against families, resulting in children being removed and making family reunification out of reach for many, is very troubling. As discussed in chapter 16 on First Nations housing, it is also a factor that is rarely something the families in question can directly control.

Low-income parents often have fewer coping mechanisms, which can lead to higher levels of substance misuse. In fact, these three risk factors are so interrelated that it is very difficult to say where one ends and the other begins. Indigenous children and their families are being punished for being faced with unacceptable living conditions that no one in Canada should have to contend with.

The legacy of over a hundred years of concerted cultural abuse, particularly directed at taking children away from their families, has taken its toll on our communities. There is no denying it. In my opinion, the question now needs to be: will Canada acknowledge this and do what it takes to redress these wrongs?

It is not enough to merely turn the system over to Aboriginal agencies, as Indigenous control alone will not solve the structural inequality that leads to the main risk factors of neglect. Adequate funding and programming are vital to support families and communities in raising healthy children. If the child-welfare system continues to merely remove Indigenous children en masse from their homes, then, regardless of good intentions, more generations will be lost.

NOTES

1. Australian Human Rights Commission, "Bringing Them Home: The Stolen Children Report (1997)," accessed November 12, 2015, https://www.humanrights.gov.au/our-work/aboriginal-and-torres-strait-islander-social-justice/publications/bringing-them-home-stolen. Here,

you will find more information about the "Bringing Them Home: The 'Stolen Generation' Report (1997)," which addressed the forced removal of Australian Aboriginal and Torres Strait Islander children from their families.

2. Virtual Law Office, "Royal Proclamation of 1763," *bloorstreet.com*, last modified January 16, 1996, http://www.bloorstreet.com/200block/rp1763.htm#1. Canadian authority is also exerted via the *Royal Proclamation of 1763*; a fantastic exploration of which can be found above.

3. Marlyn Bennett, "First Nations Fact Sheet: A General Profile on First Nations Child Welfare in Canada." First Nations Child and Family Caring Society of Canada (Ottawa, 2004), http://www.fncaringsociety.com/sites/default/files/docs/FirstNationsFS1.pdf.

4. Paul L. Chartrand, and Wendy Whitecloud, "The Sixties Scoop," *The Justice System and Aboriginal People: The Aboriginal Justice Implementation Commission Report of the Aboriginal Justice Inquiry of Manitoba* (Winnipeg, 2001), http://www.ajic.mb.ca/volumel/chapter14.html#6.

5. Royal Commission on Aboriginal Peoples, "Volume 3: Gathering Strength," *Report of the Royal Commission on Aboriginal Peoples* (Ottawa: Queen's Printer, 1997), 24–25, http://www.collectionscanada.gc.ca/webarchives/20071115053257/http://www.ainc-inac.gc.ca/ch/rcap/sg/sgmm_e.html.

6. Suzanne Fournier, and Ernie Crey, *Stolen From Our Embrace: The Abduction of First Nations Children and the Restoration of Aboriginal Communities* (Vancouver: Douglas and McIntyre, 1997).

7. See note 5, page 26.

8. Bruce DeMara, "Dispatch: Hidden Colonial Legacy: The 60's Scoop," *Toronto Star* (2012), http://www.cbc.ca/8thfire/2012/01/hidden-colonial-legacy-the-60s-scoop.html. This is a fantastic short film, available on CBC, that explores the struggle of reconnection for those taken during the Sixties Scoop.

9. Paul L. Chartrand, and Wendy Whitecloud, "The Indian Child Welfare Sub-Committee," *The Justice System and Aboriginal People: The Aboriginal Justice Implementation Commission Report of the Aboriginal Justice Inquiry of Manitoba* (Winnipeg, 2001), http://www.ajic.mb.ca/volumel/chapter14.html#7. Here, you can read more on the history of this sub-committee.

10. See note 5, page 29.

11. Paul L. Chartrand, and Wendy Whitecloud, "The Kimelman Inquiry," *The Justice System and Aboriginal People: The Aboriginal Justice Implementation Commission Report of the Aboriginal Justice Inquiry of Manitoba* (Winnipeg, 2001), accessed November 15, 2015, http://www.ajic.mb.ca/volumel/chapter14.html#9.

12. Edwin C. Kimelman, et al., *No Quiet Place, Review Committee on Indian and Metis Adoptions and Placements* (Winnipeg: Manitoba Department of Community Services, 1985), 275–276.

13. Vandna Sinha, Nico Trocmé, Barbara Fallon, Bruce MacLaurin, Elizabeth Fast, Shelley Thomas Prokop, et al., *Kiskisik Awasisak: Remember the Children: Understanding the Overrepresentation of First Nations Children in the Child Welfare System* (Ontario: Assembly of First Nations, 2011), http://cwrp.ca/sites/default/files/publications/en/FNCIS-2008_March2012_RevisedFinal.pdf.

14. Valerie J. Galley, "Summary Review of Aboriginal Over-Representation in the Child Welfare System," *Report Prepared for the Saskatchewan Child Welfare Review Panel,*

accessed November 15, 2015, http://saskchildwelfarereview.ca/Aboriginal-Over-representation-VGalley.pdf.

15. Ibid., 3.

16. *Canada (Human Rights Commission) v. Canada (Attorney General), 2012,* FC 445 – 2012-04-18, last modified November 23, 2015, http://decisions.fct-cf.gc.ca/fc-cf/decisions/en/item/60712/index.do.

17. Cindy Blackstock, "The Canadian Human Rights Tribunal on First Nations Child Welfare: Why If Canada Wins, Equality and Justice Lose," *Children and Youth Services Review* 33, no. 1 (2011): 187–194, http://chrr.info/files/CHRT-FNCW-Blackstock_2010.pdf.

18. Office of the Auditor General of Canada, "Chapter 4: First Nations Child and Family Services Program, Indian and Northern Affairs Canada," Report of the Auditor General of Canada (May 2008), last modified May 6, 2008, http://www.oag-bvg.gc.ca/internet/English/parl_oag_200805_04_e_30700.html.

19. Tim Harper, "Conservative Government Found Spying on Aboriginal Advocate: Tim Harper," *The Star,* May 29, 2013, http://www.thestar.com/news/canada/2013/05/29/conservative_government_found_spying_on_aboriginal_advocate_tim_harper.html.

20. Jorge Barrera, "Aboriginal Affairs 'Retaliated' Against First Nations Child Advocate Over Human Rights Complaint: Tribunal," *APTN.ca,* last modified June 6, 2015, http://aptn.ca/news/2015/06/06/aboriginal-affairs-retaliated-first-nations-child-advocate-human-rights-complaint-tribunal/.

21. Pamela Gough, Nico Trocme, Ivan Brown, Della Knoke, and Cindy Blackstock, "Pathways to the Overrepresentation of Aboriginal Children in Care," *Centre of Excellence for Child Welfare* (2005), http://cwrp.ca/sites/default/files/publications/en/AboriginalChildren23E.pdf.

22. China Puxley, "CFS Seizes a Manitoba Newborn a Day, First Nations Advocate Says," *CBC News,* last modified September 1, 2015, http://www.cbc.ca/news/canada/manitoba/cfs-seizes-a-manitoba-newborn-a-day-first-nations-advocate-says-1.3211451. In fact, the only reason the boy was allowed to stay with his mother for three days was he happened to be born on a Friday – he was apprehended the following Monday.

23. Douglas Quan, "Manitoba Vows to Stop Housing Foster Children in Hotels but Other Provinces Engage on Same Practice," *National Post,* last modified April 2, 2015, http://news.nationalpost.com/news/canada/manitoba-vows-to-stop-housing-foster-children-in-hotels-but-other-provinces-engage-in-same-practice.

24. Kathryn Blaze Carlson, "Manitoba Nears Deadline to Remove Foster Kids From Hotels in Wake of Sex Assault," *The Globe and Mail,* last modified May 28, 2015, http://www.theglobeandmail.com/news/national/manitoba-closing-in-on-deadline-to-move-foster-children-out-of-hotels/article24654834/.

25. Lawrence J. Barkwell, Lyle N. Longclaws, and David N. Chartrand, "Status of Métis Children Within the Child Welfare System," *Canadian Journal of Native Studies* 9, no. 1 (1989): 33–53, http://www3.brandonu.ca/library/CJNS/9.1/metis.pdf; Inuit Tuttarvingat, "Inuit Child Welfare and Family Support" (2011), accessed November 15, 2015, http://www.naho.ca/documents/it/2011_Inuit_Child_Welfare_Family_Support.pdf. A lot of this discussion focuses on First Nations children, or on Aboriginal children in general. The first source above looks at Métis children in Manitoba, while the second addresses Inuit children.

...te 13, page xix. The report says on page xviii, "It is important to note that exposure to intimate partner violence differs from the other forms of maltreatment because substantiation of this maltreatment category means that a caregiver failed to protect a child from exposure to his/her own victimization."

27. Ibid., 3.

28. Ibid., 11.

29. Office of the Auditor General of Canada, "2003 April Report of the Auditor General of Canada: Chapter 6, Federal Government Support to First Nations-Housing on Reserves," *oag-bvg.gc.ca,* last modified Apr 8, 2003, http://www.oag-bvg.gc.ca/internet/English/parl_oag_200304_06_e_12912.html.

22

Human Flagpoles
Inuit Relocation

On behalf of the Government of Canada and all Canadians, we would like to offer a full and sincere apology to Inuit for the relocation of families from Inukjuak and Pond Inlet to Grise Fiord and Resolute Bay during the 1950s. We would like to express our deepest sorrow for the extreme hardship and suffering caused by the relocation. The families were separated from their home communities and extended families by more than a thousand kilometres. They were not provided with adequate shelter and supplies. They were not properly informed of how far away and how different from Inukjuak their new homes would be, and they were not aware that they would be separated into two communities once they arrived in the High Arctic. Moreover, the Government failed to act on its promise to return anyone that did not wish to stay in the High Arctic to their old homes.[1]

Relocations of Indigenous peoples, and even of whole communities within Canada, have been a shockingly frequent event since contact. In fact, much of the history since contact has involved moving Indigenous communities from one place to another for the benefit of settlers. As the Royal Commission on Aboriginal Peoples (RCAP) report points out, the justification for these frequent relocations was often "this is for their own good."[2] Yet, RCAP goes on to explain that there are predictable results when relocation is carried out, including:

- severing Aboriginal people's relationship to the land and environment and weakening cultural bonds
- a loss of economic self-sufficiency, including, in some cases, increased dependence on government transfer payments
- a decline in standards of health
- changes in social and political relations in the relocated population[3]

Further, RCAP has this to say:

> The results of more than 25 studies around the world indicate *without exception* that the relocation, without informed consent, of low-income rural populations with strong ties to their land and homes is a traumatic experience. For the majority of those who have been moved, the profound shock of compulsory relocation is much like the bereavement caused by the death of a parent, spouse or child.[4]

Federal policy toward Inuit, both before and after Confederation, was initially markedly different than it was toward First Nations. Whereas micromanagement and assimilation were the focus for First Nations, the federal government was unwilling to take active responsibility for the Inuit, preferring instead to ensure they remained self-sufficient. While this might seem like an admirable goal, particularly when viewed in contrast with the destruction of self-sufficiency among First Nations, the desired outcome here was to avoid financial commitments. This reluctance continued even after a 1939 Supreme Court ruling clarified the federal government was constitutionally responsible for Inuit.[5] When that attitude changed, it changed in a *big* way.

Inuit relocations 1930s–1950s

The analogy of human pawns being moved on an Arctic chessboard is perhaps never more strikingly illustrated than in the instance of Devon Island. Here, there was relocation of a small group of Inuit to four new sites in succession, as it suited the experimental economic interests of the [Hudson's Bay] Company and set against the background geopolitical interests of the State.[6]

Between 1934 and 1947, Baffin Island Inuit were relocated to Devon Island, a "virgin land," according to Indian Affairs and Hudson's Bay Company (HBC) officials. Baffin Island (Qikiqtaaluk in Inuktitut) has been inhabited by Inuit for thousands of years and is home to many animals, among them caribou, polar bears, Arctic hares, foxes, and wolves, and many nesting birds. Iqaluit, the capital of Nunavut, is located on the south coast of Baffin Island.

Devon Island (Tatlurutit in Inuktitut) is much smaller, and much more northern than Baffin Island. It supports only a tiny population of muskox, and a few small birds and animals. This relocation of Inuit saw 53 people, along with their possessions and sled dogs, sent to Devon Island for two years to trap, providing furs for the HBC, as well as providing "effective occupation" in an area Canada was worried might become subject to claims from other countries.[7]

Conditions on Devon Island were extremely harsh, and the 53 Inuit originally sent there chose to leave after their "voluntary" two-year stint. Some of the families, rather than being allowed to return home, were relocated yet again to Arctic Bay (Ikpiarjuk), then on to Fort Ross (uninhabited now), and then finally to Taloyoak (formerly, Spence Bay). These families suffered years of privation and repeatedly made it clear they wished to return to their original homes, but were denied again and again.

Rather than being seen as a failure, this relocation seemed to set the stage for a succession of subsequent federal interventions. Policy shifted from one of "preservation," wherein Inuit were encouraged to remain self-sufficient within a traditional hunting economy, to one of "transformation," which saw the Inuit as being in a constant state of crisis and in need of skills to join the wage economy.

Other relocations were based on the idea that Inuit needed to be saved from the corrupt influence of settlers. In 1949, federal officials, acting without an interpreter, convinced Inuit whose territory was close to a military radio station at Ennadai Lake, to relocate to Nueltin Lake, 100 kilometres away. When the relocated Inuit decided to return to their homes, they were again moved, this time to Henik Lake. When this did not work out, Tavani became the next relocation point. After eight Inuit died (two were murdered,[8] six died of malnutrition or exposure) at Tavani, the survivors were evacuated to Arviat (formerly, Eskimo Point). Evacuations of Inuit from communities where starvation was becoming a reality began to occur more frequently.

Inuit from many communities were moved from one area to another within the Arctic, and to the south – sometimes to act as human markers, staking Canada's claim to the Arctic, sometimes because of famine, sometimes simply for bureaucratic ease. These decisions were not made in consultation with the Inuit, and it was fully believed that these relocations were in the best interests of the Inuit, who were being uprooted again and again.

Qimmiijaqtauniq: The dog slaughter

In 2000, the Qikiqtani Inuit Association (QIA) and the Makivik Corporation of Nunavik asked the federal government to launch a public inquiry into the mass killing of *qimmiit*, which are Inuit sled dogs.[9] A "comprehensive review" by the RCMP in 2005 (who were tasked with investigating themselves) found the RCMP did not engage in organized slaughter of qimmiit between 1950 and 1970.[10] The RCMP claims those qimmiit that were put down were killed for the sake of public health and safety.[11]

The slaughter of qimmiit was part of the numerous relocations experienced by Inuit between 1950 and 1970. Unsatisfied with the RCMP report, the QIA and Makivik Corporation launched the Qikiqtani Truth Commission (QTC) in 2006.[12] The QTC is Inuit-led and Inuit-sponsored, and it released its final report in 2010. The QTC report details the experiences of Inuit from the Qikiqtani (Baffin) region including relocations from *illagiit nunagivaktangat* (translated as a place used regularly or seasonally by Inuit for hunting, harvesting, and/or gather, including special places such as burial sites, or places with abundant game) to permanent settlements, the slaughter of qimmiit, and removal of Inuit children from their families for extended periods of time.[13]

The QTC report is a breathtakingly comprehensive history of the Qikiqtani region during a period of great change and settler encroachment. It incorporates Inuit testimonies and examines the way in which Inuit life was altered and impacted during the Cold War period. Most important, the entire report is rooted in an Inuit world-view, rather than being translated through an outsider's perspective.

Take, for example, this quote by Pauloosie Veevee of Pangnirtung, discussing the importance of qimmitt:

> Not all Inuit men living in traditional camps had dog teams. If an Inuk man didn't have a team of his own, it was interpreted that he was yet not quite a man…. An Inuk was judged in accordance with the dogs' performance, appearance, health and endurance… [T]his is how significantly important dogs were to Inuit.[14]

FIGURE 22.1 (pp. 194–202). "Dogs." Story and research by Hugh Goldring, art by Nicole Marie Burton (Ad Astra Comix).

Movement into permanent settlements disrupted the relationship between Inuit and qimmiit. Many qimmiit died due to disease, while others were killed because they were not allowed in the settlements, as Qallunaat (settlers) were afraid of them. Ordinances were passed that gave the RCMP the "right" to shoot loose qimmiit, and qimmiit that became sick were also killed en masse, despite the fact that Inuit knew some of the dogs would survive illnesses and provide strong stock for dog teams. According to the report:

> The killing of qimmiit has become a flash point in Inuit memories of the changes imposed on their lives by outsiders. In community after community that we visited, Inuit told me, often through tears, "I remember the day my dogs were shot," or "I remember when my father's dogs were killed." The pain still felt from these memories is a testament to the symbiotic relationship between Inuit and qimmiit, and to the fact that the loss of qimmiit was a stark challenge to their independence, self-reliance, and identity as hunters and providers for their family.[15]

Despite the way the RCMP characterized their actions as being motivated by public health and safety concerns, Inuit saw the qimmiijaqtauniq (the dog slaughter) as being a method through which Inuit were forced to remain in permanent settlements, without the possibility of returning to their traditional way of life. Thousands of dogs were slaughtered, but because the RCMP had been given authority by Canadian officials to do this, no (settler) laws were broken, and,

QIMMIT* WERE ESSENTIAL TO THE INUIT WAY OF LIFE...

...AS WELL AS BELOVED COMPANIONS.

in the eyes of Canada, no wrongs were committed. The QTC acknowledges that the qimmiijaqtauniq went on for too long to have been "the result of a secret plan or conspiracy."[16] Nonetheless, the inability or unwillingness of Canadian officials to comprehend the importance of qimmiit to Inuit culture caused great harm to Inuit communities.

The rest of the QTC report provides a thorough exploration of the stated intentions of the federal government with respect to settlement, relocation, and the removal of Inuit children for health and education reasons, along with the impact of all of these actions on Inuit people themselves.[17]

OFTEN, DOGS WERE 'DESTROYED' WHILE THEIR OWNERS WERE OUT HUNTING.—

—WITHOUT CONSULTATION, EXPLANATION, OR APOLOGY.

INUIT NOTICED THAT DOGS BELONGING TO THE POLICE OR HUDSON'S BAY COMPANY WERE RARELY SHOT.

MANY INUIT EXPERIENCED THE DOG SLAUGHTER AS A TRAUMATIC EVENT THAT DISRUPTED THEIR LIVES AND TOOK AWAY THEIR MEANS OF SUSTENANCE.

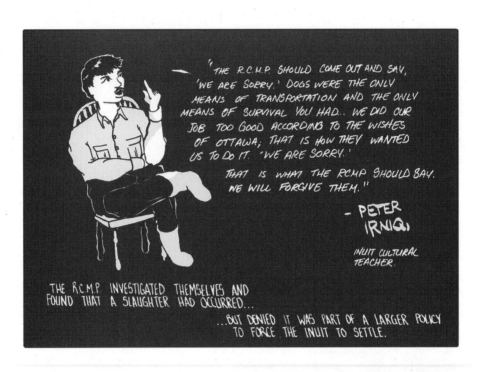

" THE R.C.M.P. SHOULD COME OUT AND SAY, 'WE ARE SORRY.' DOGS WERE THE ONLY MEANS OF TRANSPORTATION AND THE ONLY MEANS OF SURVIVAL YOU HAD.. WE DID OUR JOB TOO GOOD ACCORDING TO THE WISHES OF OTTAWA; THAT IS HOW THEY WANTED US TO DO IT. 'WE ARE SORRY.'

THAT IS WHAT THE RCMP SHOULD SAY. WE WILL FORGIVE THEM."

— PETER IRNIQ

INUIT CULTURAL TEACHER.

THE R.C.M.P. INVESTIGATED THEMSELVES AND FOUND THAT A SLAUGHTER HAD OCCURRED...

...BUT DENIED IT WAS PART OF A LARGER POLICY TO FORCE THE INUIT TO SETTLE.

SO THE INUIT IN QIKIQTAALUK SET UP THEIR OWN INQUIRY: THE QIKIQTANI TRUTH COMMISSION.

High Arctic Relocation

You may not be familiar with Nunavik; I wasn't until I moved to Quebec. I kept hearing it as Nunavut for some reason. Nunavik is an Inuit territory in the northernmost part of Quebec, home to about 11 000 Nunavimmiut.

In 1953, 87 Inuit were relocated from Inukjuak in Nunavik, to Grise Fiord (Aujuittuq) and Resolute Bay (Qausuittuq) in what is now Nunavut. Before we delve into the whys, and what happened, you need to understand the distances involved. Inukjuak sits on the 58th parallel. The families that were relocated ended up in either Resolute Bay, which is on the 74th parallel, or Grise Fiord (Ausuittuq), which is on the 76th parallel. In terms of how much farther north the Inukjuak families were, this is the equivalent of moving someone from Toronto to Whitehorse.

Three families from Pond Inlet (Mittimatalik, on the 72nd parallel) were sent to live with those from Inukjuak, ostensibly to teach them how to survive in the High Arctic.

Although the Inuit Nunangat (Inuit homelands) are all fairly northern, the differences between life in Inukjuak and life in Grise Fiord and Resolute Bay is markedly different. Inukjuak has 1333 hours of sunlight per year (compare that to 2024 hours a year in Toronto), ranging from 50 minutes of sunlight per day on average during the month of December to six and a half hours of sunlight per day in July.[18] Average temperatures are -29 degrees Celsius in December and 16 degrees Celsius in July.[19]

In contrast, Grise Fiord experiences 24 hours of darkness from October to early February, and 24 hours of sunlight from May to August! Resolute Bay has similar periods of complete darkness and 24-hour sunlight. Average temperatures are -31 degrees Celsius in January to three degrees in July.[20] All northern places are certainly *not* created equal!

It is easy, then, to imagine the despair one would experience being suddenly dropped into such a different and hostile environment. It was as unfamiliar and daunting to the Inuit of Inukjuak as it would be to families from Edmonton.

The relocation was seen as a "rehabilitation" project by the federal government, and represents the most extreme relocation experienced by Inuit. There was growing concern Inuit were becoming too reliant on welfare payments, despite being pushed to join the wage economy. The truth of the matter was that no able-bodied Inuit men in Inukjuak were the beneficiaries of government relief at the time of the High Arctic Relocation. After a bust cycle in the fur trade a few years previous, things were booming again. The cycle was related to weather and migrations, not to the presence or relocation of Inuit.[21]

Another goal of the relocation was to assert Canadian sovereignty in the High Arctic – a recurring theme between the 1950s and 1970s. Left without adequate supplies, the relocated families experienced harrowing conditions. They had been told they could return home after two years, but it wasn't until 1989 that 40 Inuit finally left Grise Fiord and Resolute Bay to return to their home communities. Others stayed behind, further fracturing kinship ties that had already been damaged by the initial relocation.

A $10 million trust fund was set up in 1996 for relocated individuals and their families, after the Royal Commission on Aboriginal Peoples released a full report on the High Arctic Relocation in 1994.[22] Families, moved in 1953, had to wait until 2010 for an apology from the federal government.[23]

Seeking saimaqatigiingniq

Saimaqatigiingniq means a new relationship when past opponents get back together, meet in the middle, and are at peace.[24] A much more nuanced term than *reconciliation*, the QTC report offers this Inuit concept as a process that could heal old wounds, create better understanding between Inuit and Qallunaat, and set a path for a healthier and more respectful relationship. Although the QTC specifically excluded the High Arctic Relocation, as it had already been addressed by RCAP, the process of saimaqatigiingniq can be as inclusive as the parties need it to be.

Unfortunately, relocation of Indigenous communities continues to be offered as a solution to a panoply of ails, everything from evacuations from natural disasters, to a cure-all for social ills. Saimaqatigiingniq cannot begin when one of the parties insists relocations are still a viable option, despite repeated experiments – all of which have had adverse impacts on Indigenous peoples. Perhaps the only way relocation will cease to be offered as a solution to the "Indian or Inuit problem" is if non-Indigenous Canadians learn about this history and recognize that abandoning a failed tactic is in the best interests of all peoples living in this country.

NOTES

1. John Duncan, "Apology of the Inuit High Arctic Relocation" (2010), last modified September 15, 2010, http://www.aadnc-aandc.gc.ca/eng/1100100016115/1100100016116. Minister of Indian Affairs, John Duncan, offered an official apology on August 18, 2010.

2. Royal Commission on Aboriginal Peoples, "Volume 1: Looking Forward, Looking Back," *Report of the Royal Commission on Aboriginal Peoples* (Ottawa: Queen's Printer, 1997), accessed November 16, 2015, http://www.collectionscanada.gc.ca/webarchives/20071124125856/ http://www.ainc-inac.gc.ca/ch/rcap/sg/sgm11_e.html. Here, you will find more on the history of some of these relocations, as well as their impacts.

3. Ibid.

4. Ibid., 415–416 (my emphasis).

5. *Re: Eskimos, 1939,* SCR 104.

6. See note 2, page 456.

7. See note 2, pages 454–466.

8. Kikkik, https://vimeo.com/18742945. In 1958, an Inuk named Kikkik was charged with murder and criminal negligence leading to the death of her child after she defended herself from the man who killed her husband, and then attempted to flee the place where she and other Inuit had been relocated to. This documentary was made by Kikkik's daughter who only learned of these events as an adult.

9. I continue using the Inuktitut word for Inuit sled dogs because the Qikiqtani Truth Commission makes a point of not using the English terms for certain things of great importance to Inuit people.

10. "Final Report: RCMP Review of Allegations Concerning Inuit Sled Dogs" (2006), accessed November 17, 2015, http://publications.gc.ca/collections/collection_2011/grc-rcmp/PS64-84-2006-eng.pdf.

11. Jim Bell, "RCMP: Dogs Killed for Health and Safety," *nunatsiaqonline.ca*, last modified December 8, 2006, http://www.nunatsiaqonline.ca/archives/61208/news/nunavut/61208_03.html.

12. Qikiqtani Truth Commission, "The Commission About Us," *qtcommission.ca,* accessed November 17, 2015, http://www.qtcommission.ca/en/about-us/the-commission.

13. Qikiqtani Truth Commission, "QTC Final Report: Achieving Saimaqatigiingniq" (Qikiqtani Inuit Association, 2010), 14, http://www.qtcommission.ca/sites/default/files/public/thematic_reports/thematic_reports_english_final_report.pdf.

14. Ibid., 38.

15. Ibid., 42.

16. Ibid., 45.

17. Sheila Watt-Cloutier, *The Right to Be Cold: One Woman's Story of Protecting Her Culture, the Arctic and the Whole Planet* (Toronto: Penguin, 2015).

18. "Sunshine and Daylight Hours in Inukjuak, Quebec, Canada," *inukjuak.climatetemps.com,* last accessed November 18, 2015, http://www.inukjuak.climatemps.com/sunlight.php.

19. "Average Weather for Inukjuak, Quebec, Canada," *weatherspark.com,* last accessed November 18, 2015, https://weatherspark.com/averages/28324/Inukjuak-Quebec-Canada.

20. Lisa Gregoire, "Grise Fiord," *Canadian Geographic Magazine,* October 2008, http://www.canadiangeographic.ca/magazine/oct08/feature_grisefiord.asp.

21. René Dussault, and George Erasmus, "The High Arctic Relocation: A Report on the 1953–55 Relocation," *Royal Commission on Aboriginal Peoples* (Toronto: Canadian Government Publishing, 1994), last accessed November 18, 2015, http://www.iqqaumavara.com/en/conclusion/. This online document highlights the conclusions of the High Arctic Relocation Report; for a summary of the Commission's conclusion see pages 135–146.

22. Ibid.

23. Melanie McGrath, *The Long Exile: A Tale of Inuit Betrayal and Survival in the High Arctic* (New York: Vintage, 2009); Zacharias Kunuk, *Exile*, directed by Zacharias Kunuk (Igloolik Isuma Productions, 2009), film, http://www.isuma.tv/isuma-productions/exile-0; Marquise Lepage, *Martha of the North* (National Film Board of Canada, 2009), https://www.nfb.ca/film/martha_of_the_north. These sources provide additional information on the High Arctic Relocation.

24. See note 12.

23
From Hunters to Farmers
Indigenous Farming on the Prairies

What do *you* know about farming among the Prairie nations?

Here's what I know. I know that after the annihilation of our main economic base, the buffalo,[1] Indigenous peoples in the Prairies were encouraged to become farmers. I know "experts" were sent by Indian Affairs to teach on-reserve populations how to farm. I know there were specific provisions in the treaties to provide the people with farming implements and seeds:

> The following articles shall be supplied... four hoes per family... two spades... one plough for every three families... one harrow... two scythes and one whetstone, and two hay forks and two reaping hooks [etc.]....
>
> For each Band, enough of wheat, barley, potatoes and oats to plant the land ... also for each Band four oxen, one bull and six cows; also, one boar and two sows, and one hand-mill....[2]

I know many people considered us "wholly unsuited to farming," believing us lazy, shiftless, and much too nomadic to prosper in such civilized pursuits. This sentiment in particular was hammered into my head and soul via a thousand comments from teachers, brief textbook descriptions, and newspaper articles that mentioned us at all. Although I believed Indigenous peoples are perfectly capable of farming (just look at the many nations that were doing this, long before settlers came along to "teach them how it's done"), I, nonetheless, half-accepted the idea that, here on the Prairies, perhaps we just weren't capable of shifting from a buffalo/trapping/fishing lifestyle to a farming lifestyle with any great ease.

Perversely, the above knowledge existed alongside my familiarity with the farming prowess of any number of Métis and First Nations families in the Treaty 6 area and beyond.[3] In fact, many Métis families pride themselves on coming from hard-working, self-sufficient, and talented farming stock, so the stories are not hard to find.[4] In addition, there is good archaeological evidence and oral history that First Nations in the Prairies were not wholly unfamiliar with farming precontact.

However, I never once read about this or any of these farming families in the textbooks, nor did I hear any "expert" admit their existence. Thus, I suppose, I felt our own understandings carried less weight. The official story supplanted my own family's history. Maybe these families were merely exceptions to the rule.

Cui bono (to whose benefit)?

An important fact that gets lost or distorted when Indigenous peoples are discussed by settler texts and educators is the issue of "to whose benefit"?

For many years, it has been asserted that virtually every government program designed and enacted by Indian Affairs was "for the benefit of the Indians." This has been the position for everything from the creation of the *Gradual Civilization Act,* to the creation of the reserve system, to the institution of residential schools. Clearly, as facts emerge and become more widely known, this official position has been altered. Officially, Canada no longer asserts that residential schooling was a positive endeavour, nor that the High Arctic Relocations were carried out in the best interests of those who endured them. Nonetheless, the belief that Canada did its best for Indigenous peoples – good intentions always at the forefront – remains deeply entrenched in the sociopolitical consciousness.

It is one thing to disbelieve this, and it is another to understand exactly to what extent "for the benefit of the Indians" is a lie. We are still taught the Numbered Treaties were signed for our benefit, to address the desperate situation so many Indigenous peoples found themselves in when the buffalo were brought to near extinction over a few decades. And if you read correspondence from First Nations leaders at that time, such as the statement of Chief Sweetgrass below, our need is absolutely evident:

> Our country is getting ruined of fur-bearing animals, hitherto our sole support, and now we are poor and want help – we want you to pity us. We want cattle, tools, agricultural implements, and assistance in everything when we come to settle – our country is no longer able to support us.
>
> Make provision for us against years of starvation. We had a great starvation the past winter, and the smallpox took away many of our people, the old, young, and children....[5]

Nonetheless, the Numbered Treaties undeniably benefited the Canadian government far more than they have ever benefited us. These treaties opened up unimaginably vast tracts of land for settlement in return for a pittance.

I do not belabour this point without reason. The question, "To whose benefit?" cannot be pushed aside or believed to be of secondary importance. Keeping this in mind, I want to turn to the push to create farmers out of the people of the Plains nations.

Lost harvests

As with so many issues facing Indigenous versus non-Indigenous peoples in this country, the level of control the government has, and had, over the lives of each must be contrasted to see a clear picture.[6]

The Prairie reserves were created in the 1870s. At that time, settlers who chose to farm had very little in the way of legislative regulation to contend with. In contrast, the *Indian Act* micromanaged reserve life to a level incomprehensible to those who have not experienced it. This micromanagement, of course, included all facets of reserve agriculture. Who benefited from this extreme control? History stands witness to the fact that it did not benefit First Nations.

What happened?

Many reserves were located in areas not suited to farming, and many grain seeds and farming implements promised to First Nations never materialized. In addition, natural phenomena such as floods and frost turned a bad situation even worse. Agriculture on the reserves took a back seat to focusing on increasing numbers of settlers flooding into the Prairies.

However, even with these impediments, farming was at first very successful in a number of First Nations communities:

> During the early 1880s ... many First Nations farmers were successful in competing in the farming economy along with the non-aboriginal farmers. Utilizing newly developed dry land farming techniques and acting as a collective, many First Nations won local prizes and awards for their crops.[7]

Stolen harvests

Despite the lack of any real effort to support reserves in implementing an agricultural lifestyle, many First Nations managed, through communal effort, to make it work. You might expect that the federal government would be pleased by this, but, instead, it went out of its way to sabotage these efforts by implementing a number of harmful policies:

- **severality** was a system of ownership in which reserve farmland was divided into 40-acre (16-hectare) plots and no one farmer could own more than 160 acres (65 hectares). The intention was to promote "individualism," directly undermining successful collective efforts. Also, any leftover land could be surrendered and made available for sale to non-Indigenous people.
- **peasant farming** was a practice in which "experts" were sent in to teach Indigenous farmers what to do. The purpose was to reduce output to subsistence levels, essentially yielding just enough to support a single family. Thus, expensive large-scale machinery would be unnecessary, and Indigenous farmers would become "more self-sufficient" by using peasant methods of production instead of the more advanced techniques they'd been using.
- **the pass and permit system** restricted the ability of First Nations peoples to leave the reserve, as well as severely curtailing their ability to sell their products or purchase farming implements. In essence, these systems ensured that Indigenous farmers could not compete with non-Indigenous farmers.[8]

The Greater Production Campaign

The early 20th century saw attention focused farther abroad as World War I broke out. At the same time, great efforts were made to first lease and then alienate reserve lands for cultivation by non-Indigenous peoples. The Greater Production Campaign was announced in 1918 at the end of the war. During this time, vast amounts of Indian lands were already being taken up and provided to settler veterans, resulting in significant erosion of Indigenous lands.[9] Indigenous veterans were denied benefits afforded to their non-Indigenous counterparts, and First Nations veterans were often left without location tickets, which would have entitled them to settle back on their home reserves.[10]

The Greater Production Campaign resulted in many amendments to the *Indian Act,* making it easier to alienate (take) lands that were not being cultivated.[11]

Can we just take a moment to think about that? The First Nations that had the least amount of success were given land unsuited to farming, or were not given the farm stock, seed, and implements promised in their treaty. When some First Nations did well despite this, an entire system was put into place to ensure their farming ability – including the methods they were able to use – would be the most ineffective and small-scale possible. After that, any lands not properly cultivated according to

Indian Affair's standards were essentially "up for grabs" because the lazy Indians just couldn't handle farming.

Oh, yes, that is bitterness in my tone.

Non-Indigenous farmers didn't care much for the Greater Production Campaign as it applied to them, and it was pretty much scrapped in 1919. It had held a mostly advisory role, anyway. On the reserves, however, Indian Affairs had absolute power via its office of the Commission for Greater Production up until 1924.

Sweeping and absolute power

In 1918, the Commissioner for Greater Production was given the power to use as much Prairie reserve land as he liked, and to spend band monies, including all the profits from decades of agricultural efforts, if he wished. The plan was threefold:

1. Lease as much reserve land as possible to non-Indigenous farmers.
2. Create government-run Greater Production farms on reserve.
3. Stimulate agricultural activity among reserve residents.[12]

No monies were expended to help individual farmers. Most of the financial focus was on the Greater Production farms. For example, a farm tractor was purchased for the Alexander reserve in Alberta, but the Commissioner for Greater Production told Alexander's Indian Agent:

> If you are under the impression that the tractor is to be used by the Indian farmers, you are quite mistaken, as this is to be run entirely separate by Mr. Laight and more as a home farm for Greater Production.[13]

All purchases desired by individual First Nations farmers came out of their own pockets or band funds and had to be approved by the Commissioner – approval that was often withheld.

Since no real effort was put into accomplishing the third goal of stimulating agricultural activity among reserve residents, it is unsurprising that it failed miserably. Some managed to find part-time work as labourers on their own reserves in the Greater Production farms. The Greater Production farms enjoyed some profits, though not princely in sum, all of which went back into Indian Affairs coffers.[14]

In addition, the lands on-reserve that were taken up for Greater Production farms were not leased to paying tenants, and that loss of potential revenue is immense. Estimates of what that rate of return would have been on a number of reserves between 1918 and 1924 are significant. For example, Blackfoot lands,

8000 acres (3200 hectares) in total, would have brought in $160,000 over four years.[15] These, and other lands, had been released for production without fee during the wartime period "as a patriotic gesture," but they continued to be used in this fashion long after the war ended.

Set up to fail

It is clear the extreme interference in First Nations agriculture in the Prairies led to conditions that made it all but impossible for Indigenous farmers to succeed and thrive. As with so many other aspects of Indigenous life in Canada, success in agriculture was met with policies that undid all those hard-won gains. When racist opinion columns allude to Indigenous laziness as a reason for current levels of poverty, these facts are never mentioned. It is doubtful the authors of such vile screeds are even aware of the history.

It is time we are all made aware of the history. It is time to put these lies to bed. I don't want another generation of Indigenous children growing up in the Prairies being told their ancestors were too lazy and stupid to survive the horrific collapse of their traditional economic base. The fact is, our peoples adapted swiftly to a set of completely new conditions, and we were damn good at it.

Our resilience and ability to adapt is constantly underestimated and glossed over. We are seen as incapable of adopting new technologies, despite the fact we have demonstrated again and again just how easily we do precisely that.

This centuries-long era of infantilization can only end when it is recognized that we were capable adults all along.

NOTES

1. My editor points out that technically, what we call buffalo are actually bison, but phrases like "Education is the new bison" simply don't sound the same, so I'm sticking with the familiar term!

2. *Treaty No. 6 between Her Majesty the Queen and the Plain and Wood Cree Indians and other Tribes of Indians at Fort Carlton, Fort Pitt and Battle River* (1876), accessed October 20, 2009, http://www.aadnc-aandc.gc.ca/eng/1100100028710/1100100028783.

3. Treaty 6 was signed on August 23, 1876, at Fort Carlton in Saskatchewan. Treaty 6 area stretches from western Alberta, into Saskatchewan and Manitoba. The Office of the Treaty Commissioner of Saskatchewan has an excellent resource on the Numbered Treaties that includes territory in Saskatchewan, as well as maps of those treaties' territories extending outside of the province.

4. Gabriel Dumont Institute, "Back to Batoche: Farm Life," last accessed November 18, 2015, http://www.virtualmuseum.ca/sgc-cms/expositions-exhibitions/batoche/docs/proof_en_metis_farmers.pdf.

5. "The Story of Treaty Six," *treaty6education.lskysd.ca,* last accessed November 18, 2015, https://treaty6education.lskysd.ca/book/export/html/4.

6. James Keith Johnson, *In Duty Bound: Men, Women, and the State in Upper Canada, 1783–1841,* vol. 227 (McGill-Queen's Press-MQUP, 2013), http://www.mqup.ca/lost-harvests-products-9780773507555.php?page_id=46.

7. Eric Tang, "Agriculture: The Relationship Between Aboriginal and Non-Aboriginal Farmers," *Western Development Museum/Saskatchewan Indian Cultural Centre Partnership Project* (2003), 5–6, http://apihtawikosisan.com/wp-content/uploads/2012/05/FNAgriculture.pdf.

8. Ibid., 5–8.

9. Sarah Carter, "'Infamous Proposal:' Prairie Indian Reserve Land and Soldier Settlement After World War I," *Manitoba History* 37 (1999): 9–21, http://www.mhs.mb.ca/docs/mb_history/37/infamousproposal.shtml.

10. Royal Commission on Aboriginal Peoples, "Volume 1: Looking Forward, Looking Back," *Report of the Royal Commission on Aboriginal Peoples* (Ottawa: Queen's Printer, 1997), http://www.collectionscanada.gc.ca/webarchives/20071211055504/http://www.ainc-inac.gc.ca/ch/rcap/sg/sg45_e.html#132.

11. Bruce Dawson, "'Better Than a Few Squirrels': The Greater Production Campaign on the First Nations Reserves of the Canadian Prairies" (master's thesis, University of Saskatchewan: 2001), http://ecommons.usask.ca/bitstream/handle/10388/etd-06052008-105240/Dawson_bruce_2001.pdf?sequence=1.

12. Ibid., 74.

13. Ibid., 77.

14. Ibid., 139.

15. Ibid., 140.

24

Dirty Water, Dirty Secrets

Drinking Water in First Nations Communities

A few years ago, a grad student in journalism at Concordia University contacted me to ask a few questions about the state of drinking water in First Nations communities. Her shock at what she had been learning reminded me, yet again, that many Canadians are totally unaware of conditions that far too many Indigenous people, particularly First Nations on-reserve, are all too familiar with.

The term *potable water* is often used when discussing various water purification initiatives in other countries. It's not a term we often use in our own homes because it is taken for granted. I think it's safe to say most Canadians would feel that access to potable water is a settled issue in this country, and every person living here has (and should have) clean drinking water. Unfortunately, such is not the case for thousands of Indigenous people. One of Canada's dirty secrets is just how bad the water situation is, and has been, for so many Indigenous communities.

While this is an issue that has predominantly affected First Nations communities up until now, the issue of access to safe water, or just access to water period, is one that has the potential to affect all communities. In 2014, more than 30 000 households in Detroit had their water supply cut off, ostensibly because of unpaid water bills.[1] The United Nation decried the situation, calling it a human-rights violation, something I think most people would agree with.[2] Bills or no bills, access to water is necessary for human life, and it should not be possible to simply deny it to anyone.

The situation is hardly unique to Detroit; early in 2015, Baltimore became the next city to see mass water shutoffs, affecting 25 000 households.[3] The cut-offs disproportionately affect Black people and non-Black people of colour, and the justifications for these shutoffs ring very hollow:

City officials...claim that residents using water without paying are to blame for the $40 million in overdue water bills. In fact... more than a third of the unpaid bills stem from just 369 businesses, who owe $15 million in revenue, while government offices and nonprofits have outstanding water bills to the tune of $10 million.[4]

This growing trend of denying a basic human need to urban households is extremely worrisome. As the People's Water Board puts it:

Water is life...We believe water is a human right and all people should have access to clean and affordable water. Water is a commons that should be held in the public trust free of privatization.[5]

tâpwê.[6]

Drinking water in Canada

Let us first take a look at the Canadian Drinking Water Guidelines put out by Health Canada:

Canadian drinking water supplies are generally of excellent quality. However, water in nature is never "pure." It picks up bits and pieces of everything it comes into contact with, including minerals, silt, vegetation, fertilizers, and agricultural run-off. While most of these substances are harmless, some may pose a health risk. To address this risk, Health Canada works with the provincial and territorial governments to develop guidelines that set out the maximum acceptable concentrations of these substances in drinking water. These drinking water guidelines are designed to protect the health of the most vulnerable members of society, such as children and the elderly.[7]

Thus, "clean" in relation to water is quantifiable. Note that while Health Canada, in its federal capacity, issues guidelines and procedural documents, the ultimate responsibility for water safety lies in the hands of the provincial and territorial governments. This, of course, makes it more difficult to get a sense of what is going on with water supplies in Canada. In addition, First Nations are a federal concern, and sometimes so are the Inuit. (The federal government has long denied responsibility for Métis, in case you were wondering.) I point these things out so you understand the following discussion is not going to be as clear, or as simple, as you may have hoped.

What is a water advisory?

According to the Health Canada, there are basically three types of water advisories:

1. **Boil Water Advisories/Orders:** Tap water should be brought to a rolling boil for at least one minute before using it for drinking or brushing teeth. This advisory is issued when there are disease-causing bacteria, viruses, or parasites in drinking-water systems.

2. **Do Not Consume Advisories/Orders:** Tap water should not be used for drinking or used for brushing teeth, cooking, washing food in, making infant formula or bathing infants/toddlers in, or for giving to pets. Adults and older children can still use it for bathing. This advisory is issued when there is a contaminant in the water that cannot be removed by boiling.

3. **Do Not Use Advisories/Orders:** Tap water should not be used for any reason. This advisory is issued when even exposure to the water could cause skin, eye, or nose irritation, and the contamination cannot be removed by boiling.[8]

The snapshot

Water advisories are not limited to First Nations. At any given time, there are upward of 1700 water advisories issued throughout Canada; a number that has not changed much since 2008.[9] That number, by the way, does not include water advisories in First Nations communities.

Water security in this country is something that should concern everyone. Nonetheless, what sets water advisories in First Nations communities apart from advisories throughout the rest of the country are severity and duration.

Health Canada reports that, as of September 30, 2015, there were 138 drinking water advisories in 94 First Nations communities.[10] This number excludes British Columbia, as Health Canada no longer reports on water advisories for First Nations in that province after turning that task over to the First Nations Health Authority in 2013. In 2012, when British Columbia was still included in these stats, 116 First Nations were under a drinking-water advisory, accounting for *nearly 20 percent of all First Nations communities.*

Between 1995 and 2007, one quarter of all water advisories in First Nations lasted longer than a year.[11] Sixty-five percent of these long-duration water advisories lasted more than two years. One of the reserves I grew up by, the Alexis Nakota Sioux First Nation, has been on a boil water advisory since 2007.

Another aspect of this problem is the fact that some First Nations do not have running water at all and, thus, are not counted when water advisories are tallied.[12] In Manitoba alone, 10 percent of First Nations have no water service. Across Canada, there are 1800 reserve homes lacking water service and 1777 homes lacking sewage service.

Since water advisories can be lifted if conditions improve even temporarily, a community can have the same water advisory in place for an extended period of time or may experience a series of advisories without the situation truly improving. Neskantaga First Nation, bordering the Ring of Fire in Northern Ontario, has been on a boil water advisory since 1995.[13]

Information is hard to come by.

In 2011, *Global News* published an interactive map showing all the water advisories in First Nations communities at that time, as well as the duration of those advisories. To create that map, *Global News* had to submit an Access to Information request. That is because, although Health Canada does keep track of water advisories that are issued throughout Canada, it does not make a list available to the public. The only way to find out if there is a water advisory in place is to track media releases or find out after the fact through Access to Information.

That would be the only way, if it weren't for Water Today, a website that tracks water advisories across the country and publishes them in an interactive map.[14] Water Today divides water advisories into four categories: do not consume, boil water, water shortage, and cyanobacteria bloom. Why we have to count on a volunteer research group to monitor this situation on a national level for us, instead of having the information consolidated on the Health Canada site, I cannot fathom.

Why is potable water out of reach for so many First Nations communities?

Hopefully, right now, you're asking yourself how this is even possible. Well, the issue has been studied intensively. In 2005, the Auditor General of Canada issued a report on drinking water in First Nations communities.[15] Basically, here's how it works:

- Indian Affairs provides the funds for designing, constructing, and maintaining water systems in First Nations.
- Health Canada helps monitor water quality (except for British Columbia, since 2013, as noted above).

- First Nations are responsible for getting the construction done and the maintenance in place.

"Aha!" you say. "So, if people still don't have clean drinking water in First Nations communities, it's because the leaders are corrupt and stole the money and didn't build anything properly!"

Well, dear reader, it's not that simple at all.

The Auditor General identified a number of problem areas:

- There are no laws and regulations governing the provision of drinking water in First Nations communities, unlike in other communities.
- The design, construction, operation, and maintenance of many water systems are still deficient.
- The technical help (including supplies like spare parts) available to First Nations to support and develop their capacity to deliver safe drinking water is fragmented.

Indian Affairs defines the construction codes and standards applicable to the design and construction of water systems in First Nations communities, and the Auditor General found these codes and standards are extremely inconsistent and the follow-up is poor. In addition, the Auditor General found water testing by Health Canada is *also* inconsistent, hampering the ability to detect problems in water quality before a crisis arises. Added to this, most of those water-treatment plant operators in First Nations are not properly trained for their position.

What has to happen?

Improving access to potable water for Indigenous peoples in Canada is going to require cooperation and commitment.

This is not a problem that can be solved with a one-pronged approach. More money has not worked, and cannot work, without addressing the regulatory gap, and ensuring capacity within the communities guarantees successful and safe operation of water-service facilities. Yet, despite a 2007 report by the Standing Senate Committee on Aboriginal Peoples saying basically the same thing, not enough progress has been made on these issues.[16] If your question is, "What needs to happen?" then let's review the Senate Committee's recommendations.

Recommendation 1:

Indian Affairs to (all in relation to the delivery of safe drinking water):

- provide a professional audit of water-system facilities and an independent-needs assessment (with First Nations representation) of:

  1. physical assets
  2. human-resource needs of individual First Nations communities

- dedicate necessary funds to provide for all identified resource needs of First Nations communities

Recommendation 2:

Indian Affairs to:

- undertake comprehensive consultation process with First Nations communities and organizations regarding legislative options with a view to developing such legislation *in collaboration*

Has any of that been done yet?

In April of 2011, Neegan Burnside provided the independent-needs assessment recommended by both the Auditor General and the Senate Committee, finally giving us a more accurate view of what the situation is and what needs exist.[17] Almost all First Nations participated in the study. Indian Affairs provided a Fact Sheet in July of 2011, laying out the summary of the report. Since people often focus on cost, here is what the report recommended:

> Having assessed the risk level of each system, the contractor identified the financial cost to meet the department's protocols for safe water and wastewater. The total estimated cost is $1.2 billion which includes, amongst other factors, the development of better management practices, improved operator training, increasing system capacity, and the construction of new infrastructure when required.
>
> The contractor also projected the cost, over 10 years, of ensuring that water and wastewater systems for First Nations are able to grow with First Nation communities. Including the aforementioned $1.2 billion to meet the department's current protocols, the contractor's projections for the cost of new servicing is $4.7 billion.[18]

Basically, we know what needs to be done, and how much it is going to cost. All we need, at this point, is the will to do it.

Problems with legislation

Bill S-11, *The Safe Water for First Nations Act*, was introduced in May of 2010. However, the much-awaited federal legislation recommended by the Auditor General and the Senate Committee met with criticism for not having been produced with actual consultation with First Nations.[19]

Bill S-11 was replaced with Bill S-8, without any substantial changes.[20] Critics of this bill pointed out that there was no funding formula included and called it a "piecemeal" approach that did not respect Aboriginal rights. The Canadian Environmental Law Association submitted a briefing note to the Senate Committee pointing out three problem areas with the proposed legislation:

1. The bill did not respect constitutionally protected Aboriginal rights.
2. There was no long-term vision for First Nations water-resource management.
3. First Nations governance structures were not being respected.[21]

A legal analysis of the bill commissioned by the Assembly of First Nations raised similar concerns, pointing out the following:

> [Bill S-8] is a legal and constitutional non-starter… [which] makes no progress towards its stated end of providing safe drinking water to First Nation communities…[and] threatens to undercut aboriginal autonomy and rights.
> [Bill S-8] shows the current government's hand-pushing for more private control, less accountability to First Nations and less responsibility to [Indian Affairs].[22]

The Ontario Native Women's Association pointed out there is still no mechanism in place to ensure that development of regulations related to water in First Nations is a joint process, rather than merely a top-down one.[23]

Nonetheless, the bill was passed into law in November of 2013.[24] No regulations were ever drafted or implemented under the Harper government, and the situation remains as dire as ever as one can tell by the stories that continue to come out of First Nations communities.[25]

This relationship has to change if things are ever going to improve.

The top-down approach reflected in this proposed legislation *has not worked*. The water crisis in First Nations communities is not some recent development, but rather a chronic problem that was caused, in great part, by the failure of the federal government to bring First Nations into this process as partners.

For years, Canada lacked a proper understanding of the scope of the problem, but that can no longer be used as an excuse. With the Neegan Burnside report, we now have the most comprehensive study ever done on the issue. We know where we need to go.

First Nations are working hard to develop a national strategy.[26] Canadians and the Canadian government need to join this process. The need is pressing, and that cannot be forgotten. All Canadians need to be aware of the severity of the problem, and I would further ask that they stand with Indigenous peoples as we ask to be consulted properly in any proposed solution.

For many years now, Indigenous women have been spearheading "water walks" to bring attention to the vital role water plays in human life.[27] In many Indigenous cultures, women are particularly tasked with the responsibility of caring for the water, and this tradition has not been forgotten. Water security is an issue everyone in this country faces, and access to clean drinking water has long been considered a basic human right. To guarantee that right, the Canadian population must become more informed on the issues and more vocal in its insistence that access to water is not sacrificed in the name of economic development. Building relationships with First Nations, Inuit, and Métis is a vital part of developing a national strategy that works for everyone.

NOTES

1. Laura Gottesdiener, "Detroit Is Ground Zero in the New Fight for Water Rights," *The Nation,* July 15, 2015, accessed December 4, 2015, http://www.thenation.com/article/detroit-is-ground-zero-in-the-new-fight-for-water-rights/.

2. "In Detroit, City-Backed Water Shut-Offs 'Contrary to Human Rights,' Say UN Expert," UN News Centre, October 20, 2014, accessed December 4, 2015, http://www.un.org/apps/news/story.asp?NewsID=49127#.VmGa2MpAEQo.

3. Carl Gibson, "This City Could Become the Next Detroit," *Think Progress,* April 4, 2015, accessed December 4, 2015, http://thinkprogress.org/economy/2015/04/04/3642935/baltimore-water-shutoffs/.

4. Ibid.

5. People's Water Board (blog), accessed December 4, 2015, http://peopleswaterboard.blogspot.ca.

6. nêhiyawêwin for: truly, this is so.

7. Health Canada, "Canadian Water Drinking Guidelines," last modified September 11, 2012, accessed December 4, 2015, http://www.hc-sc.gc.ca/ewh-semt/water-eau/drink-potab/guide/index-eng.php.

8. Health Canada, "Types of Drinking Water Advisories," last modified February 11, 2015, accessed December 4, 2015, http://www.hc-sc.gc.ca/fniah-spnia/promotion/public-publique/water-eau-eng.php#type.

9. Laura Eggertson, "Investigative Report: 1766 Boil-Water Advisories Now in Place Across Canada," *Canadian Medical Association Journal* 178, no. 10 (2008), accessed December 4, 2015, http://www.cmaj.ca/content/178/10/1261.full.

10. See note 7, http://www.hc-sc.gc.ca/fniah-spnia/promotion/public-publique/water-eau-eng.php#s2d.

11. Ibid., http://www.hc-sc.gc.ca/fniah-spnia/pubs/promotion/_environ/2009_water-qualit-eau-canada/index-eng.php#a4.1.

12. "No Running Water," *Winnipeg Free Press,* accessed December 4, 2015, http://www.winnipegfreepress.com/no-running-water/.

13. Polaris Institute with Assembly of First Nations, "Boiling Point! Six Community Profiles of the Water Crisis Facing First Nations Within Canada," May 2008, accessed December 4, 2015, https://d3n8a8pro7vhmx.cloudfront.net/polarisinstitute/pages/31/attachments/original/1411065375/Boiling_Point.pdf?1411065375. This report discusses Neskantaga and five other communities.

14. *WaterToday.ca* homepage, accessed December 8, 2015, http://www.watertoday.ca/.

15. Office of the Auditor General of Canada, "Chapter 5 – Drinking Water in First Nations Communities," *Report of the Commissioner of the Environment and Sustainable Development,* September 2005, accessed December 9, 2015, http://www.oag-bvg.gc.ca/internet/English/parl_cesd_200509_05_e_14952.html.

16. Parliament of Canada, "Safe Drinking Water for First Nations: Final Report of the Standing Senate Committee on Aboriginal Peoples," May 2007, accessed December 9, 2015, http://www.parl.gc.ca/Content/SEN/Committee/391/abor/rep/rep08jun07-e.htm.

17. Indigenous and Northern Affairs Canada (INAC), "National Assessment of First Nations Water and Wastewater Systems – National Roll-Up Report," April 2011, accessed December 9, 2015, http://www.aadnc-aandc.gc.ca/eng/1313770257504/1313770328745.

18. INAC, "Fact Sheet: The Results of the National Assessment of First Nations Water and Wastewater Systems," last modified August 19, 2011, accessed December 9, 2015, http://www.aadnc-aandc.gc.ca/eng/1313762701121/1313762778061.

19. Parliament of Canada, "Legislative Summary of Bill S-11: The Safe Drinking Water for First Nations Act," June 7, 2010, accessed December 9, 2015, http://www.parl.gc.ca/About/Parliament/LegislativeSummaries/bills_ls.asp?ls=s11&Parl=40&Ses=3&source=library_prb&Language=E.

20. Library of Parliament, "Legislative Summary: Bill S-8: The Safe Drinking Water for First Nations Act," April 19, 2012, accessed December 8, 2015, http://www.parl.gc.ca/Content/LOP/LegislativeSummaries/41/1/s8-e.pdf.

21. Canadian Environmental Law Association, "Briefing Note to the Standing Committee on Aboriginal Peoples Re: Bill S-8," June 6, 2012, accessed December 9, 2015, http://www.cela.ca/sites/cela.ca/files/846CELA_BriefingNoteBillS-8.pdf.

22. Allison Thornton, "Implications of Bill S-8 and Federal Regulation of Drinking Water in First Nations Communities," accessed December 9, 2015, http://www.afn.ca/uploads/files/parliamentary/legalanaylsis.pdf, page 7.

23. James Murray, "ONWA – Bill S-8 Fails to Address the Most Pressing Needs and Issues," *Net News Ledger,* July 16, 2012, accessed December 9, 2015, http://www.netnewsledger.com/2012/07/16/onwa-bill-s-8-fails-to-address-the-most-pressing-needs-and-issues/.

24. Accessed May 8, 2016, http://laws-lois.justice.gc.ca/eng/acts/S-1.04/index.html.

25. Joanne Levasseur, and Jacques Marcoux, "Bad Water: 'Third World' Conditions on First Nations in Canada," *cbc.ca,* October 14, 2015, accessed December 9, 2015, http://www.cbc.ca/news/canada/manitoba/bad-water-third-world-conditions-on-first-nations-in-canada-1.3269500; Gloria Galloway, "Unresolved Water Advisories Creating 'Health Emergency' for First Nations," *The Globe and Mail,* December 6, 2015, accessed December 9, 2015, http://www.theglobeandmail.com/news/national/unresolved-water-advisories-in-aboriginal-communities-creating-a-health-emergency/article27627801/; "Northern Manitoba First Nations Gather Evidence for Drinking-Water Lawsuit," *CBC News,* November 12, 2015, accessed December 9, 2015, http://www.cbc.ca/news/canada/manitoba/northern-manitoba-first-nations-gather-evidence-for-drinking-water-lawsuit-1.3315436.

26. AFN, "Honouring Water," accessed December 9, 2015, http://www.afn.ca/en/honoring-water.

27. Mother Earth Water Walk homepage, accessed December 9, 2015, http://www.motherearthwaterwalk.com/.

25

No Justice, No Peace

The Royal Commission on Aboriginal Peoples

> I believe we can do something different. *We* want to do something different. We are
> sick and tired of coming to events like this and being your conscience. Absolutely
> *sick and tired* of it. We'd love nothing more than to be able to go around and dance
> and feel good about ourselves. But, by god, we have too many real things to be
> concerned about![1]

If you've being paying attention to the voluminous endnotes, you'll have seen that I
cite the Royal Commission on Aboriginal Peoples quite frequently. There is a lot of
information contained in those five volumes, and it covers a heck of a lot of ground, so
to say I consider it a useful set of documents is a severe understatement. In fact, I am
devoting an entire chapter to why I think you ought to become more familiar with it.

What I am really trying to do with this chapter is to give you a general sense
of what is contained in the Royal Commission on Aboriginal Peoples report so you
will go and read the portions of it that interest you or that deal with questions you
have. Unfortunately, it is difficult to get a physical copy of the report, so this chapter
is heavy on the hyperlinks, which are certainly of more use in ebook versions than
in print. Nonetheless, the entire report is available online for free, and if you can't
follow the hyperlinks, I am attempting to at least get you in the general area of where
the sections I discuss can be found.

What was the Royal Commission on Aboriginal Peoples?

> Canada is a test case for a grand notion – the notion that dissimilar peoples can
> share lands, resources, power and dreams while respecting and sustaining their
> differences. The story of Canada is the story of many such peoples, trying and
> failing and trying again, to live together in peace and harmony.

But there cannot be peace or harmony unless there is justice. It was to help restore justice to the relationship between Aboriginal and non-Aboriginal people in Canada, and to propose practical solutions to stubborn problems, that the Royal Commission on Aboriginal Peoples was established.[2]

Please forgive me if I choose to quote large passages from time to time, rather than breaking it down myself. The Royal Commission on Aboriginal Peoples (RCAP – spoken aloud as "R-cap") did a fantastic job of speaking plainly, and these words have inspired me so often through the years, despite so little change in that time, that I feel it is important to share these words as they were written. Also, despite my exhortations to read the thing, I know many of you simply will not have the time or the inclination; so think of it as me drawing your attention to passages I think are particularly important.

The quote above comes from a publication that is 150 pages in length, and, in my opinion, should be mandatory reading for every single Canadian. This publication is called *Highlights from the Report of the Royal Commission on Aboriginal Peoples: People to People, Nation to Nation*.[3] If you never manage to wade through the five volumes of findings and recommendations published by RCAP, please at least make your way through the Highlights.[4]

Backing up a little, RCAP was established in 1991 and engaged in 178 days of public hearings, visiting 96 communities, commissioning research, and consulting with experts. In 1996, RCAP released a five-volume report of findings and recommendations:

> We directed our consultations to one over-riding question: *What are the foundations of a fair and honourable relationship between the Aboriginal and non-Aboriginal people of Canada?*[5]

This was the central purpose of the RCAP: to figure out what went wrong, how it went wrong, and what can be done to correct the problems identified.

Many people seem to feel lost or overwhelmed when it comes to the huge diversity of issues faced by Indigenous peoples in Canada and with the obviously dysfunctional system of relationships between Indigenous peoples and settlers. You will see this reflected in comment sections, or falling from the mouths of politicians and reporters, or yelled out in frustration over and over again whenever there is conflict between us. What you are witnessing is hopelessness. Helplessness. Confusion does this to people, and that is why I think RCAP is so incredibly powerful and important.

You see, people really do sit down and identify the problems and try to come up with solutions, and if you feel like you have no idea where to begin to address these problems, then I want you to know you have a good place to start. You don't need to reinvent the wheel here, folks. So much work has already been done to come up with practical solutions to identifiable problems, it's a damn shame most Canadians have never read a single word published by this Royal Commission. So, let's get to it, shall we?

What's the big picture here?

> Our central conclusion can be summarized simply: *The main policy direction, pursued for more than 150 years, first by colonial then by Canadian governments, has been wrong.*[6]

I know many people reading that conclusion are going to roll their eyes and say, "Well, yeah, obviously! We know that things weren't done in a fair fashion, but holy cats! Let's get over the past and live in the present already!"

Except that's not what the Commission is saying. They have not absolved current government policy or indicated that things have been fixed and now we have only historical injustices to address. Please understand this very clearly: *current government policy continues to be wrong.* RCAP was quite adamant about this when they released their final report in 1996, and not enough has changed in the 20 years since then to warrant a pat on the back for making things all better.

I recognize this is too vague for you right now, but I want you to understand it is incredibly important to simply admit this one thing. Admitting that historical and current government policy toward Indigenous peoples is wrong is no light thing. You will find strong resistance to this concept, particularly in the contemporary context. The Canadian government certainly does not accept this as true. The vast majority of Canadians probably do not accept this is true.

Before you ask the question, "Why belabour the obvious?" I want you to remember getting people to accept this premise on a wide scale is something we have yet to accomplish, and the rejection of this as truth is the number one reason we have yet to resolve our problems, people to people, nation to nation.

So, what do I need to know?

I think the first thing all Canadians need to have firmly rooted in their consciousness is that Indigenous peoples are not going away. Ever. Never, ever, ever. This, despite the fact that:

...successive governments have tried – sometimes intentionally, sometimes in ignorance – to absorb Aboriginal people into Canadian society, thus eliminating them as distinct peoples. Policies pursued over the decades have undermined – and almost erased – Aboriginal cultures and identities.

This is assimilation. It is a denial of the principles of peace, harmony and justice for which this country stands and it has failed. Aboriginal peoples remain proudly different.

Assimilation policies failed because Aboriginal people have the secret of cultural survival. They have an enduring sense of themselves as peoples with a unique heritage and the right to cultural continuity.[7]

Many Canadians are still clamouring for assimilation. Again, you can see this in all those comment sections in all of the dialogues about "how to fix the Aboriginal problem." The solutions are invariably, "Make them more like us! Private property![8] Get them out of isolated communities and into the cities with the rest of us![9] No special rights! No differences! Treat them the same!" and so on.

It's all been tried. It really has. You might not know all the history yet so perhaps you think your ideas are novel. I suggest starting with Volume 1 of the RCAP report, titled "Looking Forward, Looking Back."[10] Go ahead and skip to the sections on the *Indian Act,* residential schools, and relocation of Aboriginal communities.[11] Pretty much every suggestion currently being given to assimilate Indigenous peoples has been actively tried before with disastrous results – ultimately, a failure to assimilate us.

Stop it. It didn't work, and it isn't going to work, no matter how much cooler you think you are than the policymakers of the past. Accept the fact that we are here, and we aren't leaving, and that we recognize you aren't leaving, either. It would do us all a world of good if we could be on the same page on this one.

Where do we go from here?

After some 500 years of a relationship that has swung from partnership to domination, from mutual respect and co-operation to paternalism and attempted assimilation, Canada must now work out fair and lasting terms of coexistence with Aboriginal peoples.[12]

The truth is that the status quo isn't working. I have repeatedly talked about the need to form new relationships, but I'm not just pulling this out of thin air. This is something many people have recognized over the years as they have examined the history and the current reality of Indigenous and non-Indigenous relationships.

The Commission, quite conveniently, outlined four reasons to commit to building this new relationship:

- Canada's claim to be a fair and enlightened society depends on it.
- The life chances of Aboriginal people, which are still shamefully low, must be improved.
- Negotiations, as conducted under the current rules, have proved unequal to the task of settling grievances.
- Continued failure may well lead to violence.[13]

Don't buy that? Then, perhaps you can explain how repeating the mistakes of the past (assimilation, relocation, and so on) is a more intelligent approach? I don't know about you, but I'm definitely ready to try something different.

What did the Commission have in mind?

The first and perhaps most important element is the need to reject the principles on which the relationship has foundered over the last two centuries in particular – principles such as assimilation, control, intrusion and coercion – and do away with the remnants of the colonial era. As a beginning, we need to abandon outmoded doctrines such as terra nullius and discovery. We must reject the attitudes of racial and cultural superiority reflected in these concepts, which contributed to European nations' presumptions of sovereignty over Indigenous peoples and lands. The renewed relationship needs to be built on principles that will return us to a path of justice, co-existence and equality.[14]

I know I keep coming back to this, but it's important. The way forward needs to be guided by accepting these two related points as true:

1. The main policy direction, pursued for more than 150 years, first by colonial then by Canadian governments, has been (and continues to be) wrong.
2. We need to reject the principles on which the relationship has foundered over the last two centuries, in particular, principles such as assimilation, control, intrusion, and coercion – and do away with the remnants of the colonial era.

Until we have that firmly set in our minds, we are all going to spin our wheels, because a great many of the people coming to the table will continue to hold onto ideas that will actively sabotage any attempt to create new relationships.

But let's pretend we all agree, and move on.

Restructure the relationship? How?

Volume 2 of RCAP's final report deals with precisely this issue.[15] The Commission makes concrete suggestions about restructuring and renewing treaties, for example, to return them to living agreements rather than historical artifacts.[16] This includes changing the approach to so-called "modern" treaties that are still very much based on a model of "we talk about this once, we sign, and we never, ever discuss it again." No other kind of treaty works that way, and the Commission provides some good recommendations about how to change the process both of addressing historical treaties and approaching modern treaties.[17]

In-depth discussions and recommendations related to governance, lands and resources, and economic development can also be found in Volume 2.[18] If you are curious about any of these things, please use this resource to learn more about the issues. Again, the important thing about this report is that it does not just leave you with the problems identified (a step that is undoubtedly important), but also provides you with concrete solutions you can roll around in your head for a while to see how you feel about them.

Volume 2 is very much about building a vehicle for change.

Even if we change the relationship, how is that going to fix the problems Aboriginal communities face?

Volume 3 of RCAP is titled, "Gathering Strength."[19] It deals with many of the issues that have been raised over the past few years in the context of Attawapiskat such as housing, education, and health.[20] It also addresses family, arts and heritage, and social policy in general.[21]

Volume 3 is about how where we're going to drive that vehicle for change.

Volume 4 provides us with a diversity of Indigenous perspectives on a range of issues, providing us with historical information, current issues and needs, and recommendations for integrating these different perspectives in ways that ensure any sightseeing we do along the journey doesn't leave anyone out.[22]

What if I just want to see a roadmap for how any of this would actually work?

Volume 5 lays out a 20-year plan to implement all the recommendations of the Commission.[23] It provides the sort of cost/benefit analysis that seems to tickle some people to no end; so if that's your thing, feel free to skip straight to the nitty gritty. If you simply want to overload on practical suggestions for identified problems, mosey on over to Appendix A, which contains all 444 recommendations for change proposed by RCAP.[24]

Wait, 20-year plan? But 2016 marks the 20th anniversary of the release of RCAP; surely, we're close to implementing all these recommendations?

Ahahahahahahhaaa.......ha. No. Sadly, we have seen precious little improvement in 20 years.

The Assembly of First Nations released a Report Card 10 years after RCAP, detailing the dismal implementation record to date:[25]

> This summary analysis points to a clear lack of action on the key foundational recommendations of RCAP and a resultant lack of progress on key socio-economic indicators. *Based on our assessment, Canada has failed in terms of its action to date.*[26]

I also attended a conference in 2006 that basically discussed "Life After RCAP," which was pretty disheartening. That conference provided some very interesting information on what impact RCAP has had – even absent full implementation. So, if you want a quick discussion on the pros and cons of how the Commission went about fulfilling its mandate, and on how the report has been received nonofficially in the courts, and so on, please take a gander![27] In particular, I suggest reading the summary of Alan C. Cairn's breakdown of some of the inherent problems with the Commission's approach to nationhood. RCAP was not without its flaws.

Why hasn't there been more progress?

Aaaaand this is why I take you back to those points I kept hammering away at earlier. You know, these ones:

- The main policy direction, pursued for more than 150 years, first by colonial then by Canadian governments, has been (and continues to be) wrong.
- We need to reject the principles on which the relationship has foundered over the last two centuries – in particular, principles such as assimilation, control, intrusion, and coercion – and do away with the remnants of the colonial era.

It is my firm belief that Canada has not yet accepted these two points as true; because of this, there has been little in the way of progress.

You don't value these points if you actually believe Indigenous cultures are inferior, and you sure as heck aren't going to take them seriously. If you don't understand the history of relations between Indigenous peoples and settlers, then you aren't going to believe that current conditions faced by Indigenous peoples aren't self-imposed. If you know nothing about Indigenous governance and think *Indian Act* governance is "traditional," then you probably aren't going to have much faith in Indigenous self-government. If you don't know what has been attempted before (assimilation, relocation, and so on) then you're going to think you're coming up with something really radical when you suggest similar things in the current context.

This country is woefully ignorant on a grand scale, and we will never succeed in rebuilding relationships until we address that ignorance. I can't stress this enough: without education, there can be no justice, and until there is justice, there will be no peace.

My purpose here was to introduce people to RCAP, both as a starting point for further investigation into the many issues faced by Indigenous peoples in Canada, and also as proof positive that practical solutions have been suggested. That latter part is important because people need to stop believing there is no other way out besides just assimilating us once and for all. It might seem so much simpler to just legislate us out of existence – make us all "the same" to satisfy liberal notions of equality – but it won't actually *solve* anything. RCAP is a good place to start if you want to know why such attempts are doomed to fail, and what alternatives have been proposed.

NOTES

1. Peter Gzowski, and Georges Erasmus, *Nothing for First Nations to celebrate, says Georges Erasmus,* radio, CBC Morningside, Oct. 16, 1989, 8:34, accessed Dec. 3, 2015, http://www.cbc.ca/archives/entry/georges-erasmus-nothing-to-celebrate.

    This speech was given in 1989 to a committee planning celebrations for Canada's 125th birthday (which was in 1992) by Georges Erasmus, former National Chief of the Assembly of First Nations, and later, co-chair to the Royal Commission on Aboriginal Peoples. This speech is something you really should listen to in full, as, unfortunately, it is as relevant today as it was then. It is available at the link above, along with more resources about Georges Erasmus.

    A transcript of this speech, along with many other fantastic written pieces, is included in another invaluable learning/teaching resource: Shelagh Rogers, et al., eds., *Reconciliation and the Way Forward: Collected Essays and Personal Reflections* (Winnipeg: Aboriginal Healing Foundation, 2014), 37–41, http://www.legacyofhope.ca/downloads/reconciliation-and-the-way-forward-pdf-full.pdf.

2. Paul L. Chartrand, et al., "A Word From Commissioners," *Highlights From the Report of the Royal Commission on Aboriginal Peoples: People to People, Nation to Nation* (Ottawa, 1996), http://www.aadnc-aandc.gc.ca/eng/1100100014597/1100100014637#chp2, p.ix.

3. Ibid.

4. Institute on Governance, *Summary of the Final Report of The Royal Commission on Aboriginal Peoples* (Ottawa, April 1997), http://iog.ca/wp-content/uploads/2012/12/1997_April_rcapsum. pdf. If you want to work with something even less dense, this 51-page document summarizes the report and its main recommendations, including financial estimates for implementation of these recommendations.

5. See note 2, page 10 (my emphasis).

6. Ibid. (my emphasis).

7. Ibid. (my emphasis).

8. Tom Flanagan, Christopher Alcantara, and Andre Le Dressay, *Beyond the Indian Act: Restoring Aboriginal Property Rights* (Montreal: McGill-Queen's University Press, 2010).

9. Joseph Quesnel, *Respecting the Seventh Generation: A Voluntary Plan for Relocating Non-viable Native Reserves* (Frontier Centre for Public Policy, 2010).

10. Royal Commission on Aboriginal Peoples (RCAP), "Volume 1: Looking Forward, Looking Back," *Report of the Royal Commission on Aboriginal Peoples* (Ottawa: Queen's Printer, 1997), http://www.collectionscanada.gc.ca/webarchives/20071124125216/http://www.ainc-inac.gc.ca/ch/rcap/sg/sg1_e.html#0.

11. RCAP, "Chapter 9: The Indian Act," *Report of the Royal Commission on Aboriginal Peoples*, vol. 1, part 2, last modified February 8, 2006, http://www.collectionscanada. gc.ca/webarchives/20071124124337/http://www.ainc-inac.gc.ca/ch/rcap/sg/sgm9_e.html; RCAP, "Chapter 10: Residential Schools," *Report of the Royal Commission on Aboriginal Peoples*, vol. 1, part 2, last modified February 8, 2006, http://www.collectionscanada.gc.ca/webarchives/20071124130216/http://www.ainc-inac.gc.ca/ch/rcap/sg/sgm10_e.html; RCAP, "Chapter 11: Relocation of Aboriginal Communities," *Report of the Royal Commission on Aboriginal Peoples*, vol. 1, part 2, last modified February 8, 2006, http://www.collectionscanada.gc.ca/webarchives/20071124125856/http://www.ainc-inac.gc.ca/ch/rcap/sg/sgm11_e.html.

12. RCAP, "Volume 1: Looking Forward, Looking Back," 1.

13. See note 2, page 1.

14. RCAP, "Chapter 14: The Turning Point," vol. 1, part 3, 609.

15. RCAP, "Volume 2: Restructuring the Relationship," http://www.collectionscanada.gc.ca/webarchives/20071124125001/http://www.ainc-inac.gc.ca/ch/rcap/sg/sh1_e.html#Volume%202.

16. RCAP, "Chapter 1: Introduction," vol. 2, last modified February 8, 2006, http://www.collectionscanada.gc.ca/webarchives/20071211052559/http://www.ainc-inac.gc.ca/ch/rcap/sg/sh2_e.html#1%20Introduction.

17. RCAP, "Appendix A: Summary of the Recommendations in Volume 2, Parts One and Two," vol. 2, last modified February 8, 2006, http://www.collectionscanada.gc.ca/webarchives/20071124130607/http://www.ainc-inac.gc.ca/ch/rcap/sg/sha6a_e.html.

18. RCAP, "3: Governance," vol. 2, part 1, last modified February 8, 2006, http://www.collectionscanada.gc.ca/webarchives/20071124130703/http://www.ainc-inac.gc.ca/ch/rcap/sg/shm3_e.html; RCAP, "4: Lands and Resources," vol. 2, part 1, last modified February 8, 2006, http://www.collectionscanada.gc.ca/webarchives/20071124125812/http://www.ainc-inac.gc.ca/ch/rcap/sg/shm4_e.html; RCAP, "5: Economic Development," vol. 2, part 1, last modified

February 8, 2006, http://www.collectionscanada.gc.ca/webarchives/20071124130434/
http://www.ainc-inac.gc.ca/ch/rcap/sg/shm5_e.html.

19. RCAP, "Volume 3: Gathering Strength," http://www.collectionscanada.gc.ca/
webarchives/20071124060708/http://www.ainc-inac.gc.ca/ch/rcap/sg/si1_e.html#Volume%203.

20. RCAP, "4: Housing," vol. 3, last modified February 8, 2006, http://www.collectionscanada.
gc.ca/webarchives/20071124125633/http://www.ainc-inac.gc.ca/ch/rcap/sg/sim4_e.html;
RCAP, "5: Education," vol. 3, http://www.collectionscanada.gc.ca/webarchives/20071124125456/
http://www.ainc-inac.gc.ca/ch/rcap/sg/sim5_e.html; RCAP, "3: Health and Healing," vol. 3,
http://www.collectionscanada.gc.ca/webarchives/20071124034445/http://www.ainc-inac.gc.ca/
ch/rcap/sg/sim3_e.html.

21. RCAP, "2: The Family," vol. 3, http://www.collectionscanada.gc.ca/webarchives/
20071124125546/http://www.ainc-inac.gc.ca/ch/rcap/sg/sim2_e.html; RCAP, "6: Arts and
Heritage," vol. 3, http://www.collectionscanada.gc.ca/webarchives/20071124130346/http://
www.ainc-inac.gc.ca/ch/rcap/sg/sim6_e.html; RCAP, "1: New Directions in Social Policy,"
vol. 3, http://www.collectionscanada.gc.ca/webarchives/20071124124438/http://www.ainc-inac.
gc.ca/ch/rcap/sg/sim1_e.html.

22. RCAP, "Volume 4: Perspectives and Realities," http://www.collectionscanada.gc.ca/
webarchives/20071124125120/http://www.ainc-inac.gc.ca/ch/rcap/sg/sj1_e.html#
Perspectives%20and%20Realities.

23. RCAP, "Volume 5: Renewal: A Twenty-Year Commitment," http://www.collectionscanada.
gc.ca/webarchives/20071124125120/http://www.ainc-inac.gc.ca/ch/rcap/sg/sj1_e.
html#Perspectives%20and%20Realities.

24. RCAP, "Appendix A: Summary of Recommendations Volumes 1–5," http://www.collectionscanada.
gc.ca/webarchives/20071124130154/http://www.ainc-inac.gc.ca/ch/rcap/sg/ska5a1_e.
html#Appendix%20A:%20Summary%20of%20Recommendations,%20Volumes%201-5.

25. AFN, *Royal Commission on Aboriginal People at 10 Years: A Report Card* (Ottawa: Assembly
of First Nations, 2007), accessed December 3, 2015, http://www.turtleisland.org/resources/
afnrcap2006.pdf.

26. Ibid., 2 (original emphasis).

27. Indigenous Bar Association, "Making Aboriginal Policy: A Conference Ten Years After the
Final Report of the Royal Commission on Aboriginal Peoples," http://www.indigenousbar.
ca/pdf/2006%20IBA%20Final%20Conference%20Report.pdf; Robert K. Groves, "The Curious
Instance of the Irregular Band: A Case Study of Canada's Missing Recognition Policy,"
Saskatchewan Law Review 70 (2007): 153–459.

PART 5

Land, Learning, Law, and Treaties

26

Rights? What Rights?
Doctrines of Colonialism

You know what? I've changed my mind. Despite everything I've been saying so far, I've come to realize all of that is in the past, and it's time to move on. In fact, I want to *decimate* the past!

My whole life I have been told Indigenous peoples were conquered, defeated, never had rights, and I suppose this truth took until right this second to finally sink in! For all those people who endlessly repeat this refrain of Indigenous failure and obsolescence, don't give up; I am living proof that if you say it for long enough, it will be the only truth we need.[1]

I have spent so long on the other side of this debate that I think I have some really great arguments to lend to the cause.[2] People who argue in favour of Indigenous rights tend to rehash the same points over and over, and I am here to provide you with ironclad refutations of these ridiculous rights-based claims. Once you have finished reading this chapter, you will leave with all the ammunition you need to soldier on during those frustrating forum wars and comment section skirmishes.

Claim #1: The Doctrine of Discovery and Doctrine of Occupation (*terra nullius*) are invalid justifications for gaining sovereignty over Indigenous lands.

It would seem like common sense that discovering a nation inhabited only by Indigenous peoples would entitle Europeans to take over and assert their own sovereignty, but some Indigenous peoples and bleeding-heart settler academics contest this.[3] Quick! You need to defend the Doctrine of Discovery!

The Doctrine of Discovery is rooted in two 15th-century papal bulls called the *Dum Diversas* (1452) and the *Romanus Pontifex* (1455).[4]

The *Dum Diversas* gave Christians the right to take "pagans" (non-Christians) as perpetual slaves. This gem led directly to the transatlantic slave trade. So, if someone brings up this unsavoury history, remind them of the *Sublimes Deus* (1537), which later forbade the enslavement of Indigenous peoples of the Americas! Plenty of colonizers and conquistadors continued enslaving people from the Americas – and it was still totally legal to enslave Africans – but if no one else brings this up, you might want to consider moving on to the next papal bull.

The *Romanus Pontifex* clearly explained that since there were many people (heathens) around the world who weren't really using the land they were on, Europeans had every right to take that land and do something with it![5] Unfortunately, this papal bull also extolls the legitimacy of the enslavement of non-Christians, but since most people will not be carrying around a complete text of the *Romanus Pontifex*, it probably won't be pointed out. Besides, the *heart* of this papal bull is what matters. Judge John Catron summed it up well in *State v. Foreman,* 16 Tenn. 256 (1835). I suggest whipping this baby out when Indigenous radicals question the Doctrine of Discovery:

> We maintain, that the principle declared in the fifteenth century as the law of Christendom, that discovery gave title to assume sovereignty over, and to govern the unconverted natives of Africa, Asia, and North and South America, has been recognized as a part of the national law [Law of Nations], for nearly four centuries, and that it is now so recognized by every Christian power, in its political department and its judicial.[6]

We're talking about a very old tradition, more than 500 years old. Indigenous peoples like to talk about how our traditions are super ancient and, therefore, more important than European traditions, but come on. The Doctrine of Discovery goes way back and is still an important part of international law.[7] Besides, if Indigenous peoples didn't agree with the papal bull, we could have petitioned the pope to change it or something.[8] I'm pretty sure that by not opposing it *before* the Europeans arrived, we agreed to it. After all, ignorance of the law is no excuse!

All right, we've got the Doctrine of Discovery sewn up; let's move on!

The Doctrine of Occupation relies on a concept known as *terra nullius,* which is a Latin term that basically means "land that belongs to no one." The Doctrine of Discovery doesn't need much support beyond its obvious rightness, but *terra nullius* does help to clarify the point a little. Despite claims to the contrary, Indigenous peoples didn't believe in land ownership! Some of the refutations of the fact that Indigenous peoples never believed in owning property and, therefore, Europeans weren't stealing anything, can be found in such ridiculous decisions as *Calder* and *Delgamuukw*.[9] Be careful; Indigenous radicals love to play the "Supreme Court of Canada Agrees With Us" card. Also, some settler intellectuals and Indigenous radicals make far-out claims about Indigenous people having legal traditions that included some form of ownership of lands – but it doesn't count because it isn't a European property regime, so don't worry about it too much.[10]

Australia messed things up a lot when a bunch of liberal judges caved and said that okay, sure, Indigenous people didn't have European systems of land ownership, but this didn't mean settlers could waltz in and claim the land was unoccupied or unowned by anyone[11] – ridiculous and clearly wrong. Sounds like that Canadian *Calder* decision back in 1973: "[T]he fact is that when the settlers came, the Indians were there, organized in societies and occupying the land as their forefathers had done for centuries. This is what Indian title means."

This is the kind of thinking you're up against. But never fear! I have some really great suggestions for how you can at least get away from the radicals if they belligerently disrespect the "we've been doing this for over 500 years" argument, or they want to point to Supreme Court decisions that sort of reject the Doctrine of Discovery and the Doctrine of Occupation (via *terra nullius*):

- You should pedantically point out that the term *terra nullius* is of recent (early 20th century) origin, and, therefore, isn't even a thing you can argue against.[12] You'll have the radicals wondering whether any part of their argument is true if they got that one wrong! I suggest just dropping that bomb and walking away. Or, you may have to face the fact that, before this term became popular, international law used *res nullius* which is basically the same thing.[13] *Res nullius* is a concept based in Aristotelian notions of the need to exploit nature in order to exercise ownership over it. Failure to do so voids your ownership.
- If anyone brings up *res nullius*, merely say that *terra nullius* is a synecdoche.[14] This will confuse most people enough that they'll shut up about it. Of course, this just means international law has come to apply *res nullius* to land, but no one needs to know that. Using an obscure word most folks haven't seen since their last high-school poetry class will often buy you enough time to get out of Dodge before things get ugly.

Most important, don't let it bother you too much. The obvious fact that landing on the shores of this country gave Europeans the inherent right to claim the land for their own is still supported in domestic and even international law, at least to the extent that no one is seriously challenging underlying Crown sovereignty.[15] Well,

I mean many of us Indigenous people are, but you know what I mean. When the radicals argue this should change, I suggest merely saying, "neener neener" from a distance.

Claim #2: The Doctrine of Conquest is discredited and does not apply.

Another obvious fact is that when you conquer someone, you get their stuff. It happens all over the world and is an acceptable result of losing a battle. Everyone has been conquered at *some* point by someone else.[16] The Doctrine of Conquest states that whoever wins a war gets to claim sovereignty over the territory of the conquered. This was a recognized principle in international law until it sort of fell out of favour in the early 20th century with things like the Covenant of the League of Nations, the Kellogg-Briand Pact, the Stimson Doctrine, the United Nations Charter, and so on.[17]

Some people will argue that Europeans didn't exactly approach what is now Canada and the United States as conquerors, as evinced by things like treaties that were made with various Indigenous nations. Still, smallpox killed many more Indigenous people than settlers and so it was sort of like conquering us, right?[18] After all, if you were originally 100 percent of the population and now you're only about 4 percent, then clearly you've lost something. Besides, people are so eager to remind Indigenous peoples that we were conquered – it surely must be true in some way!

Whatever. The point isn't whether or not we were *actually* conquered. This Doctrine still totally applies and explains why Indigenous peoples lost sovereignty over these lands, and the Europeans gained it!

There are all sorts of obnoxious rejections of such principles that affirm a relationship based on treaty versus conquerors and conquered, but those only started in earnest in the 20th century, and Europeans conquered (okay, not really, but kind of) Indigenous peoples way before that.

Check and mate! If people want to reject the Doctrine of Discovery or *terra nullius,* just hit them with the fact that the Europeans "won." If anyone asks for more details, it's probably time to make your exit.

Claim #3: Other stuff about how Indigenous peoples still have rights

If you find yourself in a situation where, for whatever reason, you have not been able to successfully argue the Doctrine of Discovery, Conquest, or Occupation, fear not!

There are other Doctrines you can yank out of your back pocket like a linty caramel of Truth!

It's a pretty well-recognized principle that if you walk into someone's house and refuse to leave – living there for many years – eventually, the house is yours. Right? Exactly. This gem is called the Doctrine of Adverse Possession.[19] It requires that you live in someone else's territory for an extended period of time, and you exercise peaceful and unchallenged sovereignty over that territory.

Take Manitoba, for example. The Selkirk Settlement was established in 1811 after the Hudson's Bay Company (HBC) granted the Earl of Selkirk a concession of 300 000 square kilometres. Okay, so the HBC acknowledged Indigenous sovereignty and didn't interfere with it much because they didn't want to mess up their fur-trading business, but Selkirk definitely wanted this to be his land. Unfortunately, Selkirk's governor, Miles Macdonell, set off something called the Pemmican War, which culminated in the Battle of Seven Oaks, wherein a Métis leader, Cuthbert Grant, led a party against the governor of HBC territories, killing him and 19 of his men.[20]

Um, that might not be the best example. You can probably find *some* area in Canada that settlers lived on for a long time, over which they exercised peaceful and unchallenged sovereignty. None comes to mind, but don't let that get you down!

When all else fails, you can blurt out, "the Doctrine of Cession!" and then bask in the glow of knowing you have played your trump card, and things are well once again. Cession is the formal giving up of rights, property, or territory. This Doctrine refers to the voluntary surrender of Indigenous lands in exchange for things like five dollars a year per person in compensation in perpetuity.[21] The best thing about this Doctrine is that it is completely supported by Canadian law as the basis for sovereignty over lands covered by the Numbered Treaties 1 through 11.[22] According to Indian Affairs:

> At their base, the treaties were land surrenders on a huge scale. A total of 11 Numbered Treaties were negotiated during this period culminating with Treaty 11 in 1921. Furthermore, in the eyes of the Federal Government, the act of signing treaty brought Aboriginal people of the Northwest under the jurisdiction of the Dominion of Canada and its laws.[23]

There are hundreds of thousands of square kilometres in Canada that are not covered by these land-surrender treaties (almost all of British Columbia, for example), but why worry about that? You can circle back to laying claim to them via aforementioned Doctrines if you need to, regardless of whether or not those Doctrines have been discarded as invalid earlier on in your conversation.

You will encounter people who argue the Numbered Treaties were not land-surrender treaties, but rather were land-sharing agreements. They will say things like this:

- "The land, waters, and all life-giving forces in North America were, and are, an integral part of a sacred relationship with the Creator. The land and water could never be sold or given away by their Nations."[24]
- "With respect to land-sharing arrangements, the Elders' understanding was that the initial treaty discussions focused solely on the agricultural land requirements of the Crown, which would be used by her British subjects."[25]
- The Commissioner had said, "It is not all your land I am interested in, only the places where my people will be coming on those lands down to the depth of a plough – that is what I am asking for."[26]

These versions of the Numbered Treaties are said to be truer to the actual negotiations than what ended up written on paper, but the law is pretty clear that oral history of Indigenous peoples on this is trumped by the written word of settlers; so, what's the point of even entertaining these understandings? Why bother trying to come to some sort of agreement that respects Indigenous sovereignty when you can just take it all and benefit from all the lands and resources without ever having to share with the original inhabitants?

Anyway, that basically covers the different justifications and explanations for Canadian sovereignty over Indigenous lands in Canada, and why Indigenous peoples basically have no rights. I hope this has been a helpful tool for those of you interested in vigorously denying Indigenous rights any way you possibly can![27]

NOTES

1. Shout out to Conrad Black, Thomas Flanagan, Jonathan Kay, Christie Blatchford, Margaret Wente, and every other fellow Canadian Warrior for Justice Against the Hegemony of Indigenous Tyranny.
2. The cause is clearly the complete and total assimilation of Indigenous peoples into mainstream society, once and for all!
3. Careful! When you appeal to common sense, some people will attempt to point out you are committing the logical fallacy known as an "appeal to popularity." This logical fallacy suggests that an idea must be true because it is widely held. The appeal to popularity logical fallacy goes something like this example: (1) Most people believe in some form of a God or higher power; therefore, (2) God, or a higher power, must exist. The idea is that popular opinion can be mistaken, though we know that can only be true if popular opinion believes in things like respecting treaty rights or allowing Aboriginal title to be a thing.

4. This is a document issued by the pope or his offices. Documents issued by the pope had different names for many centuries, but they are all retroactively known as *papal bulls* now. They could range from excommunications, canonization, or declarations about the legitimacy of European global hegemony.

5. The Bull *Romanus Pontifex* (Nicholas V), January 8, 1455, last accessed November 19, 2015, http://www.nativeweb.org/pages/legal/indig-romanus-pontifex.html. Here, you can read the text of this irrefutable piece of evidence that Indigenous peoples have no claim to any lands whatsoever.

6. William Wilcox Cooke, *Reports of Cases Argued and Determined in the Supreme Court of Tennessee*, vol. 40 (Soule, Thomas, and Winsor, 1879), 256, http://tinyurl.com/qc866t2.

7. United Nations, "'Doctrine of Discovery,' Used for Centuries to Justify Seizure of Indigenous Land, Subjugate Peoples, Must Be Repudiated by United Nations, Permanent Forum Told," *un.org*, last modified May 8, 2012, http://www.un.org/press/en/2012/hr5088.doc.htm.

8. Julian Brave NoiseCat, "Indigenous Leaders Want Pope Francis to Rescind Bull Justifying Imperialism," *Huffington Post*, last modified September 27, 2015, http://www.huffingtonpost.com/entry/pope-francis-doctrine-of-discovery_56058eb9e4b0dd8503076c17.

9. *Calder et al. v. Attorney-General of British Columbia, 1973*, [1973] SCR 313, CanLII 4 (SCC), https://www.canlii.org/en/ca/scc/doc/1973/1973canlii4/1973canlii4.html; *Delgamuukw v. British Columbia, 1997*, [1997] 3 SCR 1010, http://scc-csc.lexum.com/scc-csc/scc-csc/en/item/1569/index.do.

10. Eric Dannenmaier, "Beyond Indigenous Property Rights: Exploring the Emergence of a Distinctive Connection Doctrine." *Washington University Law Review* 86 (2008): 53, http://openscholarship.wustl.edu/cgi/viewcontent.cgi?article=1114&context=law_lawreview; Val Napoleon, "Ayook: Gitksan Legal Order, Law, and Legal Theory" (PhD dissertation, University of Victoria, 2009), https://dspace.library.uvic.ca:8443/bitstream/handle/1828/1392/napoleon%20dissertation%20April%2026-09.pdf?sequence=1. Know your enemy! Here are some arguments about Indigenous property regimes and their supposed legitimacy.

11. *Mabo and Others v. Queensland* (No. 2), 1992, [1992] HCA 23; 175 CLR 1, http://www.austlii.edu.au/au/cases/cth/HCA/1992/23.html; ABC TV, *Mabo*, TV movie, produced by Blackfella Films, June 10, 2012, http://www.abc.net.au/tv/mabo/movie/. The first source is a case that found *terra nullius* does not apply to Australia. To learn more about the unfortunate events that led to undermining such an obviously true doctrine, you can watch a film (second source) about the man who brought this case to the Australian High Court.

12. Michael Connor, *The Invention of Terra Nullius: Historical and Legal Fictions on the Foundations of Australia* (Sydney: Macleay Press, 2005). Henry Reynolds attempted to refute this wonderful book in a hit piece (accessed November 18, 2015), https://www.themonthly.com.au/books-henry-reynolds-new-historical-landscape-responce-michael-connor039s-039the-invention-terra-nul.

13. Michael Duffy, "Terra Nullius – The History Wars," Interview with Andrew Fitzmaurice, Christopher Pearson, and Henry Reynolds, *Counterpoint*, ABC Radio National, August 16, 2004, http://www.abc.net.au/radionational/programs/counterpoint/terra-nullius-the-history-wars/3416432#transcript.

14. A figure of speech in which a part is used for the whole or the whole for a part, or vice versa – like how *wheels* means a vehicle.

15. Tonya Frishner, "Impact on Indigenous Peoples of the International Legal Construct Known as the Doctrine of Discovery, Which Has Served as the Foundation of the Violation of Their Human Rights," in *Preliminary Study Reported at the Ninth United Nations Permanent Forum on Indigenous Issues* (New York, 2010), 30–37, http://tinyurl.com/or9hvtg. (File opens as a document.)

16. Even though this is clearly true, saying this sometimes causes people to accuse you of using the *Tu Quoque* logical fallacy. This fallacy is committed when one assumes that just because someone else has done a thing, there is nothing wrong with doing that thing.

17. Sharon Korman, *The Right of Conquest: The Acquisition of Territory by Force in International Law and Practice* (Oxford: Clarendon Press, 1996). Korman offers a thorough discussion on how the Doctrine of Conquest has worked over the centuries.

18. Stuart C. Houston, and Stan Houston, "The First Smallpox Epidemic on the Canadian Plains: In the Fur-Traders' Words," *The Canadian Journal of Infectious Diseases* 11, no. 2 (2000): 112, http://www.ncbi.nlm.nih.gov/pmc/articles/PMC2094753/.

19. Lloyd Duhaime, "Adverse Possession – James Cooper in The Prairie Tale, 1827," http://www.duhaime.org/LegalResources/RealEstateTenancy/LawArticle-69/Adverse-Possession.aspx.

20. Chris Andersen, *Métis: Race, Recognition, and the Struggle for Indigenous Peoplehood* (Vancouver: UBC Press, 2014), 111–112.

21. Erik Anderson, "The Treaty Annuity as Livelihood Assistance and Relationship Renewal," *A History of Treaties and Policies,* volume 7, Aboriginal Policy Research series (Thomson Educational Publishing, 2010), 73, http://apr.thompsonbooks.com/vols/APR_Vol_7Ch5.pdf. Treaty annuities as carrot stick and current payments not indexed to inflation are examined in this piece. Other than in parts of Treaty 9 territory, where the annuity is four dollars, treaty payments are five dollars per person, per year.

22. *Grassy Narrows First Nation v. Ontario (Natural Resources), 2014,* [2014] SCC 48, accessed November 22, 2015, http://scc-csc.lexum.com/scc-csc/scc-csc/en/item/14274/index.do. In this case, knows as Keewatin, the Supreme Court affirmed the following: "In 1873, Treaty 3 was signed by treaty commissioners acting on behalf of the Dominion of Canada and Ojibway Chiefs from what is now Northwestern Ontario and Eastern Manitoba. The Ojibway yielded ownership of their territory, except for certain lands reserved to them."

23. Indigenous and Northern Affairs Canada (INAC), "The Numbered Treaties (1871–1921)," last modified June 4, 2013, https://www.aadnc-aandc.gc.ca/eng/1360948213124/1360948312708.

24. Harold Cardinal, and Walter Hildebrandt, *Treaty Elders of Saskatchewan: Our Dream Is That Our Peoples Will One Day Be Clearly Recognized as Nations* (Calgary: University of Calgary Press, 2000), 10.

25. Ibid., 66.

26. Ibid., 36.

27. Hopefully, it is clear this is satire – if not, my apologies. Failed satire merely replicates the offensive beliefs it is trying to mock, and that's what makes satire a bit dodgy to engage in. Nonetheless, all of the arguments I "champion" in this chapter are ones that I have actually seen people engage in, many times over. It is my hope that if folks are a bit more familiar with some of the terms and arguments in use, it will be easier to refute them. Forewarned, and forearmed, and all that.

27

Treaty Talk
The Evolution of Treaty-Making in Canada

I was at a Niigaan: In Conversation event in Ottawa a few years back, on a panel with John Borrows,[1] Shiri Pasternak,[2] and Ed Bianchi.[3] I name drop them so you can access some of the resources they have created or helped to create. Also, they're awesome people.

Anyway, we wanted to have a discussion on treaty responsibilities beyond basic 101 discussions, and it went fairly well. At the end of our panel discussion, however, a man stood up and said we had failed to reach him because he did not know what Peace and Friendship Treaties are, or the difference between those treaties and the Numbered Treaties. Basic ABCs, as he put it. He asked us to spoonfeed him and others like him. Otherwise, discussions attempting to move us forward were simply not going to work.[4]

As I pointed out in the Introduction, this entire book is meant to provide the basic 101 information people need in order to begin moving relationships forward between Indigenous and non-Indigenous people. This section of the book, specifically, is an attempt to provide people with information about the various doctrines used to justify Canadian sovereignty, as well as the kinds of treaty relationships that exist in Canada. Hopefully, the fellow who spoke up after our panel those years ago will pick up this book, like it, and recommend it to his friends.

So, let's go back in time a little.

Early treaty-making in Canada

For some time in our early relationship, Europeans dealt with Indigenous peoples on a fairly equal basis.[5] This was, of course, during a period when European numbers were low in comparison to the Indigenous population, and at a time when Europeans desperately needed help to survive these climes. Indigenous peoples were self-governing nations and had been for thousands of years.[6]

The links between Aboriginal and non-Aboriginal societies in this initial period of contact were primarily commercial and only secondarily political and military [in nature]....

They [Europeans] did not interfere in a major way with long-standing Aboriginal patterns of pursuing their livelihood and actually tended to build on Aboriginal strengths – hunting, fishing, trapping, trading, canoeing or transportation – rather than undermine them.[7]

Later on, colonial powers expanded these relationships as they sought allies among Indigenous peoples as a way of surviving the military aggression of their fellow Europeans. Treaty-making during this pre-Confederation period focused on these specific needs and were not about land so much as they were about securing military and economic aid from the eastern First Nations.

Growing up in the west, I knew very little of these kinds of treaties. My relations live mostly in Treaty 6 and Treaty 8 territory, so my understanding of treaties was very coloured by that context. The idea of treaties not being about taking land and shoving Indigenous peoples onto successfully smaller and crappier pieces of land was just something I hadn't considered as being possible.

When the wholesale acquisition of land does not even truly enter the equation via treaty, it is much more difficult to claim the original intentions were indeed "you give us everything, and we re-gift you a tiny piece back."

When Europeans arrived, Indigenous peoples were already consummate treaty-makers, with a long history of making treaties with other Indigenous nations. The Great Law of Peace is often brought forth as an example of this: a treaty that united the Oneida, Mohawk, Cayuga, Onondaga, and Seneca into the Haudenosaunee (People of the Longhouse, the Iroquois Confederacy).[8] It has 117 articles governing the relationship between five nations, is at least a thousand years old, and is still in place today.[9]

These inter-Indigenous treaties were highly sophisticated oral agreements between sovereign peoples. They covered everything from trade arrangements to the settlement of conflicts, with specific consequences for their breach, and specific ways in which these treaties would be renewed.

Renewal of treaty relationships is very much a core aspect of Indigenous treaty-making. When I talk to people about Indigenous treaties, I liken them to any other sort of relationship: you do not enter into a relationship and then simply ignore the other person afterwards; this is simply not how effective relationships work!. Relationships must be renewed with constant care, negotiation, and openness to change. So, too, treaties.

Early European arrivals understood this, and renewal was an important part of maintaining good treaty relationships with Indigenous peoples. Europeans brought their own protocols, one of which involved written documents, but they also respected Indigenous protocols. The treaty process was carried out in a way that blended Indigenous and European traditions, resulting in great diversity of process, as each Indigenous nation had its own specific procedures for making these agreements.

From the Two-Row Wampum to the Great Peace of 1701

The first formal treaties between Indigenous peoples and settlers were focused on peaceful co-existence, trade, and dispute resolution processes such as the exchange of prisoners. Europeans, at this point in history, were in an almost perpetual state of warfare with one another, competing to claim the most land and resources possible. Securing alliances among the Indigenous nations was vital to this struggle. Colonies were small in size, and vulnerable to attack and privation.

The Haudenosaunee entered into a treaty known as the Two-Row Wampum with the Dutch in 1613.[10] This was not a written treaty, but rather one that was symbolized and commemorated by a wampum belt made of quahog shells. The Two-Row Wampum is considered by the Haudenosaunee to be a foundational treaty, which remains the basis for all relationships with European powers since.[11] That relationship, which is an ongoing negotiation, not a settled issue, is captured by the term *kaswentha* (guswenta):

> *Kaswentha* emphasizes the distinct identity of the two peoples and a mutual engagement to coexist in peace without interference in the affairs of the other. The Two Row Belt, as it is commonly known, depicts the *kaswentha* relationship in visual form via a long beaded belt of white wampum with two parallel lines of purple wampum along its length – the lines symbolizing a separate-but-equal relationship between two entities based on mutual benefit and mutual respect for each party's inherent freedom of movement – neither side may attempt to "steer" the vessel of the other as it travels along its own, self-determined path.[12]

Mutual respect, peaceful coexistence, and non-interference – these are the principles at the heart of kaswentha, and at the heart of many other Indigenous nations' treaty-making process.

The Haudenosaunee went on to make a series of Covenant Chain treaties.[13] In all, between 1613 and 1842, the Haudenosaunee engaged in over 400 negotiations with other Indigenous nations, the Dutch, the English, the French, and later, the United States.[14] European nations were very familiar with Haudenosaunee protocols surrounding negotiations and treaty-making at this point in history. Annual meetings to renew alliances were seen as vital by the Haudenosaunee, and, though the British acquiesced, there were differences in opinions on the necessity of how to maintain treaty relationships:

> The British view of treaties was that once a treaty was signed it would remain in effect – more or less in a steady state – until definite action was taken by one or both sides to change it. In contrast, the Iroquoian view was that alliances were naturally in a constant state of deterioration and in need of attention.[15]

The French allied themselves with the Innu (also known as the Montagnais), Wendàt (Huron), and Algonquin in mutually beneficial commercial and military relationships against the Haudenosaunee, and later, the British, who were seeking to expand their own colonies. These alliances came about through oral treaties between the parties, respecting protocols such as gift-giving, which was a way in which the alliance was renewed over time. The fact that these treaties were not written down made them no less binding.

Written treaties between the French and Indigenous nations began as nonaggression pacts among former enemies, such as a series of agreements between the French and Haudenosaunee. These treaties were not as successful, and conflict between the French and the Haudenosaunee continued for nearly a century until the Great Peace was signed in Montreal in 1701.[16] The Great Peace of 1701 established Haudenosaunee neutrality in conflicts between the French and English for a time, ushering in a period of peace that allowed French communities in particular to flourish and grow.

Peace and friendship treaties

After 1701, the L'nu (Mi'gmaq/Micmac/Mi'kmaq) and Wolastoqiyik (Maliseet/Malecite) who were part of the Wabanaki Confederacy, entered into a series of Peace and Friendship Treaties with the British.[17] These treaties were not land surrenders, but rather established commercial trade arrangements and reflected a desire on the part of the British to have military alliances with the L'nu and others, or at least neutrality in conflicts with France. A number of these treaties were signed between 1725 and 1776.[18] Sometimes, disputes arose after a treaty was concluded, and another treaty would be negotiated to address outstanding concerns. Often, subsequent treaties were reaffirmations of issues settled in previous treaties. Despite the name, things were not all close and cozy; this was a time of great conflict and turmoil as Europeans brought their internecine warfare to the Americas.

It is important to understand that armchair interpretations of treaties are not advisable nor likely to provide you with any real understanding of the treaties. Treaties have always been more than what was written on paper, and the courts have battled mightily to interpret them over the years. If you really want to learn more about any of these treaties, you should pick up Aboriginal law texts, which include relevant court decisions, as well as commentary on how these decisions impact the understanding of the various treaty rights under discussion.[19] Keep in mind that the courts favour Canada's view of the treaties over Indigenous peoples' understandings, so you aren't exactly going to get the whole picture this way.

Treaty-making took a definite turn once the British had established supremacy in North America. Don't get me wrong. There had been differences of opinion all along as to what treaties really meant and which promises were actually binding. European powers, as they gained more of a foothold in North America, began to assert that Indigenous peoples were submitting to European rule when engaging in treaty-making. This was certainly not a point of view shared by Indigenous peoples themselves. Renewal of treaty via annual gift giving and ceremonies was seen by Indigenous peoples as central to the relationship, whereas some colonial authorities took a pragmatic approach to "humouring the Natives," without really seeing the value in these practices. Nonetheless, treaties began to be more explicitly about opening up land for use by settlers.

Pre-Confederation treaties

The pre-Confederation treaties include the Upper Canada Land Surrenders and the Robinson and Douglas treaties.[20]

The Upper Canada treaties were made to open up land for British colonists to settle. They cover very small areas of Canada, mostly in (as the name implies) Upper Canada. Between 1764 and 1783, treaties were still focused more on trade and security than on the tiny parcels of land involved. The pace of land surrenders sped up, however, and a number of treaties were negotiated between 1783 and 1812 in order to settle Loyalists after the American Revolution. The documents involved described the lands, the Indigenous peoples involved, and compensation to be received in exchange.

These were massively tumultuous times, by the way, and I am glossing over them very, very quickly.[21]

After the War of 1812, European immigration increased rapidly, and soon British attitudes toward Indigenous peoples shifted from trade, security, and land surrender for settlement to "civilizing" programs carried out by Indian Affairs.

Reserves started in 1850 with the Robinson-Huron and Robinson-Superior treaties, which created 21 reserves and opened up chunks of land for settlement. Annual annuities were established (treaty payments), and Indigenous peoples were promised they would continue to have hunting and fishing rights in the area – the first time this had been addressed in a treaty. This issue hadn't really come up before because there wasn't a question that Indigenous peoples would continue to support themselves on the land.

Treaty-making during this period was incredibly acrimonious and shady as heck. The relationship between Indigenous peoples and the British was increasingly one of conflict rather than cooperation: intrusive settlement, land speculators, disruption to traditional trade routes, relocations of entire communities (such as many Mohawk after the American Revolution), Indian Affairs asshattery – not good times at all.

Constitutional recognition

Treaties gained Constitutional recognition with their inclusion in the *Constitution Act, 1982.*

According to Section 35(1), "The existing aboriginal and treaty rights of the aboriginal peoples of Canada are hereby recognized and affirmed."[22]

So, treaty rights that already existed before 1982, as well as any treaties signed afterwards, are recognized and affirmed by the *Constitution* in section 35. This means that simply scrapping them isn't actually an option. If Canadians wanted to completely get rid of the treaties, they'd have to change the *Constitution* itself. No easy task, as we saw in Meech Lake and then Charlottetown.

But, fear not! The courts, while at times taking an expansive approach to treaty interpretation, have also been steadily eroding treaty rights since 1982.

Interpretation of treaties

Case law has fleshed out the way in which treaty interpretation should be carried out in Canadian law. Too many Canadians believe these are simply contracts, and the only binding aspects of treaties are the words written on paper. Though the Canadian courts do not fully accept Indigenous peoples' interpretation of the treaties, it is at least clear treaties must be understood outside of the four corners of a signed document.

Over the years, court cases have established the following principles of interpretation:

- Restrictions to Aboriginal rights, and extinguishments (termination) of those rights under a treaty, must be narrowly construed. These should not be rights that are easy to get rid of.
- Treaties should be liberally construed, and ambiguities resolved in favour of Aboriginal signatories.
- "Extrinsic" evidence of the historic and cultural contexts in which a treaty was made can be offered.
- The onus of proving an Aboriginal right is restricted or extinguished under treaty, falls to the party making this claim.
- Aboriginal treaties are a sacred undertaking, an exchange of solemn promises between the Crown and Aboriginal nations. The courts must hold those promises in high regard.
- Treaties must be interpreted in a manner that preserves the honour of the Crown.
- Oral promises made during the making of treaties are part of those treaties. The oral history of Aboriginal signatories has weight when figuring out what those oral promises were.
- A static approach to treaty rights should be avoided and these rights may be exercised in contemporary ways. (For example, fishing with a rod and reel instead of gill nets.)[23]

All of this sounds pretty promising, but it hasn't exactly resulted in the recognition that Indigenous peoples hoped for when the *Constitution* was repatriated in 1982.

NOTES

1. John Borrows, *Recovering Canada: The Resurgence of Indigenous Law* (Toronto: University of Toronto Press, 2002); John Borrows, *Canada's Indigenous Constitution* (Toronto: University of Toronto Press, 2010); John Borrows, *Drawing Out Law: A Spirit's Guide* (Toronto: University of Toronto Press, 2010); John Borrows, *Freedom and Indigenous Constitutionalism* (Toronto: University of Toronto Press, 2016). John Borrows (Kegedonce) is an Anishinaabe law professor specializing in Indigenous legal rights and comparative constitutional law. Basically, he studies and explains Indigenous law – the legal orders of Indigenous peoples rather than Canadian law as it relates to Indigenous peoples. If you are interested in such things, you should read his books (and other things he has written).

2. Shiri Pasternak, "The Fiscal Body of Sovereignty: To 'Make Live' in Indian Country,'" *Settler Colonial Studies* (2015), 1–22, http://www.shiripasternak.com/category/academic/. Seriously, you should read her work.

3. Ed Bianchi is a settler program manager for KAIROS, an ecumenical movement for ecological justice and human rights. KAIROS created a really fantastic (free) tool called the "Blanket Exercise," which helps "share the historic and contemporary relationship between Indigenous and non-Indigenous peoples in Canada." It has been used in many classrooms and professional settings, and I cannot recommend it highly enough as an educational tool: http://kairosblanketexercise.org/.

4. Chelsea Vowel, *Niigaan: In Conversation,* discussion with Peter Larsen, July 11, 2013, http://niigaan.ca/tag/chelsea-vowel/.

5. Royal Commission on Aboriginal Peoples, "Stage Two: Contact and Co-Operation," vol. 1, *Report of the Royal Commission on Aboriginal Peoples* (Ottawa: Queen's Printer, 1997), 99–130, accessed November 23, 2015, http://www.collectionscanada.gc.ca/webarchives/20071124124640/http://www.ainc-inac.gc.ca/ch/rcap/sg/sgm5_e.html.

6. "The Inherent Right to Self-Government Timeline," *fngovernance.org,* accessed December 3, 2015, http://www.fngovernance.org/timeline/inherent_tline. This is a wonderful interactive timeline looking at self-governance among Indigenous peoples in Canada.

7. RCAP, vol. 1, 101.

8. Tom Porter (Sakokweniónkwas), *And Grandma Said: Iroquois Teachings As Passed Down Through the Oral Tradition* (Bloomington: Xlibris Corp, 2008); Paul Wallace, *White Roots of Peace: Iroquois Book of Life* (Santa Fe: Clear Light Publishing, 1990); Tekaronianeken Jake Swamp, "Tekaronianeken Jake Swamp – Peacemaker, Part 1," YouTube video, First Nations Technical Institute, WINHEC Conference, 2009, https://www.youtube.com/watch?v=ghlqlhsoCnU; Tekaronianeken Jake Swamp, "Tekaronianeken Jake Swamp – Peacemaker, Part 2," YouTube video, First Nations Technical Institute, WINHEC Conference, 2009, https://www.youtube.com/watch?v=zfDRMgrBzgU. These are videos in a series featuring Tekaronianeken Jake Swamp, as he tells the story of the Peacemaker.

9. Robbie Robertson, *Hiawatha and the Peacemaker,* illustrated by David Shannon (New York: Abrams, 2015).

10. Neighbours of the Onondaga Nation, "Two Row Wampum Renewal Campaign," *honorthetworow.org,* accessed December 2, 2015, http://honorthetworow.org/learn-more/history/. The year 2013 marked the 400th anniversary of the Two-Row Wampum, and a number of resources were compiled to give context to the original agreement.

11. Onondaga Nation People of the Hills, "Timeline – Onondaga Nation," *onondaganation.org,* accessed November 2nd, 2015, http://www.onondaganation.org/history/timeline/. A timeline of events pertinent to the Haudenosaunee, from a specifically Onondaga perspective, can be found above.

12. Jon Parmenter, "The Meaning of Kaswentha and the Two Row Wampum Belt in Haudenosaunee (Iroquois) History: Can Indigenous Oral Tradition be Reconciled with the Documentary Record?" *Journal of Early American History* 3, no. 1 (2013): 82–109, http://honorthetworow.org/wp-content/uploads/2012/01/The-Meaning-of-Kaswentha-and-the-Two-Row.pdf. This article cites an incredible amount of sources for further study, if this is something you'd like to know more about.

13. Robert W. Venables, "Polishing the Silver Covenant: A Brief History of Some of the Symbols and Metaphors in Haudenosaunee Treaty Negotiations," part 1 (2008), http://honorthetworow.org/wp-content/uploads/2013/03/Venables-on-the-Covenant-Chain-of-Treaties.pdf; Venables, part 2, http://honorthetworow.org/wp-content/uploads/2013/03/Venables-on-the-Covenant-Chain-of-Treaties-part-2.pdf; Venables, part 3, http://honorthetworow.org/wp-content/uploads/2013/03/Venables-on-the-Covenant-Chain-of-Treaties-part-3.pdf; Venables, part 4, http://honorthetworow.org/wp-content/uploads/2013/03/Venables-on-the-Covenant-Chain-of-Treaties-part-4.pdf. This is an article in four parts that discusses the Covenant Chain treaties in great detail.

14. Ibid., parts 1, 3, accessed December 2, 2015.

15. See note 5, 123.

16. Alain Beaulieu, and Roland Viau, *The Great Peace: A Chronicle of a Diplomatic Saga,* illustrated by Francis Back (Ottawa: Canadian Museum of Civilization, 2002).

17. The Wabanaki Confederacy is comprised of the L'nu (Mi'gmaq/Micmac/Mi'kmaq), Wolastoqiyik (Maliseet/Malicite), Pestomuhkati (Passamaquoddy), Abenaki, and Penawapskewi (eastern Abenaki/Penobscot).

18. Canadian Heritage, "Speaking About Our Land-Treaty Relationship," *aboutourland.ca,* accessed December 2, 2015, http://www.aboutourland.ca/sites/default/files/files/resources/treaty%20relationship_0.pdf; Canadian Heritage, "Speaking About Our Land-Treaty Relationship," *aboutourland.ca,* accessed December 2, 2015, http://www.aboutourland.ca/search-resources/results/taxonomy%253A218. The first source is a high-resolution map with excerpts from the various Peace and Friendship Treaties and the second offers high-resolution texts of the various treaties, which can be downloaded and printed.

19. Thomas Isaac, *Aboriginal Law: Commentary, Cases and Materials,* 3rd ed. (Saskatoon: Purich Publishing, 2004). Aboriginal case law continues to evolve, so you may need to catch up on more recent decisions.

20. Indigenous Affairs and Northern Development Canada, "Historical Treaties of Canada," accessed December 3, 2015, http://www.aadnc-aandc.gc.ca/DAM/DAM-INTER-HQ/STAGING/texte-text/htoc_1100100032308_eng.pdf.

21. Anthony J. Hall, "Aboriginal Treaties," *The Canadian Encyclopedia,* June 6, 2011, http://www.thecanadianencyclopedia.ca/en/article/aboriginal-treaties/. This is a good resource for a fairly quick, yet comprehensive, overview of the historic context of various treaties I haven't covered.

22. *The Constitution Act, 1982,* Schedule B to the *Canada Act, 1982* (UK), 1982, c. 11.

23. University of British Columbia Faculty of Law, "Primer: Canadian Law on Aboriginal and Treaty Rights," accessed December 3, 2015, http://www.allard.ubc.ca/sites/www.law.ubc.ca/files/uploads/enlaw/pdfs/primer_complete_05_10_09.pdf.

28

The More Things Change, the More They Stay the Same

Numbered Treaties and Modern Treaty-Making

Aboriginal law is very frustrating to study and practice. Despite the name, Aboriginal law is not the study or practise of Indigenous legal traditions; rather, it is the way in which the Canadian state mediates its relationship with Indigenous peoples. Aboriginal law exists squarely within a legal paradigm defined solely by the Canadian state. If Canada deigns to include its interpretation of aspects of Indigenous legal traditions, then it will do so according to its own legal principles, further warping what is almost always already a poor translation to begin with.

If all this were obvious right away, then Aboriginal law would probably not be so frustrating. If it were exceedingly clear to everyone that Aboriginal law is all about a colonial nation retaining its claim to sovereignty – dedicated to shoring up its claim to title in lands throughout Canada – then that understanding alone would be a great improvement. All of us could acknowledge Canada's entire "legal" approach is based on self-interest, and certain core principles will never truly be up for negotiation as far as Canada is concerned. Those would be very important things to recognize.

It is not the case, however, that this fact is widely understood. That is because Aboriginal law is couched in liberal terms of respect and rights; and, to be fair, I think many of the lawyers and bureaucrats administering the *Indian Act* (and various other legislative or procedural regimes related to Indigenous peoples in Canada) truly believe they are doing their utmost to make things right. After all, have we not moved far beyond the day of smallpox blankets, forced relocations, military force, residential schooling, and interference?

Ha! Hahahahahahahahahahahaa….ahhhh.

The rhetoric has changed somewhat from the days when men rode around the west carrying boilerplate treaties for signing – but it hasn't changed that much. Right now, hundreds of settlements are being negotiated across the country to end various claims by First Nations over stolen lands, broken promises, damages, and so on – claims that sometimes go back hundreds of years and have been pursued doggedly by those First Nations to no avail. The way in which these settlements are being negotiated does not involve a substantially different approach from the one Canada took back in the grand old days of historic treaty-making.

The Litigation Management and Resolution Branch

If you ever get the chance to take a look at even a single claim's history, please do. It is an eye-opening experience. The Department of Justice, in cooperation with Indian Affairs, has a Litigation Management and Resolution Branch (LMRB) that conducts a risk analysis of claims against the Crown by Aboriginal peoples. This analysis often contains a lot of historical research if the claim goes back any length of time. What these documents almost invariably show is that the claim has been pursued almost without pause since the problem first arose.

In legal-sized binders, you will see copies of Band Council Resolutions sent to Ottawa to petition a resolution to the conflict; letters sent by individual chiefs or members of the community; correspondence between Indian Agents and other agencies on the matter; descriptions of protests, actions, negotiations, meetings, promises, studies, more meetings, more resolutions. Hundreds and hundreds of written documents outlining just what the community has done to press its claim, year after year, decade after decade, and, yes, sometimes century after century. It is un-fricking-believable, if you can pardon my language.

This research is undertaken in order to assess what risk Canada faces if the issue were to go to court. When it is complete, Canada may choose to negotiate a settlement, or it may decide it has a good shot at winning the case if it proceeds to litigation. The research done is not necessarily going to be handed over to you without a struggle, but many bands have copies of these document sets pertaining to their own claims, and the research is certainly reproducible if one were to try to follow the threads themselves. Of course, the Department of Justice has a lot more money and resources than the average researcher, but the documents are out there in various archives.

I bring this up because it has really brought home for me how long the struggle has gone on, to no avail. I think there is a perception out there that communities just wake up one day and decide to sue the Government for this thing or the other, but that is not reality. Most communities have long-standing grievances that simply have not been settled. Why?

For a long time, a 1927 amendment of the *Indian Act* prohibited bands from raising money or using band funds in order to pursue these claims.[1] They could not hire lawyers. They could only send letters and try to get someone's attention. Treaty 11 was signed in 1921, marking the end of the signing of the Numbered Treaties. A great many claims of treaty violations were starting to come forth, and Canada legislated away our ability to seek any recourse. The pass system, enacted in the Prairies but not written into law, helped prevent Indigenous peoples from "collaborating" to pursue grievances, as well. The pass system worked somewhat akin to a "hall pass," wherein any Indigenous person wishing to leave the reserve had to first ask the local Indian Agent for written permission, and woe to whomever was caught outside the reserve boundaries without one![2] This provision was not repealed until 1951.

The federal government also liked setting up various new hoops to jump through: a Land Claims Commission here, a new specific claims process over there – processes so labyrinthine that even the people running things didn't quite know how they worked; processes that sometimes spanned decades and often came to uncertain or discredited conclusions. All that work and effort – the research and community consultations – down the tubes, and, "Hey, here's a new process, wouldn't you folks like to try out our new and improved way of screwing you for another few decades?"

Surrender clauses

The Numbered Treaties (also sometimes just referred to as historic treaties) were full of surrender clauses. These clauses "surrender" lands and rights, giving them up in exchange for other things offered by the Crown. Here is the text of Treaty 6, which says:

> The Plain and Wood Cree Tribes of Indians, and all the other Indians inhabiting the district hereinafter described and defined, do hereby cede, release, surrender and yield up to the Government of the Dominion of Canada, for Her Majesty the Queen and Her successors forever, all their rights, titles and privileges, whatsoever, to the lands included within the following limits....[3]

Signed between 1871 and 1921, every single one of the 11 Numbered Treaties has a similar clause.[4] *Surrender, cede, release, yield* – give up your land forever and ever,

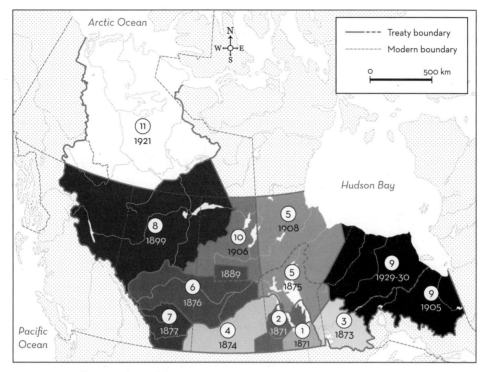

FIGURE 28.1. The Numbered Treaties, 1871–1921.

and that land now belongs to Canada; thank you very much. The entire purpose of these treaties was to open up land for settlement; so, for Canada, the issue of land became paramount.

Of course, First Nations perspectives, based on the extensive oral negotiations that went on when these treaties were made, differ considerably.

> At no time did Treaty First Nations relinquish their right to nationhood, their Inherent Right to determine their own destinies, nor did they allow any foreign government to govern them.
>
> Treaties are not static nor can they be unilaterally defined. They evolve and will continue to evolve for "…*as long as the sun shines, the rivers flow, and the grass grows….*"[5]

After the *Delgamuukw* case was heard by the Supreme Court, the Crown suddenly realized that vast tracts of lands – including almost all of present-day British Columbia, as well as huge swaths in the north, and pretty much everything east of Ontario – probably did not belong to Canada.[6] What?!

Since then, a process of modern treaty-making has swung into high gear, not just in British Columbia, but all over the country. Russ Diabo calls these the "termination tables," and for good reason, as they all seek to terminate outstanding claims.[7] In addition, there are specific claims processes, which are different from litigation negotiations, which are different from comprehensive claims, which are different than Treaty Land Entitlement processes, and so on. I am not going to explain the differences between all of those; just know that the claims landscape out there is vast, difficult to understand, and not very effective.

There are also other outstanding claims that do not quite fit into any of these categories that may still be under negotiation with Canada. Very, very few of these agreements go to court or get seen widely, but it is a process occurring in deadly earnest in the background.

Anyway, the Government of Canada claims it's moved beyond surrender clauses in its modern treaties and settlement negotiations. I suppose even they realize it's too much to say, "If you want us to finally address your longstanding concerns, you have to promise us that this land is ours forever, okay? Okay, so it might not have been up until now, but, whatever, just sign this and surrender it for all eternity so that issue can be settled. By the way, we need to extinguish all your other Aboriginal rights, too."

Does that mean the Feds have stopped trying to make sure they can say they own all the land in Canada and extinguish Aboriginal rights whenever possible? Pffft. There were surrender and extinguishment clauses in Settlement Agreements even in 2007, like this one from the Metepenagiag Mi'kmaq Nation:

> The First Nation hereby *absolutely surrenders* to Canada, pursuant to the provisions of sections 38 and 29 of the Indian Act, *all rights and interests of whatsoever kind and nature* which the First Nation and its members and their heirs, descendants, executors, successors and assigns, past, present and future, may have had, or may now have, in the lands described as follows....[8]

Na. The "kinder, gentler" negotiations are very recent.

Modern surrender clauses

Now, the Feds use new jargon. First, they make you feel good with nonderogation clauses that generally look like this one in the Yukon Northern Affairs Program Devolution Transfer Agreement:

> Nothing in this Agreement shall be construed so as to abrogate or derogate from the protection provided for existing aboriginal or treaty rights of the aboriginal peoples

of Canada by the recognition and affirmation of those rights in section 35 of the *Constitution Act, 1982.*[9]

Blah, blah, blah. Basically, this says you aren't giving up your Aboriginal rights, your section 35 rights, or any treaty rights you may have. Whew, dodged that bullet!

Except, the next phase of these newer, kinder settlement agreements often has a clause like this (from a different document):

> Notwithstanding (the non-derogation clause) the Parties agree that any person who holds or acquires any title, right or interest…shall continue to be entitled to the quiet enjoyment of their said title, right or interest…without risk of a claim, legal or otherwise, by the First nation (or any entity claiming on its behalf) based on any existing Aboriginal or treaty right to the said lands.[11]

No evil "surrender/release/cede/extinguishment" words in there; nice, hey? Except, what this is actually saying is: "You aren't giving up any Aboriginal, section 35, or treaty rights, you might have, but you agree never, ever to exercise or claim those rights once you sign this Agreement."

It's slightly more complicated than that, mind you. There is a patchwork of case law out there that regulates what rights can be exercised on Crown lands versus private lands, and what have you. Some of that could still apply, but you'd never be able to take either a private individual or the Crown to court over a violation of the rights you supposedly still have, because the courts would look at this clause you signed and say, "You promised not to do that."

You see, your rights aren't gone, they are just not exercisable. Not really an important on-the-ground difference, but much nicer sounding.

It is very important to the federal government that landowners feel confident they do actually own the land they are occupying, and that the Crown doesn't end up in court as a third party if a First Nation sues a private individual for squatting. That is the ultimate goal in these negotiations and is not something Canada is willing to give up. So, you may be trying to get compensation for various breaches, but as you negotiate for this compensation, you will face the effective extinguishment of your rights over the lands in question.

This is about relationships, not release forms.

The wording has changed, sure. It's confusing as heck and not immediately clear to anyone who reads it. Wrapped up in legal jargon and huge run-on sentences that put you to sleep, it can be difficult to notice you are effectively giving up rights in order to finally settle a grievance you've been pursuing for a hundred years – after being in a specific claims process for the last 20 of those hundred years.

I can understand why it can seem worth it. If you can settle for a few million dollars, that means immediate cash injected into your community – and there isn't a single Indigenous community in this country that doesn't need it. You can finally say to your people, "We have settled this long-standing problem. It is over." Considering the incredible time, energy, and emotional investment that go into these claims, getting closure is not something anyone can take lightly. Another option is to not sign, and eventually, limitation periods may run out and you lose your nontitle related rights because you didn't take it to court on time. Or, Canada just holds out forever and you get not one dollar for the damage that has been done. Those are real possibilities.

What bothers me about this is not that First Nations are signing these agreements. Not really. That used to bother me, but I have talked to enough people on the ground to realize no one is folding. Sometimes you go to court, sometimes you negotiate, sometimes you block roads, but you never, ever truly accept you are signing away your rights. Indigenous peoples have to do this on paper sometimes because that is what is required *to survive*. But in our hearts, we know damn well this is not going to stop us in the future from exercising those rights.

What bothers me is this: a treaty is an ongoing relationship. That's how it is in every other situation that does not involve Indigenous peoples. Treaties are nation-to-nation agreements that mediate relationships, and they can and should be revisited as the relationship progresses. Indigenous peoples know this; this is how we approach treaties and agreements with Canada. However, *Canada* does not seem to understand this. They want to settle everything and never look back. Patch up the holes in their supposed Crown title and put the whole thing to bed.

Well, it isn't that easy, folks. Canada needs to stop trying to make us go away – to stop "recognizing" our rights with one side of the mouth and restricting or extinguishing them out the other side.

That is not going to happen within the practice of Aboriginal law, however. Nope. Since *Delgamuukw* and *Marshall*,[11] Aboriginal law has been all about "reasonable justifications for infringement" of Indigenous rights instead of building a real relationship with Indigenous peoples. Canada cannot seem to kick its own bad habits.

NOTES

1. Jay Makarenko, "The Indian Act: Historical Overview," *Judicial System and Legal Issues* (2008), accessed December 9, 2015, http://mapleleafweb.com/features/the-indian-act-historical-overview.

2. *The Pass System*, Tamarack Productions, 2015. http://www.tamarackproductions.com/the-pass-system/. This film contains information on the pass system that includes interviews with Elders.

3. Indigenous and Northern Affairs, "Treaty Texts – Treaty 6," accessed December 9, 2015, http://www.aadnc-aandc.gc.ca/eng/1100100028710/1100100028783.

4. Indigenous and Northern Affairs, "Treaty Texts," accessed December 9, 2015, http://www.aadnc-aandc.gc.ca/eng/1370373165583/1370373202340.

5. The Confederacy of Treaty Six First Nations, "Fundamental Treaty Principles," accessed December 9, 2015, http://www.treatysix.org/about_principals.html (original emphasis).

6. *Delgamuukw v. British Columbia, 1997*, [1997] 3 SCR 1010.

7. Russell Diabo, "Canada: Prime Minister Harper Launches First Nations 'Termination Plan,'" accessed December 9, 2015, http://www.globalresearch.ca/canada-prime-minister-harper-launches-first-nations-termination-plan/5318362.

8. Not all Settlement Agreements are publicly available. I had access to this one when doing research on Settlement Agreements at a law firm, but I am not able to find another copy to provide proper notes. However, you can see some of the language, particularly "absolutely surrender the lands" in the Order in Council authorizing acceptance of the Settlement Agreement: http://www.pco-bcp.gc.ca/oic-ddc.asp?lang=eng&page=secretariats&dosearch=search+/+list&pg=96&viewattach=29152&blndisplayflg=1.

9. INAC, "Yukon Northern Affairs Program Devolution Transfer Agreement," §1.6, accessed December 9, 2015, http://www.aadnc-aandc.gc.ca/eng/1297283624739/1297283711723.

10. This was an actual clause from a confidential proposed Settlement Agreement that came across my desk. Keep your eye out for this sort of wording.

11. *R. v. Marshall* [1999] 3 SCR 456 (known as Marshall 1), and *R. v. Marshall* [1999] 3 SCR 533 (known as Marshall 2).

29

Why Don't First Nations Just Leave the Reserve?

Reserves Are Not the Problem

This is a question that is asked again and again whenever there is a story in the news about lack of potable water on-reserve, or housing problems, or, basically, anything to do with First Nations: "Why not move?"

As usual, before I can answer that question, we need to take a look at what reserves actually are. You might think you know this, and perhaps you're impatient to get to the point, but I've found this isn't a concept that is nearly as well understood as folks think it is.

There are almost 2300 Indian reserves in Canada, nearly half of which are in British Columbia.[1] That might sound like a lot, but keep in mind many of these are "postage stamp" reserves – very small in size. The Canyon Lake reserve, part of the Nadleh Whut'en First Nation in British Columbia, is only four hectares. Another Nadleh Whut'en reserve is six hectares.[2] To get a sense of the amount of land we're talking about here, most sports fields are nearly a hectare in size.[3] That's about 1.5 city blocks.

Many people make the mistake of thinking First Nation = reserve, but it doesn't quite work that way.

There are more than 600 First Nations in Canada, and so most First Nations have more than one reserve.[4] One First Nation might have a few reserves bordering one another, making it possible to think of these reserves as one reserve, or one piece of land. For example, Sawridge First Nation in Alberta has two reserves very close to each other: one is 906.5 hectares and the other is 1236.8 hectares. It makes sense to think of these reserves as being one piece of land even though, legally, they aren't.[5]

However, it is very common for a First Nation to have reserves that do *not* border one another. Alexis Nakota Sioux Nation in Alberta is an example of this, with four reserves. One is past Whitecourt, which is northwest of Edmonton, two are southeast of Hinton (a significant distance from Whitecourt!), and the fourth is about an hour's drive northwest of Edmonton.[6] Most members of Alexis Nakota Sioux Nation live on the reserve that is northwest of Edmonton, and the other pieces of land are used for hunting, berry and medicine picking, and so on.[7]

In total, Indian reserves comprise nearly 28 000 square kilometres, which is about the size of Belgium.[8] This may sound impressive, until you realize you can fit Belgium into Canada 326.8 times. It sounds even less impressive when you understand that reserves account for only 0.28 percent of all the land in Canada. That's just slightly more than one quarter of 1 percent – a speck.

Wow.

What's the deal with land ownership on-reserve? It's communal or something, right?

I want to make sure we're clear on how land ownership works *off*-reserve first. If you're sick of this approach already, imagine being my daughters! Whenever they ask a seemingly simple question like, "Why is the sky blue?" I end up starting with, "Well, let's talk about what the colour blue is first." It's how my mind works, and it helps me anticipate questions or misunderstandings that almost invariably arise during these kinds of explanations. My thanks for your continued patience!

Property law in Canada comes from English common law for the most part, though in Quebec there is a Civil Code regime, which originated in France. Canadian property law then has its origins in the feudal system from ye olden European days of yore. Under this system, the Crown is the real owner of all the lands in Canada, but it can grant people ownership rights to the use of land.

If you are a Canadian who owns a piece of land, you have certain ownership rights, but the land *itself* does not really belong to you. You could not, for example, declare yourself a sovereign micronation and split off from Canada.[9] Despite this legal specificity, we usually just refer to land ownership as "land ownership" rather than "a bundle of rights" and leave it at that.

The highest ownership interest possible in land is known as the "fee simple." It is an absolute estate in land marked by the fact that the land in question is alienable, divisible, and descendible. All that means is you can sell it (getting rid of your property rights), you can split the land up into pieces (sell them, rent them, whatever), and you can pass the land down to your heirs. Theoretically, your land could remain in your family's possession forever.

In Canada, that generally means you own land but not necessarily the subsurface rights to things like gravel, coal, or oil. There are exceptions to this, but work with me. So, you own the land down to a certain depth, and you can do with it what you want. You can rent it out, sell it, or pass it on to your descendants. It's yours as much as land can be in Canada.

There may be restrictions on how you can use your land, based on legislation or bylaws where you live, but the restrictions tend to be the least onerous possible to respect your property rights. The Crown can expropriate your land if it really needs to – by which I mean seize your land and kick you off it – but they must have a compelling public-interest reason to do so, and you must be compensated if this happens. If you die, and you have absolutely no heirs to pass it down to, the land reverts back to the Crown.

If you are a Canadian with fee-simple land ownership, and you want to build a home on your land, but you don't have the sôniyaws,[10] you can borrow money from the bank in the form of a mortgage. Or, say you just want a loan for something else. In both cases, the bank requires that you put your land up as collateral, meaning the bank can take your land and sell it off if you default on your mortgage or loan. It protects the bank, financially.

Another kind of property ownership arrangement that is quite common is a trust. In a trust, one person manages the property in question, but the property itself belongs to the beneficiary. The trustee is supposed to manage the property in such a way that it benefits the beneficiary (the actual owner). Confused? Well, consider Batman.

Bruce Wayne inherited a whole bunch of property when he was a child, due to the unfortunate deaths of his parents, but the court would have appointed him a trustee until he reached the age of majority. Perhaps that trustee was Alfred. Let's just pretend it was.

So, Alfred didn't actually own any of Bruce's property, but he had the right to make decisions about how to maintain and use the property – maybe rent out the guest house, or invest in topiary – and he was able to spend money from Bruce's estate to do so. Bruce would not have had any say in these decisions if Alfred chose not to listen to him. Alfred was simply managing Bruce's property, for Bruce's benefit. It goes like this:

- The Wayne Estate: The trust, the actual property.
- Little Bruce Wayne: Beneficiary, actual owner of the Wayne Estate, but unable to make decisions about what to do with it until he grows up and becomes Batman.
- Alfred: Trustee, does not own the Wayne Estate, but can make decisions about what to do with it, as long as those decisions are to the benefit of young Bruce Wayne.

Cool. I'm clear. So, what about reserves?

Reserve lands are not fee simple, and despite the way the *Indian Act* words things, they are not held in trust, either.

Reserves are set aside for the exclusive use of a First Nation. They are actually a kind of private property, and you can be charged under section 30 of the *Indian Act* for trespass if you enter a reserve without permission.[11] However, the *Indian Act* also makes it clear that "no Indian is lawfully in possession of land in a reserve," so this is not the kind of private property you may be thinking of.[12]

Reserve lands *cannot* be put up as collateral for loans or anything else, because they cannot be seized. They are not owned individually, so they cannot be sold off. Of course, this causes all sorts of problems when someone wants to get a loan to build a house, or start a business, but there are various ways around this, including Ministerial Loan Guarantees and so on. While these complications can be frustrating, they have helped prevent further erosion of a land base for First Nations.

Remember that fee-simple lands are "alienable, divisible, and descendible." Reserve lands cannot be alienated (sold or given away) to anyone *except* the Crown. They are not divisible in that they cannot be split up among members in a permanent way that changes the nature of their use from communal to individual. They are not descendible in the sense that they cannot be permanently passed down to specific descendants. The right to use and benefit from the land belongs to the band, not to specific people within the band.

Now, look at the *Indian Act* definition of reserves:

> …reserves are held by Her Majesty *for the use and benefit* of the respective bands for which they were set apart, and subject to this Act and to the terms of any treaty or surrender, the Governor in Council may determine whether any purpose for which lands in a reserve are used or are to be used is for the use and benefit of the band.[13]

"For the use and benefit" sounds an awful lot like a trust relationship, where the Crown would be holding reserve lands for the benefit of First Nations, but First Nations themselves actually own the land. Canadian law, however, says this is not how it works. Neither fee simple nor a trust, reserve lands (like so many things having to do with Indigenous peoples) are in a special category called *sui generis,* which basically just means "unique" and "we'll figure it out as we go."

Reserve lands are lands "set aside." Set aside from what, you might ask? Well, as you saw in chapter 27, the Crown laid claim to all of the lands in Canada, but is very sketchy on the details as to how this claim actually came about or can continue to be defended. Nonetheless, this claim is at the foundation of the Canadian state, and, therefore, is not seriously questioned in any way by the Canadian state itself. So, when Canada talks about "setting aside" lands for the use of First Nations, this means Canada believes it owns all the land and has the right to reserve little areas for First Nations to live on.

Let's review, because this is a bit odd. Reserves are located on Crown land (land owned by Canada). The Crown holds these lands for the use and benefit of Indians, meaning First Nations people have the right to live on and use those lands. However, the Crown is the one calling the shots when it comes to how those lands are managed. First Nations do not have legal title to those lands (which they would, if this were actually a trust relationship).

Basically, First Nations only have control over reserves if the Crown chooses to give them that control. Which – as anyone who was asked as a child, "Do you want to wear the red pyjamas or the blue pyjamas?" knows – isn't really control at all.

Originally, reserves were set up as a civilizing project, forcing First Nations to settle in one place (chosen by the Crown) so they could turn their attention and labour toward whatever the Crown chose – like farming and going to church. This, coincidentally, freed up all sorts of lands for settlers to move onto. On the other hand, it also ensured there were some lands First Nations could still cling to.

Much of the land promised for reserves was never actually put to this use, and, instead, ended up owned by land speculators and Indian agents themselves. Frank Oliver, for example, used his political power to help remove the Papaschase Band from their traditional territory in Edmonton, and later became Superintendent of Indian Affairs. A staunch anti-Black racist and proud anti-immigrant bigot, he has a whole neighbourhood in Edmonton named after him.[14]

Reserve lands that were actually set aside were often eroded by expropriations and shady "surrenders" to benefit the expansion of municipalities. This is a big reason we're talking about 0.28 percent of the land in Canada instead of something that makes a bit more sense as a land base.

Creating reserves made it much easier to manage First Nations and, ultimately, to disrupt kinship and governance systems, as well as removing First Nations from their traditional economies and sources of food. The reserve system was essential to the settlement of Canada and was particularly vital to opening up the Plains for that purpose. Disease and starvation, deliberately weaponized against Indigenous peoples on the Plains, helped to force them onto reserves.[15]

That sounds horrible! Why do First Nations want to keep living on reserves?!

It was horrible. In some cases, reserves at the time were likened to open-air prisons.[16] However, despite the way reserves were created, and the way in which they have been and continue to be used to control First Nations in various ways, they are also places where First Nations culture continues to thrive. It is very important for Canadians to recognize what even this minuscule land base means to First Nations beyond "poverty and despair."

The *Indian Act* ushered in administrative systems in First Nations communities that displaced traditional leaders. Just because these administrative systems are given the name Chief and Council does not mean they reflect the original sociopolitical governance systems of those First Nations. These are purely Canadian creations, and First Nations people have been given no choice in their design or implementation.

Despite this, in many First Nations communities, traditional governance systems *do* continue to exist – although they are not recognized by Canada as being legitimate. They may not always be recognizable to Canadians, because they are rooted in fundamentally different traditions. Nonetheless, having even a tiny land base for communities to remain together upon has helped these traditional governance systems continue to exist.

Reserves continue to be physical places where First Nations cultures are practised. Some First Nations are culturally healthier than others, but reserves play an important part in providing a space for First Nations to resist the erosion that colonization demands. They also provide a "place to go back to" for those who want to reconnect.

First Nations people can become disconnected from their communities for many reasons. They may have been "scooped" or adopted out. They may have been seized by child welfare and raised in foster care. They may have left with family members who were experiencing abuse. They may have lost status or been forced out by membership codes. Children and grandchildren of those who have had to leave their community experience many difficulties when it comes to reconnecting with their home community – if they are able to even identify it. However, if those communities ceased to exist because they were considered "unviable," reconnection would become next to impossible.

As I pointed out, most First Nations have more than one reserve, and it is often the case that one reserve is for living on, while other reserves are used for traditional activities. In the more crowded south, many First Nations find themselves hemmed in on all sides by urban centres and cottagers, resulting in a loss of access to land.

With reserves, there is still some guarantee of being able to access materials and relationships central to Indigenous spirituality.

On a more practical level, these lands continue to provide First Nations people with food, though environmental degradation and pollution are directly threatening the health of plants, animals, and the humans who rely on them. First Nations people have certain Aboriginal rights to hunt and gather foods off-reserve, as well; but as more and more land is taken up for industry and settlement, those rights become increasingly limited. While few First Nations families are able to subsist entirely on country food anymore, reserves remain an important element of food security.

Indigenous languages have been in serious decline due to forced assimilation in residential schools, as well as to urbanization and lack of support for Indigenous languages. There are only a handful of off-reserve schools that teach children in an Indigenous language. It is rarer still to find health or social services in an Indigenous language. Moving away from the reserve often means language loss and subsequent loss of culture and identity. Reserves remain linguistic homelands for many, and their physical dissolution would be disastrous for Indigenous-language survival.

Above all, reserves are communities with histories, families, and aspirations. They experience challenging social and economic conditions. But it is vital to recognize they also create conditions for resilience.

When people ask First Nations people to abandon the reserves as a gesture of "freedom," they are really asking First Nations to abandon the places that have helped them resist complete assimilation. If assimilation is something you are championing, then do it honestly, without couching your arguments in progressive-sounding rhetoric.

NOTES

1. Indian Affairs and Northern Development, "Search by Reserve/Settlement/Village," accessed November 20, 2015, http://pse5-esd5.ainc-inac.gc.ca/fnp/Main/Search/SearchRV.aspx?lang=eng.
2. See note 1, search "Nadleh Whuten." Nadleh Whut'en First Nation has six reserves for a total of 969 hectares.
3. A hectare is 10 000 square metres. That's 100 metres by 100 metres. If you understand acres better, an acre is 0.4047 hectares, so one hectare contains about 2.47 acres.
4. See note 1.
5. See note 1, search "Sawridge."
6. See note 1, search "Alexis." It is listed as Alexis Nakota First Nation on the site.

7. Alexis Nakota First Nation, "Land Use," accessed November 30, 2015, http://www.ansn.ca/business-economy/land-use/#overview.

8. INAC, "Resolving Aboriginal Claims: A Practical Guide to Canadian Experiences" (Ottawa, 2003), 2, accessed November 30, 2015, http://www.aadnc-aandc.gc.ca/DAM/DAM-INTER-HQ/STAGING/texte-text/rul_1100100014175_eng.pdf.

9. John Ryan, George Dunford, and Simon Sellars, *Micronations: The Lonely Planet Guide to Home-Made Nations* (London: Lonely Planet, 2006). Micronations are entities claiming to be independent nations or states, but without global recognition as such. They tend to be tiny islands claimed by European settlers who want independence from whatever nation they are living in. The history and legality of micronations is actually quite fascinating. There is a strange and interesting little micronation wiki available here (accessed November 27, 2015): http://mw.micronation.org/wiki/Main_Page. There are also numerous journal articles discussing the micronations in international law that might tickle your fancy, but those are easy enough to find.

10. One of the Cree words for money is sôniyaw.

11. *Indian Act,* RSC 1985, c I-5. s. 30. "A person who trespasses on a reserve is guilty of an offence and liable on summary conviction to a fine not exceeding fifty dollars or to imprisonment for a term not exceeding one month or to both."

12. Ibid., s. 20.

13. Ibid., s. 18 (my emphasis).

14. Papaschase First Nation, "A Brief History of the Papaschase Band," accessed November 27, 2015, http://www.papaschase.ca/history.html; K. Toni Hallihan, "'A Break Upon the Wheel': Frank Oliver and the Creation of the Immigration Act of 1906," accessed November 27, 2015, http://tinyurl.com/nttrs3q; Sarah-Jane Mathieu, *North of the Color Line: Migration and Black Resistance in Canada, 1870* (1955; repr., Chapel Hill: University of North Carolina Press, 2010), 25, 32–33, 38–41, 48, 56–57. These sources refer to Oliver's role in dispossessing the Papaschase band, his immigration policy, and his anti-Black perspective, respectively.

15. James Daschuk, *Clearing the Plains: Disease, Politics of Starvation and the Loss of Aboriginal Life* (Regina: University of Regina Press, 2013). This is not a conspiracy theory – it has been proven as fact.

16. Alex William, *The Pass System* (Tamarack Productions, 2015), documentary film, http://www.tamarackproductions.com/the-pass-system/.

30

White Paper, What Paper?

More Attempts to Assimilate Indigenous Peoples

If you hang around Indigenous people long enough, you'll probably hear references to white paper, and it might have you scratching your head. What's so awful about white paper? Don't Indigenous people prefer some sort of birchbark concoction?

The trick is to capitalize the words. They're talking about *the* White Paper. Now, that still won't clarify much for you. A White Paper is essentially a federal government policy document presented by a minister. It is intended to "state and explain the government's policy on a certain issue."[1] There are green papers, too, by the way, "issued by government to invite public comment and discussion on an issue *prior* to policy formulation."[2]

White Papers are often persuasive in nature, intended to mark a shift in policy before any legislation is actually enacted. They are put out to literally stir the waters, and to see what public reaction is likely to be, though the planning stages have already been fleshed out fairly thoroughly. Green Papers tend to be issued before that level of planning has been done. Anyway, we're not really talking about Green Papers right now.

Unsurprisingly, the notorious document being discussed is a very specific one: the White Paper of 1969, officially titled, "Statement of the Government on Indian Policy."[3] It was put out by then Minister of Indian Affairs, Jean Chrétien. Remember him? Yeah, he was prime minister from 1993 to 2003. Not a lot of Indigenous people really trusted that guy, for reasons you'll soon see.

Okay, so why the grim faces when anyone mentions the White Paper?

First, it is important to understand the context. In 1966, the Hawthorn Report was released.[4] It was a federally commissioned investigation of the social conditions faced by Indigenous peoples, which found that Indigenous peoples were the most disadvantaged among the Canadian population. The report stated these social conditions were a *direct* result of federal policy (in particular the residential-school system), and Indigenous peoples needed resources and opportunities to exercise self-determination, if there was any hope of improving their situation.

Chrétien, as Minister of Indian Affairs, decided to launch a nationwide series of consultations with First Nations communities across Canada, with the intention of amending the *Indian Act*. First Nations representatives expressed their concerns with Aboriginal and treaty rights, title to land, and the various struggles First Nations communities experienced accessing services like education and health care. A lot of time and energy went into these meetings, and there was a sense that, after the Hawthorn Report, it was clear the assimilationist policy was a failure and something new must be tried.

Yet, after all that – after a report that clearly stated the assimilationist policies of the past had failed and were actively harmful and should be rejected completely, and after First Nations in good faith engaged in numerous discussions with the government – what did Chrétien, et al. do?

They ignored all of this, issued the White Paper, and attempted to finalize the assimilation project by stating their desire to:

- eliminate Indian status
- abolish the *Indian Act*
- get rid of the Department of Indian Affairs
- *convert communally held reserve land to private property that could be sold by a First Nation or its members, "Indian control of Indian lands" (a fee-simple regime)*[5]
- transfer responsibility toward "Indians and lands reserved for Indians" from the federal government to provincial governments
- appoint a commissioner to address any outstanding land claims, ending this issue
- gradually terminate existing treaties

Can you imagine how frustrating this must have been for Indigenous peoples? Why commission a report if you aren't going to pay attention to its findings? Why even bother to hold nationwide consultations? Why not just do what you obviously intended to do all along? Sadly, this is not a one-off situation. This exact progression of events has been replicated too many times – studies, reports, recommendations, consultation, inaction. It's unacceptable and infuriating.

In essence, the federal government wanted to get rid of the category of Indian altogether. This might not seem like a bad idea to a great many Canadians; in fact, many people continue to suggest that doing this would solve all the problems experienced by Indigenous communities.

That is precisely why understanding the history of policies toward Indigenous peoples in this country is so vital. So many of what are suggested today as "solutions" have been tried – not only failing, but causing horrific damage along the way. Repeating these social experiments in the face of that history and the evidence available makes absolutely no sense. Harold Cardinal coined the fantastic term *buckskin curtain* in reference to exactly this sort of indifference and ignorance that continues to exist when it comes to Indigenous peoples, and that curtain has certainly not been drawn back yet.[6]

The White Paper causes grim looks because it was grim business. Couched in terms of *equality* and *dignity*, the White Paper proposed to pave over the colonial history of Canada and pretend none of it happened, or mattered. It reflected a government intent on doing away, once and for all, with what Duncan Campbell Scott called the "Indian Problem."

In response, 24-year-old Harold Cardinal and the Indian Chiefs of Alberta published what was dubbed the Red Paper (ha, get it?) in opposition; it was also known as "Citizens Plus."[7] It countered with the following points:

- Indian status and rights must be maintained; changes should only occur via negotiation with Indians.
- The *Indian Act* should remain in place, to be reviewed and changed only with the consent of Indians *after* treaty issues resolved.
- The Department of Indian Affairs needs to be modernized, and truly responsive to Indian needs, with a focus on ensuring treaty and land-rights promises are kept.
- "Indian control of Indian lands" must be recognized as meaning something other than Eurocentric notions of property (i.e., not a fee-simple regime). Also, reserves are already Indian lands; they are held in trust by the Crown for the benefit of the actual owners, who are Indian people.
- The federal government cannot abdicate its Constitutional responsibility toward Indians by transferring that responsibility to the provincial governments.
- The spirit and intent of the treaties must be respected and treaties modernized.[8]

The name of this counterpolicy paper is explained by a quote from the Hawthorn Report: "Indians should be regarded as 'Citizens Plus.' In addition to the rights and duties of citizenship, Indians possess certain additional rights as charter members of the Canadian community."[9]

If any of this sounds dry and boring, you absolutely need to read Arthur Manuel's description of the events surrounding the White and Red Papers, because it is anything but![10] In fact, his book *Unsettling Canada* is, in my opinion, one of the most accessible and important resources available to people living in Canada for understanding Indigenous activism and federal policy toward Indigenous peoples over the past half a century. I usually save these kinds of recommendations for the endnotes, so believe me when I tell you how important I think it is that you read this book!

The White Paper was scrapped, and, hey, it's ancient history, right? That was 1969, and this is now. Things have completely changed! Indigenous peoples have constitutional rights now, there have been apologies for residential schools and the High Arctic Relocation, and all sorts of things are just super better. The '60s and '70s were different times, friends. Let bygones be bygones.

Wait a minute; that doesn't sound like you at all…

You're right, and I'm sorry. Sometimes, I let my sarcasm get the better of me.

When the Red Paper was delivered to Pierre Trudeau, Arthur Manuel noted that the prime minister defended his government against accusations of dishonesty, claiming that they were simply trying to find a solution to a very old problem. Manuel goes on to explain:

> It was an interesting response, but the real problem hadn't been that the government was being dishonest. It was that they were moving ahead, quite openly in fact, to rob our peoples of our homelands and our heritage.
>
> The dishonesty came later. While the government officially buried the White Paper, Chrétien told my father unofficially, in private, that they "were withdrawing the White Paper but they would hold it aside for the generations of leaders who will accept it."[11]

Okay, I'll be up front about this. The reason I'm talking about the White Paper is because of a piece of legislation that was proposed in 2009 by Manny Jules, Chief Commissioner of the First Nations Tax Commission,[12] called the *First Nations Property Ownership Act* (FNPOA). Jules was chief, for a time, of the Tk'emlúps te Secwépemc (formerly known as the Kamloops Indian Band) and had been pushing the First Nations Property Ownership Initiative since 2006.[13] The FNPOA was revived in a big way in 2012, and again in 2013, when the Harper government made it known they wanted to introduce this piece of legislation.[14] It ended up not being introduced, but it is certainly not dead in the water, and will come up again at any moment.

I think people need to take another look at the 1969 White Paper and ask themselves whether or not there has actually been change in the rhetoric being used.

Take a look at this stirring speech used to introduce the FNPOA:

> To be a First Nations person is to be a human, with all a human's needs and abilities. To be a First Nations person is also to be different. It is to speak different languages, draw different pictures, tell different tales and to rely on a set of values developed in a different world.
>
> Canada is richer for its Aboriginal component, although there have been times when diversity seemed of little value to many Canadians.
>
> But to be a First Nations person today is to be someone different in another way. It is to be someone apart – apart in law, apart in the provision of government services and, too often, apart in social contacts.
>
> To be a First Nations person is to lack power – the power to act as owner of your lands, the power to spend your own money and, too often, the power to change your own condition.
>
> Not always, but too often, to be a First Nations person is to be without – without a job, a good house, or running water; without knowledge, training or technical skill and, above all, without those feelings of dignity and self-confidence that a man must have if he is to walk with his head held high.
>
> All these conditions of First Nations people are the product of history and have nothing to do with their abilities and capacities. Aboriginal relations with other Canadians began with special treatment by government and society, and special treatment has been the rule since Europeans first settled in Canada. Special treatment has made First Nations people a community disadvantaged and apart.
>
> Obviously, the course of history must be changed.
>
> To be a First Nations person must be to be free – free to develop Aboriginal cultures in an environment of legal, social, and economic equality with other Canadians.

Now wait a damn minute, I actually have a copy of the 1969 White Paper right here in my hands, and that quote is from the introduction to it!

Oops, caught me. You're right; I copied and pasted the opening statement from the White Paper, changing some of the terminology from "Indian" to more politically accepted terms like *First Nations* and *Aboriginal*.[15] I admit it.

Now that you've read it, though, does it sound terribly different from present-day rhetoric? I mean, it *sounds* great! And yet, this is the opening to a proposal that would have seen the unilateral violation of treaties made with Indigenous nations and the destructive forced assimilation of Indigenous peoples into the Canadian politic.

The White Paper dealt with much more than the privatization of reserve land, so perhaps I should narrow the comparison between it and the FNPOA somewhat. What you should really do is compare the "Indian Lands" portion of the White Paper with what the FNPO Initiative has to say.[16] The two proposals are essentially the same.

Now, it's true that just because the wording is very similar in 2015 to what it was in 1969, this does not mean the FNPOA is about complete assimilation the way the White Paper was. On the other hand, what lends credibility to the idea that this is exactly what it intends is the fact that it is being championed and promoted by people who support complete assimilation.

Take Tom Flanagan, for example. Former advisor to Harper, he wrote a book in 2000 delightfully titled, *First Nations? Second Thoughts.* In it, Flanagan clarifies his position on the assimilation of Indigenous peoples: "Call it assimilation, call it integration, call it adaptation, call it whatever you want: it has to happen."[17]

This champion of property rights on-reserve also argues the following:

- Indigenous peoples are simply prior immigrants with no real rights (to the land or otherwise).
- European colonization was inevitable and justifiable because of the "tremendous gap in civilization" between Indigenous peoples and Europeans.
- Indigenous peoples in Canada can't have sovereignty because they didn't achieve statehood recognizable to Europeans prior to contact.
- Indigenous peoples cannot have nations because they are just tribal communities and must remain subordinate.
- Indigenous government, in practice, "produces wasteful, destructive, familistic factions."
- Indigenous title as currently defined is impossible to use in a modern economy.
- The historic treaties must not be re-evaluated.
- Indigenous peoples can only find prosperity by integrating into the economy, "which means, among other things, a willingness to move."[18]

There are plenty of refutations to all of these claims, but the point of this is to sketch out Flanagan's approach to First Nations issues. Why am I harping on Flanagan? Well, this fine fellow coauthored another book called *Beyond the Indian Act: Restoring Aboriginal Property Rights,* which Manny Jules (Chief Commissioner of the FNPO Initiative) wrote a foreword to, and both men are great supporters (and co-architects, perhaps?) of the FNPOA.[19] That book reads a heck of a lot like both the White Paper and the discussion of the FNPOA – both of which basically assert that the only rights Indigenous peoples should have are private-property rights.

So, pardon me if I'm skeptical in the extreme of a plan that was virulently opposed by First Nations when it was first proposed in 1969; a plan couched in Western liberal notions of human dignity and freedom of choice just like it is today, over four decades later. Just because they found a First Nation face to slap on top of the FNPOA makes no difference when the attitudes are exactly the same.

So, let's call this property-rights-specific proposal what it really is: The White Paper Lite.

NOTES

1. Parliament of Canada, "White Papers: Introduction," *parl.gc.ca,* last modified December 16, 2009, http://www.parl.gc.ca/parlinfo/Pages/WhitePapers.aspx. Here, you will find more information on White Papers, as well as a list of those published since 1939.

2. Parliament of Canada, "Green Papers: Introduction," *parl.gc.ca,* last modified February 23, 2009, http://www.parl.gc.ca/parlinfo/Pages/GreenPapers.aspx. (My emphasis.)

3. Jean Chrétien, "Statement of the Government of Canada on Indian Policy, 1969," (1969), http://www.aadnc-aandc.gc.ca/eng/1100100010189/1100100010191.

4. Harry Hawthorn, ed., "A Survey of the Contemporary Indians of Canada: Economic, Political, Educational Needs and Policies," 2 vols. (Ottawa: Queen's Printer Press, 1966–1967). Accessed November 26, 2015, http://www.ainc-inac.gc.ca/ai/arp/ls/phi-eng.asp.

5. Yes, I italicized this for a reason. This part is going to come up again, later in this chapter. Muahahahaha!

6. Harold Cardinal, *The Unjust Society* (Vancouver: Douglas & McIntyre, 1969; 1999).

7. Indian Association of Alberta, *Citizens Plus* ["The Red Paper"] (Edmonton: Indian Association of Alberta, 1970), https://ejournals.library.ualberta.ca/index.php/aps/article/view/11690/8926.

8. Here, I use the term *Indians* because that is the language of the Red Paper. You may have noted I did not do this when summarizing the White Paper. It's one of those prickly "insider versus outsider" uses of language I refer to in chapter 1, and is just how I felt like approaching it.

9. See note 4.

10. Arthur Manuel, and Ronald M. Derrickson, *Unsettling Canada: A National Wake-up Call* (Toronto: Between the Lines, 2015), 29–36.

11. Ibid., 35.

12. You can find the First Nations Tax Commission webpage here: http://fntc.ca/.

13. You can access the First Nations Property Ownership Initiative webpage here: http://fnpo.ca.

14. Pam Palmater, "Flanagan National Petroleum Ownership Act: Stop Big Oil Land Grab," *Indigenous Nationhood* (blog), August 7, 2012, http://indigenousnationhood.blogspot.ca/2012/08/flanagan-national-petroleum-ownership.html. Here, you can read Pam Palmater's vociferous challenge to the proposal on her blog.

15. Jean Chrétien, "Statement of the Government of Canada on Indian Policy, 1969," (1969), http://www.aadnc-aandc.gc.ca/eng/1100100010189/1100100010191#chp1.

16. Jean Chrétien, "Statement of the Government of Canada on Indian Policy, 1969," (1969), http://www.aadnc-aandc.gc.ca/eng/1100100010189/1100100010191#chp14; First Nations Property Ownership Initiative, "Proposal: In Summary," *fnpo.ca,* last modified 2012, http://fnpo.ca/Proposal.aspx.

17. Thomas Flanagan, *First Nations? Second Thoughts* (Montreal: McGill-Queen's University Press, 2000), 196.

18. Ibid., chapter 1. Flanagan uses the constitutional term *Aboriginal*, but I prefer to use *Indigenous* unless I'm referring specifically to the Constitution.

19. Tom Flanagan, Christopher Alcantara, and Andre Le Dressay, *Beyond the Indian Act: Restoring Aboriginal Property Rights* (Montreal: McGill-Queen's University Press, 2010).

31

Our Children, Our Schools

*Fighting for Control Over
Indigenous Education*

Education is widely seen as a key component to future success not only for the individual children who receive that education, but also for the society to which they belong, as a whole. We use graduation rates and postsecondary degree attainment numbers to help determine the efficacy and accessibility of a system of education. These numbers give us fundamental information about the overall health of a society, rather than simply telling us how many individuals are meeting educational standards.

There is no Indigenous system of education in Canada. This fact is sometimes obscured by misunderstandings of reserve or band schools, or even charter schools that may provide "Indigenous content." Nonetheless, the system of education that exists in Canada is wholly Canadian, both legislatively and in terms of provision.

Another important fact is that the Canadian system of education is failing Indigenous peoples. Regardless of personal opinion, the grim statistics paint a very clear picture. When examining access, graduation rates, and postsecondary-degree attainment in other countries, we do not blame individuals for egregiously poor outcomes. We do not do this because education is a social undertaking that transcends individuals and even minority groups. It requires mobilization of all levels of government, and it affects every single person living within the boundaries of that system of education.

The stats: outcomes

- A sizeable gap in student performance between Indigenous and non-Indigenous students is already present by grade 4, with a widening of the gap by grade 7.[1]

- Forty (40) percent of Indigenous peoples aged 20–24 do not have a high-school diploma compared to 13 percent of non-Indigenous peoples.[2]
- High-school non-completion rates are even more pronounced on reserves (61 percent) and among Inuit in remote communities (68 percent).[3]
- Ten (10) percent of the Indigenous population have a university degree compared to 26 percent among non-Indigenous students.[4]
- Sixty-three (63) percent of Indigenous university graduates are women.[5]

The stats: funding

- Non-Indigenous funding is provided by the provinces. Indigenous education is funded federally. Non-status Indians and Métis students receive provincial funding only.
- The federal funding formula for on-reserve schools has been capped at 2-percent growth per year since 1996, despite the need having increased by 6.3 percent per year, creating a $1.5 billion shortfall between 1996 and 2008 for instructional services alone.[6]
- Only 57 percent of federal funding for First Nations students is allocated to First Nations schools. The rest goes to support students attending off-reserve schools.[7]
- Unlike their provincial counterparts, First Nations schools receive no funding for library books, librarians' salaries, construction or maintenance costs of school libraries, nor funding for vocational training, information and communication technologies, or sports and recreation.[8]
- In 2007, there was a need for 69 new First Nations schools across Canada and an additional 27 needed major renovations. Funding was provided for only 21 new schools and 16 renovation projects.[9]
- Despite claims by Indian Affairs to the contrary,[10] a recent federal report confirms there are severe funding gaps in First Nations education that must be addressed immediately in the short term, and long-term improvements must be made with the active participation of First Nations stakeholders.[11]
- Postsecondary funding (available only to status Indians and Inuit) has been historically inadequate when meeting funding needs, and has created a backlog of 10 589 students who were denied funding between 2001 and 2006.[12]

The First Nations control of First Nations Education Act: the top-down approach again

Despite a plethora of reports that recommend the federal government cease acting unilaterally and without consultation with First Nations, the Harper government introduced a draft First Nations Education Act in October of 2013, after minimal engagement with Indigenous communities.[13]

Even in draft form, First Nations leaders and educators were vociferous in their dissatisfaction with the proposal, and with the engagement process.[14] Consultation leading up to the draft was comprised of eight consultation sessions, about 30 teleconferences, and some online activities. Eventually, in Orwellian fashion, the draft was rebranded the First Nations Control of First Nations Education Act (Bill C-33) and given its first reading April of 2014.[15]

Despite promising $1.9 billion in funding (to be spread out over several years), many people identified serious flaws in the proposed legislation – aside from the fact it had not truly been developed in consultation with First Nations.

In particular, despite the name, this act would not have given control over First Nations education to First Nations themselves. In fact, even more control would be put in the hands of Indigenous Affairs appointees. The Act did not even mention Aboriginal or treaty rights to education, which is something First Nations communities have demanded recognition of in any such legislation. Schools that were not "up to the standards" of the Act could be taken over by Indigenous Affairs appointees, with no recourse, and absolutely no liability possible on the part of Indigenous Affairs if things went horribly wrong. Even worse, there was no mechanism to fix the underfunding experienced by First Nations students on-reserve.

The tabling of Bill C-33 created a lot of tension in First Nations communities. New funding is desperately needed, and $1.9 billion sounds like a lot of money; at least until you start breaking it up over several years and realize it was not going to be enough to build the new schools needed or maintain the ones already built, much less bring per-student funding up to par. However, then Minister of Indigenous, Affairs, Bernard Valcourt, insisted it was this or nothing. After some major upheavals, which included the resignation of the Assembly of First Nations National Chief, Shawn Atleo, the bill was shelved.[16]

Indigenous education means Indigenous planning, development, and control.

Canada needs to finally listen to what Indigenous peoples have been demanding for years: our cultures and languages must be given more importance in our systems of education. This focus has been supported by so many publications including (but not limited to):[17]

- Indian Control of Indian Education, 1972[18]
- Royal Commission on Aboriginal Peoples Report, 1996[19]
- Final Report of the Minister's Working Group on Education, 2002[20]
- United Nations Declaration on the Rights of Indigenous Peoples, 2007[21]
- First Nation Control of First Nation Education, 2010[22]
- Report of the Senate Standing Committee on Aboriginal Peoples, 2011[23]
- Joint FNEC-NAN-FSIN Report, 2011[24]
- Report of the National Panel, 2012[25]

Every community wants to have a say in the education of its children. Indigenous peoples want to be able to develop their own standards and programs, along with other governance structures, and this includes the ability to use a pedagogical approach rooted in Indigenous world-views.[26] These are not mere aspirations; a lot of work has been done by Indigenous educators on specific frameworks based within specific Indigenous cultures.[27]

First Nations schools, in particular, need:

- school facilities to be located *in* the community, so students no longer have to leave their homes to study elsewhere (a practice that has been a factor in the tragic deaths of too many First Nations students over the years)[28]
- adequate funding that ensures cultural and linguistic needs are met
- the possibility of a modern education context – meaning access to libraries, technology, sports and recreation, and other resources available to off-reserve students
- funding to ensure competitive working conditions so communities do not need to rely on unseasoned staff (or even people who fake their qualifications),[29] and an unsustainably high turnover among staff[30]

Above all, funding must be stable and predictable. The design and implementation of Indigenous education must be in the hands of Indigenous communities.

Not an impossible task; some First Nations are already doing it!

Freedom Schools originated in the 1964 Mississippi Summer Project, as part of a wider Black civil-rights movement.[31] In the early 1970s, building on the model of the freedom schools, the American Indian Movement (AIM) opened two survival schools: Heart of the Earth and Red School House in Minneapolis and St. Paul, respectively.[32] Survival schools sprung up all throughout Indian country after this, though many were forced to close their doors for lack of funds and support in the mid-1980s and 1990s.

Here in Canada, in 1978 and 1979, the Mohawk communities of Kahnawake and Akwesasne opened their own schools, respectively named the Kahnawake Survival School (high school) and the Akwesasne Freedom School (elementary, junior high). Both schools are still going strong. Focusing on cultural and linguistic immersion and academic excellence, these schools are community funded, the infrastructure was built by the community, and each school has created its own curriculum. In essence, these are private schools that have had to form relationships with provincial authorities to ensure their students graduate with recognized credentials that will be accepted in postsecondary institutions.

In 1999, Mi'kmaq communities in Nova Scotia took control of their schooling through the *Mi'kmaq Education Act* after tripartite negotiations between the federal government, the province, and First Nations.[33] It is a self-governance act and it created the Mi'kmaw Kina'matnewey (MK), a Mi'kmaq education authority, which has 12 member communities and more than 3000 students.[34] It operates somewhat like a school board, except rather than directing the activities of community schools it is accountable *to* those schools.

In addition to prioritizing language and culture, the MK has also focused on hiring Mi'kmaq educators, boasting a 50 percent rate by the 2010–2011 school year. By 2014, the MK had a graduation rate of 88 percent, compared to 25 percent of First Nations students nationwide.[35] Don't read that stat too quickly and accidentally miss it! That is a huge difference! MK students are even outperforming the rest of Canada, which has an average graduation rate of 85 percent.[36]

In 2015, University nuhelot'įne thaiyots'į nistameyimâkanak Blue Quills (UnBQ) became the first Indigenous-controlled university in Canada.[37] Formerly Blue Quills College, the new university is housed in a former residential school in Alberta (in Treaty 6 territory), and is governed and owned by seven First Nations. It has operated under Indigenous control since 1971, building partnerships with various postsecondary institutions to co-deliver degrees. Now, the UnBQ will also be able to offer its own degree programs.[38]

These examples embody the implementation of recommendations in numerous federal reports, as well as the stated needs and aspirations of Indigenous communities. It can be done, it has been done, and it can continue to be done.

They are not the only examples of solutions created and implemented by Indigenous peoples, but the fact remains that the Canadian system of education does not provide adequate space for the widespread development of an Indigenous system of education. This has to change.

Indigenous communities as a whole simply do not have the internal resources to create an entire system of private schooling to rectify the horrendous gap that has always existed between Indigenous and non-Indigenous student outcomes. If you can judge a society by its system of education, then Canada stands clearly guilty of discriminating against Indigenous peoples by allowing this situation to continue.

NOTES

1. John Richards, Jennifer Hove, and Kemi Afolabi, "Understanding the Aboriginal/Non-Aboriginal Gap in Student Performance: Lessons from British Columbia" (C.D. Howe Institute Commentary, December 2008), 4, accessed December 9, 2015, https://www.cdhowe.org/pdf/commentary_276.pdf.

2. Congress of Aboriginal Peoples, "Staying in School: Engaging Aboriginal Students" (2010), 3, accessed December 9, 2015, https://neaoinfo.files.wordpress.com/2014/07/aboriginal-education-congress-of-aboriginal-peoples.pdf.

3. Ibid.

4. Indigenous and Northern Affairs Canada, "Fact Sheet – 2011 National Household Survey Aboriginal Demographics, Educational Attainment and Labour Market Outcomes," last modified August 18, 2015, accessed December 9, 2015, https://www.aadnc-aandc.gc.ca/eng/1376329205785/1376329233875.

5. Vivian O'Donnell, and Susan Wallace, "Aboriginal Women Less Likely to Have a University Degree," *First Nations, Inuit and Metis Women,* last modified November 30, 2015, accessed December 9, 2015, http://www.statcan.gc.ca/pub/89-503-x/2010001/article/11442-eng.htm#a31.

6. Chiefs Assembly on Education, "Federal Funding for First Nations Schools," last modified October 3, 2012, accessed December 9, 2015, http://www.afn.ca/uploads/files/events/fact_sheet-ccoe-8.pdf; Tim Fontaine, "First Nations Welcome Lifting of Despised 2% Funding Cap," *cbc.ca,* last modified December 12, 2015, accessed December 11, 2015. Prime Minister Trudeau announced on December 11, 2015 that his government would be lifting the 2-percent cap in their first budget but as of writing this piece, it is not known if funding will be increased to address the deficiencies that cap has caused.

7. First Nations Education Council, "Paper on First Nations Education Funding," 13, last modified February 2009, accessed December 9, 2015, http://www.cepn-fnec.com/PDF/etudes_documents/education_funding.pdf.

8. Ibid., 20.

9. Ibid., 24.

10. "First Nations Education Not Underfunded, Figures Suggest," *cbc.ca,* last modified October 2, 2012, accessed December 9, 2015, http://www.cbc.ca/news/politics/first-nations-education-not-underfunded-figures-suggest-1.1143430.

11. INAC, "Summative Evaluation of the Elementary/Secondary Education Program on Reserve," June 2012, accessed December 9, 2015, http://www.aadnc-aandc.gc.ca/eng/1365183942467/136518 4080356.

12. See note 7, page 34.

13. INAC, "First Nations Education Act," last modified 2014, accessed December 10, 2015, http://actionplan.gc.ca/en/initiative/first-nations-education-act.

14. Tyler Clark, "PAGC Rejects Feds' Education Act," *Prince Albert Daily Herald,* September 19, 2013, accessed December 10, 2015, http://www.paherald.sk.ca/News/Local/2013-09-19/ article-3395710/PAGC-rejects-feds%26rsquo%3B-education-act/1.

15. Parliament of Canada, "Bill C-33," April 10, 2014, accessed December 10, 2015, http://www.parl.gc.ca/ HousePublications/Publication.aspx?Language=E&Mode=1&DocId=6532106.

16. Ontario Native Education Counselling Association (ONECA), "First Nations Education Act," 2012, http://www.oneca.com/first-nation-education-act.html. Here, ONECA provides more of the background on the life of this Bill, including Indigenous Affairs' take on it.

17. First Nations Education Council, "Quality Education for All First Nations Citizens," March 27, 2013, accessed December 10, 2015, http://www.cepn-fnec.com/PDF/APNQL/Position_du_ CEPN_eng.pdf accessed Dec. 10, 2015. See this report for a comprehensive list of studies and reports addressing First Nations education, as well as how specifically those resources addressed the issue.

18. National Indian Brotherhood/Assembly of First Nations, "Indian Control of Indian Education," policy paper presented to Indian Affairs and Northern Development, 1972, accessed December 9, 2015, http://www.oneca.com/IndianControlofIndianEducation.pdf.

19. INAC, *Report of the Royal Commission on Aboriginal Peoples, 1996,* accessed December 9, 2015, http://www.collectionscanada.gc.ca/webarchives/20071115053257/http://www.ainc-inac.gc.ca/ ch/rcap/sg/sgmm_e.html.

20. Minister's National Working Group on Education, "Our Children – Keepers of the Sacred Knowledge: Final Report of the Minister's National Working Group on Education," commissioned by Indigenous and Northern Affairs Canada, December 2002, accessed December 9, 2015, http://www.afn.ca/uploads/files/education/23._2002_dec_jeffrey_and_jette_ final_report_to_min_national_working_group_ourchildrenkeepersofthesacredknowledge.pdf.

21. United Nations, Declaration on the Rights of Indigenous Peoples, September 13, 2007, accessed December 9, 2015, http://www.un.org/esa/socdev/unpfii/documents/DRIPS_en.pdf.

22. Assembly of First Nations (AFM), "First Nations Control of First Nations Education; It's Our Vision, It's Our Time," July 2010, accessed December 9, 2015, http://www.afn.ca/uploads/ files/education/3._2010_july_afn_first_nations_control_of_first_nations_education_final_ eng.pdf.

23. Gerry St. Germain, and Lilian Eva Dyck, "Report of the Senate Standing Committee on Aboriginal Peoples," December 2011, accessed December 9, 2015, http://www.parl.gc.ca/ content/sen/committee/411/appa/rep/rep03dec11-e.pdf.

24. "Report on Priority Actions in View of Improving First Nations Education," presented by First Nations Education Council, Nishnawbe Aski Nation, and Federation of Saskatchewan Indian Nations, November 2011, accessed December 9, 2015, http://www.cepn-fnec.com/PDF/etudes_ documents/Report-Priority-Actions-View-Improving-FN-Education-November-2011_eng.pdf.

25. National Panel on First Nation Elementary and Secondary Education for Students on Reserve, "Nurturing the Learning Spirit of First Nation Students: The Report of the National Panel on First Nation Elementary and Secondary Education for Students on Reserve," 2012, accessed December 9, 2015, https://www.aadnc-aandc.gc.ca/DAM/DAM-INTER-HQ-EDU/STAGING/texte-text/nat_panel_final_report_1373997803969_eng.pdf.

26. Linda M. Goulet, and Keith N. Goulet, *Teaching Each Other: Nehinuw Concepts and Indigenous Pedagogies* (Vancouver: University of British Columbia Press, 2014). This example comes from a Cree perspective.

27. See, for example, from a Mi'kmaq perspective: Marie Battiste, *Decolonizing Education: Nourishing the Learning Spirit* (Saskatoon: Purich Publishing, 2013).

28. Jody Porter, "First Nation Student Death Inquest: 5 Things Revealed So Far," *cbc.ca,* last modified November 16, 2015, accessed December 10, 2015, http://www.cbc.ca/news/canada/thunder-bay/first-nation-student-deaths-inquest-5-things-revealed-so-far-1.3318357.

29. "First Nations Schools Vulnerable to Teacher Impersonators, Educator Says," *cbc.ca,* last modified November 11, 2015, accessed December 10, 2015, http://www.cbc.ca/news/canada/manitoba/first-nations-schools-vulnerable-to-teacher-impersonators-educator-says-1.3315029.

30. Robin Mueller, Sheila Carr-Stewart, Larry Steeves, and Jim Marshall, "Teacher Recruitment and Retention in Select First Nations Schools," *In Education* 17, no. 3 (2011), accessed December 10, 2015, http://ineducation.ca/ineducation/article/view/72/553.

31. Charles M. Payne, *I've Got the Light of Freedom: The Organizing Tradition and the Mississippi Freedom Struggle* (Los Angeles: University of California Press, 2007).

32. Julie L. Davis, *Survival Schools: The American Indian Movement and Community Education in the Twin Cities* (Minneapolis: University of Minnesota Press, 2013).

33. Government of Canada, *Mi'kmaq Education Act,* June 18, 1998, http://laws-lois.justice.gc.ca/eng/acts/M-7.6/page-1.html#docCont.

34. Mi'kmaw Kina'matnewey website, last updated March 1, 2016, http://kinu.ca/.

35. Linda Simon, "Mi'kmaw Kina'matnewey – Supporting Student Success," September 2014, accessed December 10, 2015, http://indspire.ca/wp-content/uploads/2015/03/indspire-nurturing-capacity-mk-2014-en.pdf. Here, you will find an in-depth profile of Mi'kmaw Kina'matnewey schools.

36. Arik Motskin, and Zack Gallinger, "The Vast Disparity in Canada's High School Graduation Rates," The 10 and 3 website, August 12, 2015, accessed December 10, 2015, http://www.the10and3.com/the-vast-disparity-in-canadas-high-school-graduation-rates-00016/.

37. nuhelot'įne thaiyots'į is the Dene name for UnBQ; nistameyimâkanak is the Cree name. The combined Dene/Cree name reflects the First Nations that own and govern the university.

38. University nuhelot'įne thaiyots'į – nistameyimâkanak Blue Quills, "About Us," accessed December 1, 2015, http://www.bluequills.ca/welcome/about-us/.

Index

Interim Métis Harvesting Agreement (IMHA), 42–43, 52n15, 166
Into the West (tv series), 173
Inuit
  identity and facts about, 55–58
  importance of hunting to, 60–61
  and *Indian Act,* 28
  in Montreal, 71
  names for Black people, 19
  names for settlers, 20–21
  relocation of, 191–193, 202–204
  stories, 95–96
  on use of as term of address, 11
Inuit Nunangat, 56–57
Inuit Qaujimajatuqangit (IQ), 60–61
Inukjuak, 202–203
Ipellie, Alootook, 60

J
James Bay and Northern Quebec Agreement (JBNQA), 62–63
Japanese symbols, 87–88
Johnson, Anguti, 55
The Journals of Knud Rasmussen, 56
Jules, Manny, 271, 273

K
KAIROS, 177, 250n3
Kalluak, Mark, 96
Kaskaskia, 53n27
kaswentha, 245
Khelsilem, 110
Kimelman, Edwin C., 183
Kiskisik Awasisak report, 185–187
Klassen, Karin, 117–118
Klein, Ralph, 42, 166
Kress, Nancy, 74, 75–76, 78
Kunuk, Zacharias, 55–56

L
ladder theory, 163
land owning, 247–248, 261–266
language, 65, 106–108, 266
Lee, Erica Violet, 174
Lewis, Brian, 101–102
liberalism, 127–132
Litigation Management and Resolution Branch (LMRB), 253

loaded terms, 8
Loyer, Louis Divertissant, **40**

M
Macdonnell, Miles, 239
maiko, 87–88
Makivik Corporation, 193–194
Manitoba Indian Brotherhood (MIB), 183
Manuel, Arthur, 271
Maori symbols, 85–86
Maracle, Brian, 156
market-based housing, 145–147
McIvor, Sharon, 31
McNickle, Lettia, 87
media, 88–89, 117–119
membership, 26, 31–32
metabolization of alcohol, 152–154
Metcalfe, Jessica, 103
Métis
  author's attempt to describe her heritage, 36–37, 39, 40–41
  definition, 39, 41–42, 47–48, 50
  as farmers, 206–207
  and federal government, 214
  history of, 39–40
  impact of *Daniels v. Canada* on, 49–51
  and *Indian Act,* 28
  Interim Métis Harvesting Agreement, 42–43, 52n15, 166
  non-Indigenous misidentifying as, 42–47
  organizations misidentifying as, 46–47, 53n27
  as racial and sociopolitical identity, 37–39, 40–41
  symbols of, 84–85
  on use of as term of address, 11
  use of to mean mixed culture, 43, 52n16
Métis in Space (podcast), 79n8
Métis Nation of Alberta (MNA), 42–43
Métissage, 44–45
Mi'kmaq, 280
Mi'kmaw Kina'matnewey (MK), 280
millenial scoop, 184–187
Ministerial Loan Guarantees, 146–147, 263
Mohawk Kahnawake, 139, 280
Montreal, 71
Morgan, Cora, 185
Morissette, Réjean, 118

Image Credits

Cover, pp. 5, 23, 115, 169, 233: © Nadya Kwandibens/Red Works Photography from the series Concrete Indians.

p. 40: Figure 4.1 – Photo of Angelique Callihoo and Louis Divertissant Loyer. From the family collection of Crystal Hayes. Used by permission.

p. 63: Figure 6.1 – Map (adapted) of Eeyou Istchee Territory courtesy of Eeyou Istchee/Grand Council of the Crees.

p. 111: Figure 12.1 – Poster from the Native Youth Sexual Health Network at: http://nativeyouthsexualhealth.com, reprinted by permission.

pp. 194–202: Figure 22.1 – DOGS is © by Nicole Burton and Hugh Goldring, Ad Astra Comix, 2015. See more at the Qikiqtani Truth Commission website: http://www.qtcommission.ca, reprinted by permission.

 THE DEBWE SERIES

The Debwe Series features exceptional Indigenous writing from across Canada. Named for the Anishinaabe concept debwe, meaning "to speak the truth," the series showcases both established and new Indigenous writers and editors producing and publishing stories from their communities, experiences, and cultures.

Series Editor: Niigaanwewidam Sinclair, PhD, Assistant Professor, Department of Native Studies, University of Manitoba

Titles in this series:

A Blanket of Butterflies, by Richard Van Camp
Fire Starters, by Jen Storm
The Gift Is in the Making: Anishinaabeg Stories, by Leanne Simpson
Manitowapow: Aboriginal Writings from the Land of Water, Niigaanwewidam
    James Sinclair and Warren Cariou, editors
The Stone Collection, by Kateri Akiwenzie-Damm
Three Feathers, by Richard Van Camp